THOMAS G. SIMONS

HOLY PEOPLE HOLY PLACE

RITES FOR THE CHURCH'S HOUSE

LITURGY
TRAINING
PUBLICATIONS

Acknowledgments

Excerpts from *Environment and Art in Catholic Worship* © 1978, United States Catholic Conference (USCC); *Committee on the Liturgy Newsletter,* vol. 24, © 1988, USCC. Used with permission. All rights reserved.

The English translation of *Dedication of a Church and an Altar* © 1978, International Committee on English in the Liturgy, Inc. (ICEL); excerpts from the English translation of *Documents on the Liturgy 1963–1979: Conciliar, Papal, and Curial Texts,* © 1982, ICEL; excerpts from the English translation of *Rite of Reconciliation of a Profaned Church* (draft text), © 1983, ICEL; excerpts from the English translation of *Book of Blessings,* © 1988, ICEL; excerpts from the English translation of *Ceremonial of Bishops,* © 1989, ICEL. All rights reserved.

The scripture quotations contained herein are from the New Revised Standard Version Bible, © 1993 and 1989 by the Division of Christian Education of the National Council of the Churches of Christ in the U.S.A. Used by permission. All rights reserved.

Copyright © 1998 Archdiocese of Chicago: Liturgy Training Publications, 1800 North Hermitage Avenue, Chicago IL 60622-1101; 1-800-933-1800; fax 1-800-933-7094; e-mail orders@ltp.org. All rights reserved.

This book was edited by David Philippart and designed by Barb Rohm, with assistance from Anna Manhart. Audrey Novak Riley was the production editor with assistance from Theresa Houston. Typesetting was by Mark Hollopeter in Garamond and Frutiger.

Photographs of Blessed Padre Serra Church, Camarillo, California (Archdiocese of Los Angeles), on pages 4 and 9 by Linda Ekstrom, on page 16 by Ron LeBlanc. Photographs of St. Marcelline Church, Schaumburg, Illinois (Archdiocese of Chicago), on pages 12, 21, 48, 97 and 104 by David Kathrein. Photograph of Most Holy Trinity Church, Saco, Maine (Diocese of Portland), on page 30 by Brian Vanden Brink, courtesy of Barbara Chenicek, OP, and Rita Schiltz, OP. Photograph of St. Agnes Church, Chicago Heights, Illinois (Archdiocese of Chicago), on page 37 by Regina Kuehn. The book was printed by Bawden Printing of Eldridge, Iowa.

Library of Congress Cataloging-in-Publication Data
Simons, Thomas G.
   Holy people, holy place: rites for the church's house/Thomas G. Simons.
      p.   cm.
   ISBN 1-56854-095-7
   1. Church dedication. 2. Catholic Church — Liturgy — Texts.
I. Title
BX2302.S57   1998
264'.020992 — dc21

97-49362
CIP

ISBN 1-56854-095-7
DED/CH

Contents

iv   *Introduction*

1   *Chapter 1*   Church and church
                          Ecclesiology and the Rite as Metaphor

15   *Chapter 2*   Making Holy the Place
                          Evolution and Overview of Rites of Dedication

25   *Chapter 3*   The Rite Reformed
                          The 1977 Rite of Dedication of a Church and an Altar

31   *Chapter 4*   Initiating the Church's House
                          Studying and Preparing to Celebrate the Rite

59   *Chapter 5*   Holy Rites, Holy Places
                          Other Liturgies of Blessing, Prayer and Thanksgiving
                             Laying the Foundation Stone or Groundbreaking
                             Rituals for Renovated Churches
                             Leave-taking before a Renovation
                             Celebrating the Anniversary of Dedication
                             Celebrating the Titular of the Community
                             Anniversary of the Dedication of the Cathedral
                             A Service for Burning the Mortgage
                             Blessings for Particular Spaces and Furnishings
                             Public Prayer after the Desecration of a Church
                             Rituals for the Closing of a Church

107   *Resources*   Selected Bibliography

113   *Text*   Dedication of a Church and an Altar

Introduction

It is said "You are what you eat." And "You are a product of your environment." Nowhere is this more evident than in the *Rite of Dedication of a Church and an Altar.* Through the words, gestures and symbols in this rite, it is abundantly clear that the people of God are the Church that is being dedicated. The introduction to the rite reminds us that the Church is the temple of God built of living stones, where the Father is worshiped in spirit and in truth. In the Church every person becomes by baptism a member of Christ and, at the same time, a temple of the Holy Spirit in which the Father and the Son make their dwelling.

Though God can be worshiped anywhere, the local community builds a "house of the Church" *(domus ecclesiae)* for the benefit and use of all the faithful, where sacred celebrations take place, where each one may find a "house of prayer" that is a place of peace and reflection and where all are commissioned to go forth and make real God's justice and peace. From earliest times, that building was called a "church" in which the Christian community, assembled by its pastors, met to hear the word of God, to pray together and to celebrate the sacraments, especially the eucharist. A physical place, the house of the Church is a sacred sign of the pilgrim Church on earth. It also points to the Church's dwelling in heaven which, in a sacramental way, it shows forth and anticipates.

Likewise, from earliest times, rituals for the dedication of these places have evolved as an act of the local Church. The rite we have today presents a compelling and renewed sense of the pre-eminence of the worshiping community as the primary liturgical symbol. As baptism initiates us into the pilgrimage of a life lived in faith, so the initiation of this place creates a space in which we realize our continuing call to conversion in Christ. As we recognize our being "set apart" (anointed), so we anoint this place and set it apart. As the eucharist sustains and continues our life of conversion, so the celebration of the eucharist ultimately dedicates this place to God. The rite of dedication is a many-layered symbol that intends the renewal of the Church as it inaugurates the use of its church.

In ritual celebration we not only seek to express who we are, we press on to become what we are not yet. The celebration of the dedication of a church is a commitment on the part of the community to follow in the footsteps of Christ. The church building is our house of prayer, but one in which we are never fully at home. Our true and eternal home is yet to come. The church building is a tent, a bridge, a ship, a workshop in which God's people assemble, cross over and connect, begin the journey and are built up. In the workshop that is the church, Christ is formed in us, because it is in the church *as the Church* that we do the work of the people, the work of the new creation. Since the eucharist is the work of Christians and the church building is the worksite of the eucharist, the dedication of the church takes place essentially within a celebration of the eucharist.

As the eucharist is the sacrament for the achievement of full Christian identity, it is also the eucharist that effects the dedication of a church: its designation as a holy place. The eucharist makes the church building a house of God *(domus Dei)* because it makes the Church, the people, the temple of God's presence. In the church building, more than in any other place, the Christian is shaped into Christ. But since Christian identity is always an eschatological possibility that the Church strains to achieve, all eucharist is viaticum, and all church buildings are provisional (see Revelation 21:22), mere resting stations on our pilgrimage to God.

While an examination of the *Rite of Dedication of a Church and an Altar* is the central purpose of this book, I also wanted to show the relationship of other rituals to the place we call church. Therefore, other liturgies of blessing (laying the foundation stone, groundbreaking, renovated or restored spaces, particular spaces and church furnishings), prayer (celebrating the anniversaries of name and dedication, public prayer after the desecration of a church) and thanksgiving (the closing or consolidation of a church) are also included. The entire work presented here is offered essentially from a pastoral perspective. Other studies of the subject treat more fully, for example, the historical development of the rites of dedication and their critical analysis.

We now have had twenty years of experience with this rite. Pastoral experience is showing us areas that will eventually need to be adapted or expanded. The rite itself is not experienced often, and when it is celebrated it is a historic event for a community. It remains one of our most complex liturgies, somewhat like the Easter Vigil. It is my hope that this work will help all who are preparing to celebrate the rite to come to know its richness. All involved with this rite — bishop, clergy, ministers and assembly — need to be fully aware of its depth and spirituality.

This work has been in preparation for almost five years and was finally completed during a sabbatical in the winter and spring of 1996.

I am very grateful to Ignazio Calabuig, OSM, rector of the Pontifical Theological Faculty of the Marianum in Rome. Father Calabuig served as a leading member of the working group that prepared the Latin edition of the rite published in 1977. So instrumental was his work in the ordering of the rite and the composition of original texts that he rightly merits the title "father of the post–Vatican II rite of dedication." He would never claim that title, but the truth remains that he was the driving force behind the reformation and restoration of this rite. He was very helpful to me with his assistance and guidance.

I am also grateful to Luke Chengalikavil, OSB, who completed his doctoral thesis in liturgy on the subject of the rite of dedication. While I was in Rome, he shared with me his research and insights into the rite. I have tried to persuade him to publish his excellent historical research on the subject and hope that we have the benefit of it some day.

I am most grateful to Father J. D. Crichton, former parish priest of Pershore, Worcestershire, England, and a well-known lecturer and writer in liturgy. His insights and commentary have greatly contributed to this book.

I am also indebted to the late Robert J. Flinn, SVD, for his valuable assistance in coordinating the translation of some research materials. His wit and wisdom will always be appreciated and remembered.

I am grateful to many individuals who shared their experience and stories of the rite of dedication and other rituals related to the church building.

There is a song that is very popular these days at the dedication of a church, as evidenced by the many orders of service I have examined. Written by Marty Haugen, published in 1994 by GIA Publications in Chicago, "All Are Welcome" has the Church sing: "Let us build a house where love is found in water, wine and wheat; a banquet hall on holy ground, where peace and justice meet. Here the love of God, through Jesus, is revealed in time and space. As we share in Christ the feast that frees us: All are welcome, all are welcome, all are welcome in this place." May all our efforts at being the Church and dedicating churches make it so!

Thomas G. Simons

Church and church
Ecclesiology and the Rite as Metaphor

When a community constructs a new church building or renovates an older one, the basic question in the process is, "Who is the Church?" From this follows another question, "What is a church building?" To respond to these fundamental questions, a community should give serious consideration to three documents in particular.

The *Constitution on the Sacred Liturgy,* the first document of the Second Vatican Council, was promulgated on December 4, 1963. It has been said that this document—in its style, content, and development—paved the way for the *Dogmatic Constitution on the Church,* promulgated on November 21, 1964. Thirteen years after that, appropriately on Pentecost, May 29, 1977, the Congregation for the Sacraments and Divine Worship published that part of the Roman Pontifical known as the *Dedication of a Church and an Altar.*

These three documents should be read and understood together, almost as a unit. They build one upon the other and are dependent upon each other. The *Constitution on the Sacred Liturgy* redefined worship as the work of people, as the action of the whole Church. This in turn caused us to look more closely at ourselves precisely as Church: the people of God, the body of Christ, the gathered community of the Holy Spirit—all these images are expressed and reaffirmed powerfully in the *Constitution on the Church.* These two documents then give practical shape to the ritual expression for dedicating the house of the Church in the *Rite of Dedication.*

If we believe in the age-old wisdom that "the rule of praying establishes the rule of believing," then the rites of dedication both express and form a part of the liturgical spirituality that is a key ingredient in giving shape to a place for worship of God's holy people. Theology, specifically the theology of what it means to be the Church (ecclesiology), and liturgy are intertwined in this rite. It follows that the rite should inform the preparation, prayer and process that lead to a physical building that we call a church.

CHURCH AS PEOPLE

The *Rite of Dedication of a Church and an Altar* begins to answer the questions "Who is the Church?" and "What is a church?" with a number of theological statements:

Through his death and resurrection, Christ became the true and perfect temple of the New Covenant and gathered together a people to be his own.

This holy people, made one as the Father, Son, and Holy Spirit are one, is the Church, that is, the temple of God built of living stones, where the Father is worshiped in spirit and in truth.

Rightly, then, from early times the name "church" has also been given to the building in which the Christian community gathers to hear the word of God, to pray together, to receive the sacraments, and to celebrate the eucharist. (chapter 2, 1)

The vision of the Church offered here is deep and rich. The true temple of God is Jesus. The real Church is the body of Christ and even the heavenly Jerusalem is not a building: "I saw no temple in the city, for its temple is the Lord God the Almighty and the Lamb. And the city has no need of sun or moon to shine on it, for the glory of God is its light, and its lamp is the Lamb" (Revelation 21:22–23). And for all its glory, the heavenly Jerusalem bears the marks of the passion of Christ, the Lamb who was slain. It was by Christ's passion, death and resurrection that the Church is called into existence.

So the people are the place where God is worshiped in spirit and in truth. It is they who, through Christ, are the temple of the living God; it is they who are set apart; it is they who are the royal priesthood offering to God sacrifices that are acceptable because they are offered through Christ (see 1 Peter 2:4–9).

Throughout the rite of dedication, the emphasis is on the Church as a people, the body of Christ. In the bishop's first address to the people, after recalling the purpose for which the church building exists (namely, to be a place for the Church to hear the word of God, to baptize, to be fed at the table of the Lord), the bishop prays that the community may grow into a spiritual temple and be made one by God's love as they gather around the altar (chapter 2, 30). Likewise, when he blesses the water, he speaks of the people who die with Christ in the waters of baptism and who are thereby made members and co-heirs with Christ in everlasting life. The water is blessed and sprinkled on the people and the walls so that both may be "a sign of the saving waters of baptism, by which we become one in Christ, the temple of your Spirit" (chapter 2, 48). In the invitation to the Litany of the Saints, the bishop tells the assembly to ask the saints to support its prayer to God, who makes "the hearts of [God's] people faithful temples of his Spirit" (chapter 2, 57).

But it is in the splendid prayer of dedication (chapter 2, 62) that the rite unfolds the nature of the Church, of which the church building is but a metaphor:

Here is reflected the mystery of the Church.

The Church is fruitful,
made holy by the blood of Christ:

a bride made radiant with his glory,
a virgin splendid in the wholeness of her faith,
a mother blessed through the power of the Spirit.

The Church is holy,
your chosen vineyard:
its branches envelop the world,
its tendrils, carried on the tree of the cross,
reach up to the kingdom of heaven.

The Church is favored,
the dwelling place of God on earth:
a temple built of living stones,
founded on the apostles
with Jesus Christ its corner stone.

The Church is exalted,
a city set on a mountain:
a beacon to the whole world,
bright with the glory of the Lamb
and echoing the prayers of her saints.

The entire prayer is rich with scriptural references, proclaiming a theology of a Church that is at the same time a faithful virgin and a mother made fruitful by the power of the Holy Spirit. The Church is a vineyard no longer restricted to one people, but open to the whole world. Existing here on earth, it is also in union with the heavenly city. Like the temple of old, it is the sign of God's presence, but that presence is now actualized in this place, because it is a structure in which Christ dwells, holding it together by the life that his Holy Spirit communicates to it. It is visible — that is, in the world now for all to see — but its foundations are the apostles, the twelve who represent the people, the biblical Israel, which now consists of the whole people of God who are the living members of Christ. Even here it can be described as "a city set on a hill" for all to see, for penetrating it from above is the light that is the Light of the World. The Lamb is not only the city's light (see Revelation); Christ is also the lamb of sacrifice who created this Church by his passion, death and resurrection. As yet, however, it is but a pilgrim Church painfully making its way to the heavenly city, where it will be transformed and will be "without a spot or a wrinkle or anything of the kind . . . holy and without blemish" (Ephesians 5:27).

 The image of the Church presented in the dedication prayer is vast and complex — as the mystery of the Church is vast and complex. But the dedication prayer says no more than the scriptures. The church building itself is only an image

The people gather outside of the new church in order to enter in procession on the day of dedication. Two important rites then occur: the handing over of the building to the bishop and the sprinkling of the people and the building with holy water.

or metaphor of this deeper reality called the Church. It is a high expectation of a building to reflect this deeper reality. No symbol can ever represent adequately the reality of which it is the symbol. All it can be is an approximation of it. No church building, however carefully thought out and constructed, can do justice to the underlying reality. This is an important consideration for those whose task it is to design a church.

BUILDING AS SYMBOL

The dedication prayer goes on to say that because the church building is the symbol of the Church, it can be made holy and dedicated: "Lord, send your Spirit from heaven to make this church an ever-holy place, and this altar a ready table for the sacrifice of Christ." It will be an "ever-holy place" because it becomes the image or symbol of the whole Church. This is the only text in the rite of dedication that refers to the church building as a "holy place," a dramatic change of emphasis from the former view of church buildings. The same emphasis is made throughout the rite, where the word "dedicate" is used instead of the word "consecrate," which occurs only twice. The word "consecrate" was formerly used with the sense of "setting apart" a place exclusively for worship. Though this sense is apparent in the reformed texts, it is not where the emphasis falls.

In the early stages of humanity's religious development, people thought of the whole world as sacred, but, as they came to realize that there were forces hostile to the sacred in the world, places and spaces were set apart where worship could take place and where those forces could be kept away and excluded. In pagan cultic practice, the place, or later the building, usually regarded as the shrine of the god became sacred and inviolable. For unclean or unpriestly hands to touch or violate the temple was sacrilege. The effect was sometimes deadly (see 2 Samuel 6:1–7).

In the rite of dedication, the church is "made a sacred place" as a symbol, and, as the prayer of dedication indicates, because of what goes on in it.

In the next portion of the prayer of dedication, the church building is described as the place where "the waters of baptism overwhelm the shame of sin . . . your people die to sin and live again through grace as your children . . . [and where] gathered around your altar, [they] celebrate the memorial of the Paschal Lamb, and [are] fed at the table of Christ's word and Christ's body." Here, "prayer, the Church's banquet," is made, and continual prayer for the salvation of the world ascends to God. Again, the church building is holy because of the praise of God's holy people in it.

The concluding petition of the dedication prayer focuses the praying community on its mission and asks that God allow this place to become a sanctuary in the fullest sense: "Here may the poor find justice, the victims of oppression, true freedom. From here may the whole world clothed in the dignity of the children of God, enter with gladness your city of peace." The implication is that the care of the poor and the oppressed begins in the building. If it does not, it is difficult to see how the building could be a symbol of the serving Church.

In the Middle Ages, certain churches extended sanctuary to those accused or even guilty of crimes — inside the building, such people were beyond the reach of the authorities. In our own day some churches, especially in inner-city areas, provide night shelters for the homeless or refuge for undocumented immigrants. Many churches house soup kitchens and other social services. These things are necessary if the church is going to serve the Church. At the very least the prayer seems to suggest that the church building should be more varied in its design than it used to be, more varied in the possibilities that it offers to the local community for its own needs and for the service of others.

NEW UNDERSTANDING, NEW RITE

Set side by side, the new and the former prayers of dedication illustrate not only changed understandings of the church building, but a new self-understanding of the Church itself. First is the former prayer of dedication, translated from the Latin.

Be present to our prayers,
be present to the sacraments

be present also to the holy works of your servants,
and to us who beg your mercy.

Pouring out the richness of his seven-fold grace,
let your Holy Spirit come down into this church
which, by invocation of your Holy Name,
in honor of the holy Cross
on which your coeternal Son,
our Lord Jesus Christ,
suffered for the redemption of the world,
and in memory of St. *Name,*
we, your unworthy servants consecrate,
so that, whenever your holy Name is called upon
in this house
the prayers of those who invoke it
will be heard by you, O loving Lord.

O blessed and holy Trinity,
who purify all things
cleanse all things
adorn all things!

O blessed majesty of God,
who fill all things,
contain all things,
dispose all things!

O blessed and holy hand of God
who sanctify all things,
bless all things
increase all things!

O God, holy of holies,
with deepest devotion we beseech your mercy
that through our lowly service,
you will purify, bless and consecrate this church
with the fullness of perpetual sanctification;
in honor of your holy and triumphant Cross
and in memory of St. *Name.*

May priests here offer you sacrifices of praise;
may the faithful here fulfill their commitments;

may the burden of sins be here relieved;
and the fallen-away be reconciled.

In this house, O Lord, by the grace of the Holy Spirit,
may the sick be healed
the weak have their strength restored,
the lame begin to run,
the lepers be cleansed,
the blind be made to see,
and demons expelled.

By your gift, may all these sufferings be relieved,
and every bond of sin absolved,
so that all who enter this temple
to present their honest petitions,
may rejoice to have all their prayers answered,
and, receiving from you the mercy they had begged,
they may be perpetually engaged
in glorifying your generosity.

(Translation published in *Assembly* [Notre Dame Center for Pastoral Liturgy] 10:2 [1983]: 230.)

Following is the prayer of dedication from the 1977 *Rite of Dedication of a Church and an Altar.*

Father in heaven,
source of holiness and true purpose,
it is right that we praise and glorify your name.

For today we come before you,
to dedicate to your lasting service
this house of prayer, this temple of worship,
this home in which we are nourished by your word and your sacraments.

Here is reflected the mystery of the Church.

The Church is fruitful,
made holy by the blood of Christ;
a bride made radiant with his glory,
a virgin splendid in the wholeness of her faith,
a mother blessed through the power of the Spirit.

The Church is holy,
your chosen vineyard:

its branches envelop the world,
its tendrils, carried on the tree of the cross,
reach up to the kingdom of heaven.

The Church is favored,
the dwelling place of God on earth:
a temple built of living stones,
founded on the apostles
with Jesus Christ its corner stone.

The Church is exalted,
a city set on a mountain:
a beacon to the whole world,
bright with the glory of the Lamb,
and echoing the prayers of her saints.

Lord,
send your Spirit from heaven
to make this church an ever-holy place,
and this altar a ready table for the sacrifice of Christ.

Here may the waters of baptism
overwhelm the shame of sin;
here may your people die to sin
and live again through grace as your children.

Here may your children,
gathered around your altar,
celebrate the memorial of the Paschal Lamb,
and be fed at the table
of Christ's word and Christ's body.

Here may prayer, the Church's banquet,
resound through heaven and earth
as a plea for the world's salvation.

Here may the poor find justice,
the victims of oppression, true freedom.

From here may the whole world
clothed in the dignity of the children of God,
enter with gladness your city of peace.

At the door, representatives of those who designed and built the structure symbolically hand it over to the bishop by giving the bishop a set of drawings, a ceremonial key or some other sign.

The church building, in addition to being a symbol of the Church, is also a place of celebration (baptism, eucharist and prayer) and a place of loving service to those in need. The rite expresses in a full and powerful way our Christian ecclesiology; those who design churches are challenged to find ways to embody all of this.

CONSTRUCTING A SYMBOL

How does one construct a building that is a symbol of the redeemed people who are making their pilgrim way to the heavenly Jerusalem, whose splendor is to be discerned even in the earthly Church? And it is just as difficult, if not more, to construct a building that will be a symbol of all the loving service that is of the essence of the Christian life.

This portion of the dedication prayer seems to respond, in some way, to the question often raised in a church building process about spending considerable sums of money on a building when there are so many human needs today that cry out for justice and compassion. It is the dilemma of splendor versus austerity, of magnificence versus humility, of the immense inner richness of the Church as opposed to the inadequacy of material things of any kind to symbolize it. It is the tension that always exists between the symbol and the reality symbolized.

In the Christian scheme of things, the latter is always infinitely greater than the former. Thus, no church, no matter how splendid in its appearance, no matter how large or lofty, no matter how impressive its furnishings, can ever convey the inexhaustible richness of the Church that reaches up to the heavenly city, which is resplendent with the light and life of God. This tension is recognized in the *Constitution on the Sacred Liturgy,* which says that the Church's rituals should be distinguished by a "noble simplicity" (34). The Church is encouraged to favor and seek sacred art for its "noble beauty rather than sumptuous display" (124). This orientation is reflected in the prayers of the rite of dedication.

Likewise, the General Instruction of the Roman Missal (the introduction to the sacramentary, the book that contains the prayers for Mass) provides a direction for design when it states, "The general plan of the sacred edifice should be such that in some way it conveys the image of the gathered assembly. It should also allow the participants to take the place most appropriate to them and assist all to carry out their individual functions properly" (257). The nature and the needs of the people who are to use the church, as well as the liturgy that they enact in it, are always the foremost consideration shaping the architecture.

The people who assemble in the church are a redeemed people, "bought at a great price," with the blood of Christ. They constitute a royal priesthood. But because they are a people still on pilgrimage, they still bear the marks of sin and, indeed, include within their number sinners. And they are a community whose members in some parts of the world are oppressed or persecuted. As followers of Christ, they recall that he lived in poverty and had "nowhere to lay his head" (Matthew 8:20). So if the building is going to act as a honest symbol of *this* people, there is no room for triumphalism in design. Rather, the building must take into account Christ's poverty and the Church's shortcomings.

Perhaps the word "poverty" is misleading. Poverty of design, poverty of materials and especially poverty of imagination will not produce any sort of sign, except in circumstances where nothing else can be obtained. The eucharistic celebration in the poor shack of an impoverished community is just as worthy as that celebrated in a grand cathedral. In such a circumstance, the rite itself and the devotion of the people must bear the whole weight of the symbolism, as has been done throughout the ages and still is done in many parts of the world.

AUTHENTICITY

Perhaps a better word to capture the tone or direction of church design is authenticity or genuineness. This goal is articulated in the 1978 document of the United States Bishops' Committee on the Liturgy, *Environment and Art in Catholic Worship:* "Our response must be one of depth and totality, of authenticity, genuineness, and care with respect to everything we use and do in liturgical celebration" (13).

Whatever is done must be as well done as possible, and whatever is used should always be genuine. For example, stone, of however humble a quality, must appear to be stone. This kind of authenticity and honesty is necessary if the Church is to be credible in this age of Hollywood special effects, political deception and entertainment-based culture.

Does this suggest that the rite of dedication favors multi-purpose church buildings as a solution to conflicting values? As the term has been understood in recent years, perhaps not; but the question of whether the only right way is to build a church exclusively for worship should continue to be asked. Should so much emphasis be put on a building that will only be used for a restricted number of hours in the week — buildings that cost a great deal of money to maintain and that by their design and provision serve no other purpose? It is a question that will, and must, continue to be raised.

A particular form of this concern was raised in November of 1987 when the Holy See issued a circular letter on "Concerts in Churches" (see "Concerts in Churches," dated November 5, 1987, Bishops' Committee on the Liturgy *Newsletter,* 24 [January 1988]: 97–100). This letter to bishops provides "some observations and interpretations" about the character and purpose of churches and the use of churches for various kinds of music. The document states that, "according to tradition as expressed in the *Rite* [*for the*] *Dedication of a Church and an Altar,* churches are primarily places where the people of God gather. . . . [C]hurches, however, cannot be considered simply as public places for any kind of meeting. They are sacred places, that is, 'set apart' in a permanent way for Divine Worship by their dedication and blessing" (5).

The letter goes on to say that "as visible constructions, churches are signs of the pilgrim Church on earth; they are images that proclaim the heavenly Jerusalem, places in which are actualized the mystery of the communion between [human beings] and God. . . . It remains a sacred place, even when no liturgical celebration is taking place" (5). In a world filled with noise, especially in urban areas, churches are often an "oasis" where people can gather in silence and prayer, to "seek peace of soul and the light of faith" (5). The letter warns that "when churches are used for ends other than those for which they were built, their role as a sign of the Christian mystery is put at risk, with more or less serious harm to the teaching of the faith and to the sensitivity of the People of God, according to the Lord's words: 'My house is a house of prayer' (Luke 19:46)" (5). (For more on this letter, see John Huels, "Canonical Comments on Concerts in Churches," *Worship* [March 1988]: 165–172; and *Pastoral Music* [April–May 1988] devoted to the letter.)

With careful planning, the church building could be made more a center of life and not merely of one part, however important, of life, namely worship. It should not be impossible to suggest something of the transcendence of God by the shape and arrangement of the church building and the immanence of God by the accommodation, integrated into the whole, that it provides for the needs of the human

The rite envisions that the procession of all into the building is the first time that the parish has come inside the new church — a ritual first entry encouraging surprise and wonder. "Let us go rejoicing to the house of God!"

community in whom God is present. Is this not what the New Testament suggests in its understanding of the Christian people as the new temple? (See, for example, 1 Corinthians 3:6 – 9, 2 Corinthians 6:16, Ephesians 2:19 – 22 and 1 Peter 2:4 – 9.)

One inference we can draw from the prayer of dedication is that, if the church building is to symbolize the Church in its richness and diversity, its design will have to be a great deal more varied than church designs have been in the past.

An additional factor raises the same question: the mobility of people. The vast number of urban churches built in another age to serve large Catholic populations whose descendants have now moved to other areas should serve as motivation for carefully thinking through what kind of building is needed and where it will be placed.

The reason that multi-purpose church buildings have been regarded so negatively in the past is because they did not adequately embody the rich symbol of the Church as articulated in the prayer of dedication, for example. They were often drab buildings where formal worship seemed to be an occasional, secondary and even casual event. But as with any church building, the result depends on the quality of design and construction. A multi-purpose church building need not be an ugly or inadequate one. If it has the marks of transitoriness, it will be a symbol of the pilgrim people of which the rite speaks. It will reflect the fact that God's chosen people worshiped in a tent during their desert sojourn. It will remind us that even when, at last, the chosen people had a magnificent and more permanent Temple in which to worship, the furnishings were mostly movable, so that they could once again move on if necessary. Our early Christian history shows that our ancestors worshiped in homes, and later, places of worship were set up in vast public buildings that were given to them, buildings that had known other uses.

Again, it must be said that no building, whether a conventional church or a multipurpose one, can be a wholly adequate symbol of the Church. What message a particular building conveys will be determined by the community in collaboration with the architect and artists, and will reflect their understanding of Catholic worship.

BUILDING FOR WORSHIP

Worship is the response to the transcendent God who is Emmanuel, "God is with us." Worship is the response of that redeemed people who, in one way or another, bear the marks of the crucified Christ. Worship is the embodied response of the Christian people whom God has approached through the embodiment of Christ, who became human that we might become divine. The building is simply the embodiment or incarnation of that people who give an embodied or sacramental worship to the Father, through the Son, in the Spirit. Worship is the expression of the love that the redeemed people have for one another. That love must be expressed if they are to manifest the love of God that is poured into human hearts by the Holy Spirit. Of this, too, the building must be the sign and symbol.

The General Instruction of the Roman Missal rightly emphasizes the symbolic function of the church building:

> For the celebration of the eucharist, the people of God normally assemble in a church or, if there is none, in some other fitting place worthy of so great a mystery. Churches and other places of worship should therefore be suited to celebrating the liturgy and to ensuring the active participation of the faithful. Further, the places and requisites for worship should be truly worthy and beautiful, signs and symbols of heavenly realities. (253)

> The faithful should give due honor to the cathedral of their diocese and to their own church as symbols of the spiritual Church that their Christian vocation commits them to build up and extend (255).

And the deeper reality to which the church building as symbol points is the Church itself, the body of Christ assembled to worship. The General Instruction makes it clear:

> The people of God assembled at Mass possess an organic and hierarchical structure, expressed by the various ministries and actions for each part

of the celebration. The general plan of the sacred edifice should be such that in some way it conveys the image of the gathered assembly (257).

This is amplified in *Environment and Art in Catholic Worship:*

> To speak of environmental and artistic requirements in Catholic worship, we have to begin with ourselves — we who are the Church, the baptized, the initiated. (27)

> Among the symbols with which liturgy deals, none is more important than this assembly of believers. It is common to use the same name to speak of the building in which those persons worship, but that use is misleading. In the words of ancient Christians, the building used for worship is called *domus ecclesiae*, the house of the church. (28)

TRANSCENDENCE AND IMMANENCE

It is possible to discern in these instructions the delicate balance between transcendence and immanence that the Christian church should suggest. If the basic design of the building truly embraces the people for whom it is intended, it will suggest that they are the community of faith bonded in Christ. If the same building, through the articulation of its various parts, is to accommodate the different functions of the celebrants who together make *leitourgia* (the work of the people), it will at the same time suggest the various roles in the Christian assembly. If all this can be oriented to the altar, which should be the natural focus of attention of the assembly (see the General Instruction of the Roman Missal, 262), then the building will have begun to symbolize the Church as the community that is gathered by Christ and directed toward something beyond itself. The place itself will proclaim God-with-us as well as God-yet-to-come.

Making Holy the Place
Evolution and Overview of Rites of Dedication

Christians hold many sorts of places sacred, including cities, geographical territories, shrines and churches. Some of these are places where miracles are believed to have taken place. Most are actual geographical locations — Jerusalem, Rome, Lourdes or a local church or shrine. But some belong to the realm of belief and hope, and must be imagined. It is very easy to discuss sacred places that can be located on ancient or modern maps, but much more difficult to talk about those places that we cannot visit literally. The Garden of Eden and heaven are two obvious examples.

IDEAL SACRED PLACES
When Christians talk about these places we use language in a special way, often without realizing it. When that language happens to be from the scriptures, some hold a literal interpretation while others see the scriptures as poetic, metaphorical or theological expressions of belief. This approach, of course, is not new to Christianity. Saint Augustine, in the 5th century, devoted an entire chapter of his remarkable work, *The City of God,* to the question of whether the Garden of Eden stories in Genesis should be interpreted in allegorical terms or in a more literal sense to refer to a real place. He concluded that it was perfectly acceptable to use the stories to derive additional meanings, "provided that the history of the true and local paradise be firmly believed" (see book 13, chapter 21). Augustine was happy with the idea that Eden could represent the bliss of the saints or could stand for the Church itself, or that the four rivers flowing from Eden could be seen as the four gospels, but whatever else was said, he believed that Eden was an actual place where actual people lived. Thus he understood the original sacred place in both literal and metaphoric terms.

JERUSALEM
One of the best examples of this literal and metaphorical interpretation of sacred places is Jerusalem, a city that appears in the Bible as the capital of Judah and the site of the Temple — the ultimate holy place of the Jews. As such, it plays an important part in the history underlying the scriptures and the account of God leading the Jews into the land divinely promised to them: Zion. In the sixth century before Christ, Jerusalem fell to the Chaldeans and many of its citizens were deported to Babylon. Psalm 137 expresses the hopelessness of the exiles in Babylon:

By the rivers of Babylon —
   there we sat down and there
   we wept
   when we remembered Zion.
On the willows there
   we hung our harps.
For there our captors
   asked us for songs,
and our tormentors asked for
   mirth, saying,
   "Sing us one of the songs
of Zion!"

They ask, miserably, "How could we sing the Lord's song in a foreign land?" In this poignant psalm Babylon symbolizes alienation from the sacred place of Jerusalem. After the Exile, Jerusalem was rebuilt, and its second Temple served as an important center for worship and a focus of Israel's identity. Yet further political disaster led to this Temple being profaned in the second century before the common era. The third Temple was established in the generation before Jesus

The bishop anoints the altar with chrism, first pouring the sacred oil onto the mensa, then rubbing it in. The altar now stands in our midst as a sign of Christ, the Anointed One.

and plays a significant part in the New Testament accounts of his life. This Temple was destroyed by the Romans in 70 CE, an event that marked the end of any centralized Jewish sacrificial worship. To this day the Western or "Wailing" Wall, all that remains of Solomon's Temple, serves as a sacred place for prayer and lamentation over the downfall of Israel's Temples. The site of the last Temple is now partly covered by the Dome of the Rock, a sacred place for Muslims, who believe that it covers the rock from which Muhammad ascended to heaven.

The idea of a heavenly Jerusalem in Christian thought offers a dramatic example of the way an actual place comes to function symbolically as an expression of faith and hope.

In the Book of Revelation, there is a vision of "a new heaven and a new earth," and of "the holy city, the new Jerusalem, coming down out of heaven from God" (Revelation 21: 1–2). This image united two ideas in previous scripture: the image of the sky as heaven (Genesis 1:8) and the abode of God (Ecclesiastes 5:2), and the image of Jerusalem as the earthly city where God dwelt in some symbolic way. By the first century of the common era, heaven was widely seen as the place where

God reigns and the faithful find their ultimate life (Matthew 5:12). Numerous other references occur in the New Testament (see, for one example, 2 Corinthians 12:2–4) and are perhaps best summarized in the opening words of the Lord's Prayer in the gospel of Matthew: "Our Father in heaven" (Matthew 6:9). The link between the Christian idea of heaven and the image of Jerusalem is one of the strongest indications that Christianity emerged out of Judaism. This link developed among later Christians to the point that heaven came to be viewed as an actual place into which people passed after death. This belief has been enshrined in many Christian liturgies, hymns and prayers over the centuries. In all these texts and hymns there is a kind of supernatural geography, a territory of faith, wherein believers see themselves as part of the great community of believers down the years all moving toward God's ultimate sacred place. On the way they encounter, are encouraged by and are nourished in local sacred places that help them to their goal.

EARLY CHRISTIAN PLACES

Christianity does not require a sacred building or place in which to worship. In fact, the first two centuries of Christianity show that the followers of Jesus had no particular places set aside for this purpose. Early Christians consciously resisted using the word "church" to refer to a building or the phrase "going to church" in the sense of going to a place. This can be seen in the writings of such people as Clement of Alexandria who wrote around the year 200: "It is not the place but the assembly I call the Church," and Hippolytus of Rome who wrote around 230: "It is not a place that is called Church nor a house made of stones and earth. What then is the Church? It is the assembly of those who live in righteousness."

Various references in the Acts of the Apostles, particularly Acts 20, indicate that the eucharist was celebrated in the homes of members of the Christian community. These were probably very small homes, though the house where Paul preached and celebrated the eucharist for a long time was a building of three stories, evidently of some size (see Acts 20:7–12). Celebrating the eucharist in ordinary homes lasted until the freedom of the Church in 313, though by then the "house church" was already well-organized. Well-known examples in Rome are the churches of St. John, St. Paul and St. Clement. In St. Clement there is the ancient house, the fourth-century church on top of it and over that again the twelfth-century basilica of today. The stories of early Christians gathering for the eucharist in the secluded confinement of the catacombs have been dispelled as unlikely by most historians. In the comparative safety of the second half of the third century, there were certainly fully constituted church buildings. One that has survived is at Dura Europos, on the banks of the Euphrates River, near present-day Baghdad.

THE FIRST SEVEN CENTURIES

The first recorded instance of the dedication of a Christian church edifice was documented by the historian Eusebius (*Ecclesiastical History, Book 10,* 3–5, translated by G.A. Williamson [New York: Penguin, 1965], 383–400). He describes the dedication of the basilica of Tyre in 314 under Constantine. The church was dedicated simply by the celebration of the eucharist, without any additional rituals. This festive occasion, with numerous bishops present, was an example of dedications that took place in the cities. Thus civil authorities recognized publicly the ecclesiastical use of a royal building (basilica).

Consecration by celebration of the eucharist remained the rite of dedication until the sixth century. Pope Vigilius (537–555) mentioned in a letter to Profuturus of Braga a sprinkling of the edifice with water, but he insisted that a church was to be considered dedicated once the eucharist had been celebrated in it. From his letter it appears that sprinkling the building with holy water was done in some places, perhaps in Rome itself. He also mentioned the depositing of relics in the church, a practice that had developed out of the custom of celebrating the eucharist over the tombs of martyrs. The first known instance of the use of relics was in Africa in 359, though this seems to have been a special case.

In Rome, so-called cemetery churches were held at the tombs of local martyrs whose memorial was being kept, the relics being buried under the altar along with a fragment of the True Cross, earth from "the Promised Land" and some sort of relics of Saints Peter and Paul (see L. Duchesne, *Origines du culte chrétien* [Paris, 1903 ed. 402, n. 1). Cemetery churches became places of popular pilgrimage, and buildings *(martyria)* were erected to accommodate the crowds. These often resembled the mausolea that pagans built to honor their dead. When the body of a martyr was not already within the building, there was the solemn "translation" of relics to the site. Such an example occurred in Milan in 386. Ambrose had previously dedicated a church with relics obtained from Rome. (The relics were almost certainly objects that had touched the tombs of the apostles and martyrs. The dismemberment of martyrs' bodies was at that time strictly forbidden.) It was evidently a popular move, and the people asked for a repetition of the ritual. Ambrose replied that he would provide one if he could find some martyrs' relics. The bodies of Saints Gervase and Protase were discovered, exhumed, and, after a vigil, transferred and buried in the new basilica. Ambrose wrote of all this in a letter to his sister, Marcellina. It is interesting that the ceremonies connected with the relics were the result of popular demand.

THE EIGHTH TO TENTH CENTURIES

In Rome, at this time, neither the use of holy water nor the burial of relics was regarded as essential, though relics were sometimes buried at the inaugural celebration of the eucharist. By the time of Pope Gregory the Great (590–604), a rite of exorcism by lustration (sprinkling) had become a standard practice, especially when dedicating former pagan temples. Gregory ordered Bishop Mellitus in England to exorcise with holy water churches that had been pagan temples. There seems to have been no fixed rite of dedication apart from the celebration of the eucharist in the sixth and seventh centuries. From the seventh century on, however, there was a fusion of rites. A Roman book, the Gelasian Sacramentary, seems to demonstrate a Gallican influence. There is a prayer of consecration, the blessing of water mixed with wine, the anointing of the altar with that mixture, the sprinkling of it seven times, the offering of burning incense on the altar and the prayer of blessing. There follows the blessing of the altar cloths, chalice and paten. A Mass of dedication, for which several texts are provided, concludes the service. Some have described this form of the rite as a funerary model, where the church is the mausoleum of a saint, the altar a tomb, the deposition of relics a burial and the Mass a funeral requiem.

What is more important than the details of the ritual is the change of emphasis. What was originally dedication by eucharist is now a series of preliminary rites prefacing the celebration of the eucharist. The prayer for the blessing of the altar asks that it may be blessed so that the offerings placed on it may be blessed, a complete reversal of the original practice where the offerings (the eucharist) blessed the altar. This is one source of the elaborate ceremonial that eventually surrounded the dedication of the altar.

The liturgy of dedication in Spain and Gaul, influenced by the Eastern liturgy and strong on symbolism, inspired by Old Testament sources, produced a Gallican form. By the end of the fifth century it had adopted from Constantinople the rite of anointing with chrism the "tomb" of the relics, that is, the altar, the doors and the walls of the church. The climax of the service was the anointing of the altar, rather than the burial of the relics beneath it. From the East, too, the Gallican Church took the rite of multiple incensations of the altar and of other parts of the building.

The service of dedication took this shape by the middle of the eighth century:

1. A vigil is kept with the relics of the martyrs on the eve of dedication.

2. The bishop strikes the door three times with the pastoral staff while all sing Psalm 24, followed by the entrance into the church.

3. The litany of the saints is sung.

4. The bishop traces two alphabets with his staff, one in Greek and one in Latin. (Though this was recorded for the first time in the ninth century, the practice is believed to be older. It may have come from the Celtic Churches, from the classical Roman practice of taking possession of a piece of land by marking out its boundaries. Or the Celts may have seen in the alphabet a certain symbolic and perhaps almost magical value.) The alphabets were traced in a St. Andrew's cross, suggesting a *chi rho* monogram written on the floor of the church to sanctify the foundation in the name of Christ.

5. "Gregorian water" (water mixed with salt and wine) is blessed, and the bishop makes a triple circumambulation, sprinkling the outside and inside walls of the building, and sprinkling the altar.

6. The prayer of consecration is said.

7. The altar and the walls of the church are anointed.

8. The altar cloths and liturgical vessels are blessed.

9. The relics are translated into the church: They are carried in procession and placed in the "tomb" of the altar along with particles of the eucharist and incense. During this time, a veil is drawn between the altar and the people so that all is done out of their view.

10. The lamps are lighted (the illumination rite).

11. The eucharist is celebrated.

It is clear that the rites had already become rather complicated, making use of some symbols that many no longer understand. Underlying this rite, however, was a line of thought that made sense of the multiplicity of ceremonies and texts. This was an initiatory model. The sprinklings of the floor and of the outside and inside of the church were a symbol of baptism, and the anointing of the door posts and the walls was a symbol of confirmation. The altar was clothed in white like a neophyte and given light. It was as if the building were being baptized and confirmed and readied to receive the body and blood of the Lord — the paschal sacraments. The funerary imagery — the relics of the martyrs and seeing the altar as a tomb — is likewise paschal.

The ritual and texts seem at first to be directed to the building, but they were in fact directed to the people. The final implication of the rite was that the people were being reconsecrated for worship in the new building. Nowhere was this more explicit than in the only gospel passage prescribed for the rite: "Today salvation has come to this house" (Luke 19:9). And the "house" is the "house of the Church."

THE FOURTEENTH CENTURY TO 1961

The Gallican rite described above, with certain additions, was incorporated into the pontifical that was revised in Germany in the tenth century and brought to Rome under the influence of the Ottonian emperors. It was a fusion of the funerary and initiatory models. This in turn was further elaborated by William Durandus, bishop of Mende (southern France) in the thirteenth century, and became substantially the service found in the Roman pontificals until the first revision of 1961. The elaboration of the rite can be seen in this synopsis:

1. There is a vigil, usually from the Office of Martyrs.

2. The next morning, the bishop, with ministers, servers and cantors, arrives at the west door of the church. The litany of the saints is sung while the bishop blesses water.

The bishop anoints the walls of the new building with chrism, assisted perhaps by priests or deacons. Four crosses on four walls (representing the cardinal directions) are anointed, or twelve crosses around the perimeter (representing the twelve apostles, the foundations of the New Jerusalem) are anointed.

3. The bishop goes around the church three times, sprinkling the upper and lower walls.

4. Each time, he returns to the door and strikes it with the foot of his pastoral staff, while verses of Psalm 24 are sung—the first two times without response from within the church building. The third time, a lone deacon in the otherwise empty church replies: "Who is the King of glory?" The bishop responds, "The Lord, who is virtuous, is the King of glory." Then the doors are opened.

5. The singing of the *Veni creator* (introduced by Durandus) follows and, for a second time, the litany of the saints.

6. The bishop traces the alphabet on the floor.

7. He blesses the Gregorian water, sometimes called "water of consecration," now consisting of water and small amounts of wine, salt and ashes. Then he sprinkles the walls of the church, going around the room three times, sprinkles the floor at the four directions of the compass and finally sprinkles the altar.

8. The prayer of dedication (as in the Gelasian sacramentary) is said.

9. The bishop and the ministers go to the place where the relics are exposed and bring them back in solemn procession after carrying them all around the outside of the church.

10. The "tomb" of the relics is prepared: It is anointed inside with chrism, the receptacle placed in it and the tomb sealed.

11. The bishop incenses the altar: the table, the base and the sides. When he has done this, he hands the censer to a priest, who continues to walk around the altar incensing it for the rest of the ceremony.

12. The bishop anoints the table of the altar three times, in five places: twice with the oil of catechumens (used in baptism), the third time with chrism (used in baptism and confirmation).

a. In the tenth century, the anointing of the mensa all over with chrism is added. In the thirteenth century, the chrism is mixed with oil of catechumens.

b. The anointing is eventually extended to the walls, which were marked in twelve places with chrism. In the thirteenth century, Durandus added this elaboration: candle-holders with candles are affixed to these places.

13. Incense is burned on the five places on the altar's mensa that were anointed: the center and four corners. Meanwhile, the bishop recites the formula of consecration.

14. Finally, the front of the altar is anointed (beginning in the twelfth century), and the four joints of the altar, where the table meets the supports, are also anointed (added by Durandus in the thirteenth century).

15. The altar cloths are blessed and the altar vested; the chalice and paten are then consecrated.

16. The Mass of dedication takes place.

This description omits most of the many chants and prayers that interpreted the rites.

The whole service was one of great complexity. The chants taxed the resources of even the most skilled musicians. The continual additions of rites and texts obscured the main line of the rite and prevented an intelligent understanding. All, of course, was said and sung in Latin, while the people watched; they were not even admitted into the church until a good deal of the rite was over. The whole service took an inordinate amount of time, and after three or four hours the consecrating prelate retired exhausted. According to the Roman Pontifical of 1888, he was to go to the sacristy where he would take off his cope. The rubric goes on to say that "if he wished to celebrate" the eucharist, he was to put on all the pontifical vestments, return to the altar and begin the Mass with the prayers at the foot of the altar as if nothing had happened previously (see Ignazio M. Calabuig, OSM, *The Dedication of a Church and an Altar: A Theological Commentary* [Washington: United States Catholic Conference, 1980] 33).

THE REFORM OF 1961

A revised and simplified rite of dedication was included in the reformed edition of Part Two of the Roman Pontifical, authorized by the Congregation of Rites on April 13, 1961. The revision divided the rite into four parts:

1. The lustration and taking possession.
2. The burial of the relics.
3. The consecration of the church and altar.
4. The Mass of dedication.

The lustration or sprinkling signified the expulsion of every evil power from the house of God, which is set aside for worship alone. The bishop stood before the locked and empty church and prayed to the Trinity. He commenced the lustration in front of the door, and proceeded around the edifice, sprinkling the walls with Gregorian water. Psalm 86 was sung during the procession and concluded with an oration. In response to the bishop's request that the door be opened, a deacon unlocked the door. Then followed the entrance into the church by the bishop, clergy and people. During the procession into the church, the litany of the saints was sung. The lustration of the interior of the church followed, and finally there was the lustration of the altar. The bishop then formally took possession of the church. With his crozier, he inscribed the Latin and Greek alphabets on the beam of a St. Andrew's cross that had been traced with sand or ashes on the floor of the presbyterium or nave. The rite of the alphabets was diminished to the area that the sand or ash cross covered — no longer the whole length of the building — and thus lost a great part of its significance. (Frederick R. McManus, who was a *peritus* at the Second Vatican Council and is familiar with the history of this revision, has said that the only reason this rite was kept was because Pope John XXIII said he liked it.) This was followed by a solemn prayer and a preface that spoke of the power of prayer in God's house.

The rite of the entombment of the relics consisted of a procession with the relics and their entombment in the altar, accompanied by various antiphons. The rite concluded with an oration.

At twelve places along the walls of the church that had been previously marked with consecration crosses, the bishop anointed the walls with sacred chrism. These crosses symbolize the twelve apostles, the foundation stones of the heavenly Jerusalem (an allusion to Revelation 21:14). When the bishop arrived at the church door, he anointed the door posts. Each of the consecration crosses on the walls was incensed and a candle was lighted before each. The consecration of the church concluded with an oration.

The consecration of the altar followed. The altar table and supports were anointed while Psalm 43 was sung. Then the altar was incensed and a symbolic sacrifice of incense was burned on it. The consecration of the altar was concluded by a solemn prayer and the consecrating preface of the dedication. While Psalm 95 was chanted, the altar was prepared for Mass. The Mass concluding the dedication was normally celebrated by the bishop himself, using the proper Mass for the dedication of a church.

Even though this 1961 revision simplified the rite, it remained burdened with centuries of development and ceremonial accretions that smothered the pastoral-liturgical fundamentals with a multitude of secondary symbols.

THE REFORM OF THE SECOND VATICAN COUNCIL

The liturgical reform begun before the Council and taken up as the Council's first order of business was certainly looking toward such rituals as the dedication of a church when the Council stated, "The rites should be marked by a noble simplicity;

they should be short, clear, and unencumbered by useless repetitions; they should be within the people's powers of comprehension and as a rule not require much explanation" (*Constitution on the Sacred Liturgy,* 34). The 1970 General Instruction of the Roman Missal states: "All churches are to be solemnly dedicated or at least blessed. But cathedral and parish churches are always to be dedicated" (255).

Thus, the *Constitution on the Sacred Liturgy* and the *Constitution on the Church,* and the reform of Church and worship that they helped bring about paved the way for a new rite of dedication that would confirm the ancient saying, "The rule of praying establishes the rule of believing."

The Rite Reformed
The 1977 Rite of Dedication of a Church and an Altar

As we have seen, the first rite of dedication of a church was simply the celebration of the eucharist in the new building. In a sense, the revised rite of 1977 returns to this tradition. The most significant change is that the whole rite is now enclosed within the celebration of the eucharist. The entrance rite, rather than being a mystifying liturgy before the liturgy, is simply a more solemn and significant beginning of the eucharist. The order of the Mass is followed: the Gloria, opening prayer and liturgy of the word are all in their familiar places. The rite of dedication itself takes place after the homily, the same point in the liturgy where baptism, ordination, marriage and other sacramental acts take place. It moves without a break into the celebration of the eucharist, with the preface of the Mass referring to the dedication, and the inauguration of the blessed sacrament chapel taking place before the final blessing and dismissal. The eucharist is clearly the heart of the entire celebration. This fundamental change, more than any other that has preceded it since the earliest times, gives the rite a clear focus. At the same time, the rite is still somewhat elaborate, retaining from previous times some features that are seen only on the occasion of the dedication of a church.

HISTORY OF THE 1977 RITE

How was the new rite shaped? Ignazio Calabuig, osm, who guided much of the work, is the source of many of the insights that follow. Archbishop Annibale Bugnini, considered the architect of post-conciliar liturgical reform, has also provided insights in his liturgical memoirs.

On the feast of Pentecost, May 29, 1977, the *Rite for the Dedication of a Church and an Altar* was promulgated by decree of Cardinal James Knox, prefect of the Sacred Congregation for the Sacraments and Divine Worship. The document is part of *The Roman Pontifical* as revised by decree of the Second Vatican Council and published by the authority of Pope Paul VI.

The 1977 rite developed in two directions. It continued in part the reform of the pontifical, which had appeared in a revised edition in 1961, on the eve of the

The altar is then incensed as the bishop prays, "As this building is filled with fragrance, so may your Church fill the world with the fragrance of Christ."

Council. In Book II of that edition, the *Rite for the Dedication of a Church* had been carefully revised. Swiftly-moving events showed that the 1961 revision was no more than a first step toward a definitive reordering of the system.

The 1977 rite was part of the restoration and revision of all the Roman liturgical books. This task, promulgated originally by the Sacred Congregation of Rites working with the Consilium for Implementing the Constitution on the Sacred Liturgy, the Sacred Congregation for Divine Worship (as it was then called), and by the Sacred Congregation for the Sacraments and Divine Worship (as it is now called), began in 1968.

In May 1970, Study Group XXI was formed within the Congregation for Divine Worship and given the responsibility of restoring and revising the rites of Book II of the pontifical. Pierre Jounel of France was appointed relator, the one in charge of the group. Other members of the group included Ignazio Calabuig, OSM, of Spain, Andre Rose, OSB, of Belgium, Domenico Sartore of Italy as secretary, and Rosella Barbieri of Italy, a Latinist. Calabuig eventually became secretary of the group and was chiefly responsible for the new texts and the majority of the work accomplished (see Annibale Bugnini, *The Reform of the Liturgy 1948–1975* [Collegeville: Liturgical Press, 1990], 792–797).

A careful theological, historical and pastoral study had to be made in order to answer several questions. Which of the often venerable and impressive signs in the pontifical could be kept as still meaningful? What structure should the celebrations have? What new elements should be introduced? The most important decision was that the proper liturgical focus of the dedication is the celebration of the eucharist. The last point had to receive the greatest emphasis. Within the celebration of eucharist there would be a discreet presence of the traditional elements of the rite: sprinkling with holy water, honoring with incense and lighting the building with candles.

The effort of the committee concluded with a proposal for the revision of book II, which was approved by the plenary session of the Sacred Congregation in March 1972. The proofs of the draft manuscript appeared the following spring and were sent for response to conferences of bishops, centers for liturgical studies and liturgical experts. After many insistent requests, the rite for the dedication of a church was sent to many bishops for experimental use. Perhaps the first use of the provisional rite in the United States was on July 25, 1976, when Edmund Szoka, then first bishop of the diocese of Gaylord, dedicated the newly built Cathedral of St. Mary in Gaylord, Michigan. Archbishop Jean Jadot, then apostolic delegate to the United States, provided him with the rite. The provisional rite enabled a celebration marked by the full, conscious and active participation of the whole Christian community because it displayed the same simplicity as the other rites reformed by Vatican II.

The Content of the Provisional Rite

The provisional rite contained an introduction and the following rites:

    I. A rite for laying the cornerstone or beginning work on the construction of a church.

    II. A rite for the dedication of a church.

    III. A rite for the dedication of an altar.

    IV. A rite for the blessing of a church

    V. A rite for the blessing of a movable altar.

    VI. A rite of inauguration of a place intended for liturgical celebrations and other uses.

    VII. A rite for the blessing of a chalice and paten.

    VIII. A rite for the blessing of a new cross to be displayed for the veneration of the faithful.

    IX. A rite for the blessing of a bell.

    X. A rite for the blessing of a cemetery.

    XI. A rite for public supplication when a church has been the place of a serious offense.

    XII. A rite for the crowning of a statue of the Blessed Virgin Mary.

As a result of the responses of the liturgical experts and others who had received copies of the draft, the texts were revised once more, and some additions were made. Two of these should be noted:

1. Many cases were cited in which a church was dedicated after it had already been in use for a period of time (sometimes years) because of necessity or some other reason, or in which old churches were inaugurated again after a complete restoration. It was asked that suitable celebrations be provided for these occasions. The study group therefore prepared a "rite for the dedication of a church already in general use for sacred celebrations."

2. Others saw benefit in having a rite for the inauguration of a baptistry, since this plays an important part in the life of a Christian community.

After these additions, the new rites were studied by the various curial agencies, especially the Congregation for the Doctrine of the Faith (which examined the entire set of rites) and the Secretariats for Christian Unity and for Non-Christians, which took under consideration the not unusual situation in which one place of worship is used by various Christian confessions or is even shared by Christians and non-Christians. That situation seemed to call for doctrinal, pastoral and liturgical clarification.

Agreement was reached on all points. The Congregation for Divine Worship sent confidential copies of the entire work to the international translation committees, so that they might begin their work while the Latin original was making its way through the publication process. The final printer's proofs were just ready to be sent to the pope for his definitive approval when the Congregation for Divine Worship was suddenly suppressed as part of a curial reform.

Two years passed. Nothing further was heard of the work. Then, by a decree dated May 29, 1977, the Congregations for the Sacraments and Divine Worship published a part of the complete work: the rites for laying the cornerstone of a church, for the dedication and blessing of a church and an altar, and for the blessing of a chalice and paten, or chapters I–V and VII of the list above, along with the first addition. No one knows why these parts were chosen for publication. The other items eventually found their way into the new *Book of Blessings* or were published separately (such as the *Order for the Crowning of an Image of the Blessed Virgin Mary*).

The introduction to the rite, especially the doctrinal part that explains the meaning of the dedication of a church and an altar, was, according to Bugnini, "seriously mutilated, at times in a clumsy way" (795). According to Calabuig, "The doctrinal element, in this particular case, is not formally developed at length. Rather than confine it to the necessary tight forms of the introductions, the editors decided to let the rich theological content of the texts speak for itself" (Ignazio M. Calabuig, OSM, *The Dedication of a Church and an Altar: A Theological Commentary* [Washington: United States Catholic Conference, 1980], 5).

After the altar is incensed, the whole room is incensed by assisting ministers: "From the hand of the angel, clouds of incense rose in the presence of the Lord."

The renewal of the rite is not a concession to changing fashions, but a recognition and discernment of authentic and legitimate ecclesial needs. Furthermore, the renewed rite is able to incorporate into the ancient structure of the Roman liturgy the valid contributions of other cultures. The renewed rite allows the dedication to be celebrated with the full understanding and participation of the Christian community; it displays the same simplicity of ritual that marks the other reformed liturgical actions. The way in which particular problems were solved, as well as the animating spirit of the work, make clear the criteria for renewing the rite of dedication.

CRITERIA FOR THE RENEWAL

The dedication of a church, like baptism and confirmation, is a rite that is enacted but once. And just as rites of initiation make or attest to essential phases in Christian life, so the dedication of a church points to a unique and characteristic moment in the life of a local Church. A Church may exist without literal and physical walls. Christ is the reason for its existence, and the Holy Spirit is the wellspring of its life. Yet, since the pilgrim Church on earth cannot exist outside the limits of space and time, it usually erects buildings that are the visible counterparts of the invisible "house of God" (1 Corinthians 3:9), the place where the faithful meet in their worship or in holy assembly.

The dedication of a church, consequently, is the occasion for joy in the completion of a work that required effort, sacrifice and unremitting toil. The dedication of a church also provides the opportunity for the local Church to see itself as the true "temple of God," to renew its obligation to be built up as the Church and to increase its membership, its "living stones." In building itself in the midst of other buildings in the temporal city, the Church can ponder the meaning of its presence in the world, the value of its services to humanity.

The *Rite of Dedication of a Church and an Altar* can contribute much to this end, provided the pastoral preparation is adequate, and provided the liturgy is understood and celebrated in all its eloquence and straightforwardness. Architects and artists, parish planning groups, clergy and all who are involved in the process that will lead to a new or renewed church building need to

After the altar candles are lit for the first time, candles at the crosses on the spots where the walls were anointed are lit for the first time: "Light of Christ, shine forth in the Church!"

become intimately familiar with the rite and its texts from the very beginning of the planning. Planning sessions should include a generous time for prayer, making use of scriptural and liturgical texts drawn from the rite. The celebration of the rite should never be merely tacked on at the end of the process, but should be at the heart of the process from its inception. Only when this awareness is a pastoral priority will the rite, in all its richness, speak to the entire community that knows itself as Church while it shapes for itself a place we also call church.

Initiating the Church's House
Studying and Preparing to Celebrate the Rite

The *Rite of Dedication of a Church,* like all the rituals that have been reformed since the Second Vatican Council, includes a pastoral introduction as a preface to the rite itself. The introduction and the directives of the rite are discussed in detail in this chapter. The introduction and the rite together make up Chapter 2 of the *Rite of Dedication of a Church and an Altar.*

PASTORAL INTRODUCTION

The introduction is mostly concerned with the order of the rite and the preparations necessary for it. There are seven divisions in the introduction, as follows:

Nature and Dignity of Churches
Titular of a Church and the Relics of the Saints to be Placed in it
Celebration of the Dedication
> Minister of the Rite
> Choice of Day
> Mass of Dedication
> Office of the Dedication
> Parts of the Rite

Adaptation of the Rite
> Adaptation within the Competence of the Conferences of Bishops
> Decisions within the Competence of the Ministers

Pastoral Preparation
Requisites for the Dedication of a Church
Anniversary of the Dedication
> Anniversary of the Dedication of the Cathedral Church
> Anniversary of the Dedication of a Particular Church

Nature and Dignity of Churches (paragraphs 1–3)

These three paragraphs summarize the purpose of a church building in a theological framework. The nature of a church building "demands that it be suited to sacred celebrations, dignified, evincing a noble beauty, not mere costly display, and it should stand as a sign and symbol of heavenly realities" (3). The norms of the General Instruction of the Roman Missal and of the celebration of the sacraments, especially baptism and penance, are to be taken into account in the planning of churches. The implication is that the physical requirements of celebrations such as those of Holy Week (for example, processions, and beginning or ending the liturgy in another space) and the Triduum (for example, the blessing of the new fire, a font for the immersion of the elect) should be taken into account when planning for a new church building. This will prevent later difficulties that could have been avoided from the start.

The Titular of a Church and the Relics (paragraphs 4 – 5)

The instruction here is the same as in the 1961 rite except that now a church may have only one title, unless the dedication is under the invocation of saints who are always linked in the calendar (for example, Saints Peter and Paul). A church may not be named for a *beatus,* a person who has been beatified but not yet canonized, without an indult from the Holy See. Dedications to a divine person coupled with a saint or saints are no longer allowed.

Canon 1218 of the Code of Canon Law states: "Each church is to have its title which cannot be changed after its dedication." This canon would seem to refer as well to churches that are only blessed rather than dedicated (see *The Code of Canon Law: A Text and Commentary* [New York: Paulist Press, 1985], 848 – 849).

Parishes today are much more involved in the selection of a name or title for a church than in the past. It seems to be a common practice to select several possibilities which are then submitted to the bishop for final determination or confirmation. The choice of a name for a church can be an occasion for growth in understanding of the titles of Christ, Mary, the apostles and the witness of the martyrs and saints. Research, particularly into the lives of the saints, can be a deeply enriching experience for the members of a community. Ecumenical consultation can also be a means of fostering church unity and common witness.

A discussion of the relics to be placed in the altar of the church may be found below, beginning on page 44.

Celebration of the Dedication (paragraphs 6 –17)

Minister of the Rite

It is fitting that the bishop who is the ordinary of the diocese, as shepherd of the local Church, dedicates churches in the diocese and presides at the celebration. If the bishop is unable to preside, an auxiliary bishop of the diocese or another bishop may preside. Paragraph 6, as well as Canon 1206 of the Code of Canon Law, indicates that a bishop may commission, "in altogether special circumstances," a priest to preside at the dedication.

The whole of the rite is a concelebration of ministries, involving readers, cantors, musicians, deacons and priests united with the bishop, who presides over all. The assembly has its role, and from the assembly come representatives who will hand over the church to the bishop and others who will present the gifts at the altar for the eucharist. It is a common practice to invite ministers and members of neighboring local churches or faith communities to participate in the celebration as well.

The directives indicate that the priests who will concelebrate in the rite should be chosen from those who are associated with the bishop and those who have the pastoral care of "the parish or the community for which the church has been built" (9).

Choice of Day

The day chosen for the dedication should be a day when "as many of the people as possible can participate" (7), preferably a Sunday. Dedications, however, ought not coincide with the great feasts of the Church, such as the Easter Triduum, Christmas, Epiphany, Ascension, Pentecost, Ash Wednesday, the weekdays of Holy Week, and All Souls. Many of these days are already solemnities, and the "day on which a church is dedicated is kept as a solemnity" in that church thereafter (10).

Mass of Dedication and Office of the Dedication

The rite of dedication has its own texts (see the Common for the Dedication of a Church in both the lectionary and sacramentary), which are always to be used. The rite is inseparably bound up with the eucharist — a single, continuous celebration — and the texts proper to the rite should be used (8).

The *Liturgy of the Hours* provides a celebration of a "Common of the Dedication of a Church," beginning with Evening Prayer I. When there is a rite of the deposition of relics, a vigil consisting of the Office of Readings, in accordance with the instruction of the *Liturgy of the Hours* (70–73), should be celebrated.

Carefully review all the texts that may be used, and include them as part of the prayers with the planning process that will lead to a new church building.

The rite of dedication no longer requires fasting in preparation for the dedication, but that does not mean a fast may not be observed or encouraged. Some communities keep vigil with fasting, leading to first vespers or the Office of Readings. There may also be concerts, dances, plays, contests, parades, fireworks and festivals to celebrate the dedication in the days or weeks surrounding the event.

Perhaps we might draw upon some of the wisdom we have gained from our experience with the Rite of Christian Initiation of Adults about the journey toward the day of initiation. There is a separation from the past: leaving the old place of worship. There is a time of ordeal: worshiping in a hall while waiting for the new or existing church to be finished — that is a kind of fasting! There is rebirth: a new font to wash in, a new door to walk through, a new name to call the church by, new furniture to sit on, the smell of flowers, fragrant incense, candle wax. Lights go on, the place is "enlightened" and we become beacons to the world. There is food and drink and joy. Attentive preparation should be made for to the days surrounding the dedication itself, and other times of gathering and festivity. Thought should be directed to the whole spirit of the occasion.

Parts of the Rite (paragraphs 11–17)
See the detailed examination of the elements of the rite later in this chapter, beginning on page 38.

Adaptation of the Rite (paragraphs 18–19)

As in most of the other reformed rites, provision is made for adaptation "to the character of each region" in the celebration of the rite of dedication. The instruction directs that two particular points be observed: First, that the celebration of the eucharist with its "proper preface and prayer for a dedication must never be omitted" and second, that rites with "a special meaning and force from liturgical tradition be retained, unless weighty reasons stand in the way, but the wording may be suitably adapted if necessary" (18).

Various choices and options are left to the discretion of the bishop and the local community, including the ritual form of the entrance into the church, the manner of handing over the new church to the bishop and the decision whether to include the depositing of relics of the saints.

In June 1990, this author conducted an informal survey of 25 liturgical consultants listed in the Federation of Diocesan Liturgical Commissions *Liturgical Consultants' Directory*. One of the questions asked was, "What, in your view and experience, areas of the rite need adaptation?" Among the suggestions made by the liturgical consultants were these:

First, the name of the rite needs to be reconsidered. The name, "Rite of Dedication of a Church and an Altar," may emphasize the altar in a way that recalls a pre–Vatican II notion of the altar as a ritual object that unified word and eucharist, and also as the place where the eucharist was both confected and stored. The altar at one time had its "epistle side" and "gospel side," in addition to being the table of the eucharist. That is no longer the case today. The ambo and altar are separate furnishings and symbols, where the power and mystery of word and sacrament are celebrated in related but distinct ways. Due to a pastoral need to acknowledge the importance of the ambo, the name of the rite of dedication needs to be expanded. There is precedence for this in the renaming of the rites of anointing — now called the Pastoral Care of the Sick, and of funerals — now called the Order of Christian Funerals.

Second, some furnishings that have taken on new or renewed prominence in our worship spaces need some form of ritual recognition. These would include the font, the repository for the holy oils, the reconciliation and weekday chapels, and the organ and other musical instruments. Blessings for some of these are provided in the *Book of Blessings* and the American additions to that book. But these are better suited for other circumstances than the dedication of a new or renovated building. How can we include a better recognition of these elements at the time of dedication, to avoid a disjointed multiplication of blessings once again?

Third, the rite makes no adequate provision for churches that have been renovated. Even though such spaces were previously dedicated, the drastic changes that sometimes take place seem to call for a ritual that celebrates this newness and change. We need to provide a form with a variety of options that will meet this ongoing need.

Finally, our use of the rite and our adaptations of it need to be more attentive to the basic anthropological and non-verbal elements connected with the story of dedicating a place for access to the Other who is essential to life. There is a fine line here. We may be tempted to explain everything away with needless commentary. Does the rite speak for itself? What is the difference between instruction and story? These things need careful and loving attention in view of our almost twenty years of experience with the rite.

Pastoral Preparation (paragraph 20)
This brief section is as important as any of the others in the introduction. The rite of dedication is a complex rite, celebrated rarely. Most people will experience it only once in their lives. Therefore, it is right and necessary to prepare the people for the celebration. Echoing the often-quoted directive of the *Constitution on the Sacred Liturgy* that liturgy requires participation that is full, conscious and active, paragraph 20 states that the people "are to be instructed" so that "they may take an active, intelligent and devout part" in the dedication.

The subject matter of the preparation in general is to be the "spiritual, ecclesial, and missionary power" of the rite (20). Clearly, it is to be related first to the spiritual life of the participants. Second, the vision of the Church expressed in the rite should be shared with the community by every means possible during the building process in order to assist everyone in grasping the nature of the Church of which we are members. Finally, the missionary dimension to which the introduction refers is most important. It is one more sign that the rite has people foremost in mind, people who are to be dedicated or rededicated to the vocation that is theirs by baptism and confirmation — the vocation of spreading the gospel.

Some communities have exemplified this missionary dimension by setting aside a tithe or portion of their building fundraising for works of social justice. A portion of the collection on the day of dedication could be earmarked for works of mercy. There are many ways of embodying this value.

The process of preparing the community should also include catechesis on the church building itself and the meaning and use of its different parts. As the rite makes clear, the church has many purposes. As well as being the place of the celebration of the eucharist, it is the place of teaching, the place of baptizing, the place of prayer (both public and private) and the place where people assemble as society and as the people of God. Although in many places churches are no longer the focal points of community life that they once were, they still serve important needs, especially in inner-city and rural areas. This is another illustration of the missionary dimension of the rite.

In the instruction or formation process, the rites, texts and symbols of the whole service should be made familiar to people. The biblical basis of the symbols (oil and anointing, light, incense) should be brought out in their richness and fullness so that their significance will be experienced and appreciated in the service. Early in the process of planning and building, the community should learn the hymns and songs that will be used in the dedication rite. The people should know why particular psalms are used on this occasion.

It would be easy to make all this instruction or formation a cerebral experience. We could satisfy ourselves by giving a few explanations and distributing a few leaflets. But it is better to use the many means available to help the members of the community see, hear, touch, taste and smell the stuff of the rite, to feel truly connected to it. Many people have never touched an altar, have never smelled chrism or know what incense is made of. We can counter the functionalism and minimalism of our age, and bring to the people the fullness and richness of our Christian signs and symbols.

Who is to give this instruction and when is it to be given? Formation should be part of the church building process from the start, carefully organized and well prepared. The architect and artists, the liturgical consultant, the pastor, clergy and parish staff members, members of the pastoral council and building committee, and perhaps members of the diocesan liturgical commission or liturgy office may all participate. Members of the community who work in fields such as communications and the arts, advertising and education can contribute to a practical plan to assist the whole of the community in its learning experience. Some parishes have had a retreat or a mission for this purpose, using the texts and music of the rite as part of the prayer.

Requisites for the Dedication of a Church (paragraphs 21–25)

This section lists the furnishings and appointments needed for the celebration of the rite. Well in advance, look over the inventory provided (21–24). Budget for these needs from the beginning. Pay close attention to the quality and appropriateness of the objects necessary for the ritual. Engage artisans in the community to provide handsome, well-made vessels for sprinkling, anointing, incensing and communion. Weavers and fabric artists should become familiar with the new space in order to provide appropriate hangings, coverings and vesture. Consult florists for the appropriate placement of flowers and plants throughout the space at different times and seasons. What kind of bread and wine will be presented and offered? Are the liturgical books in good condition, particularly the lectionary? Give careful attention to the dedication crosses and candles so that they are well-made and complement the architecture and design of the building (22).

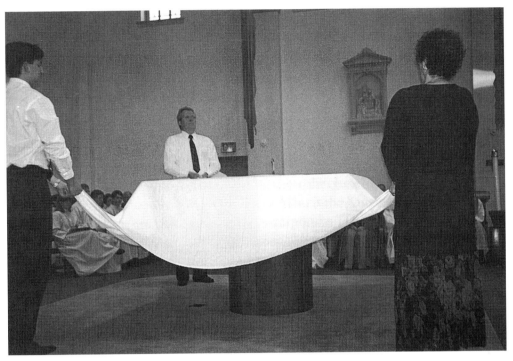

The altar is dressed for the sacrificial supper, robed in fine linen after having been washed with water, anointed with chrism and surrounded with candles.

The dedication of a church is a historic event in a parish or community. An appropriate record of the event should be made (25; see also Canons 1208 and 1209 of the Code of Canon Law). Two copies of the record of the dedication of the church are to be made, both signed by the bishop, the rector of the church and representatives of the community. One copy is to be kept in the diocesan archives and the other in the archives of the newly dedicated church.

When there is a deposition of relics under the altar, a third copy is to be included in the vessel containing the relics. This document should record the year, month and day of dedication, the name of the bishop who celebrated the rite, the title of the church and, if necessary, the names of the martyrs or saints whose relics are placed under the altar.

In the church itself there should be a visible inscription in some convenient place bearing the date of the event, the title of the church and the name of the bishop who celebrated the rite.

Anniversary of the Dedication (paragraphs 26 – 27)

The instruction notes that the anniversary of the dedication of the diocesan cathedral is to be observed as a solemnity in the cathedral itself and as a feast in the other churches of the diocese. If it is not always possible to observe this particular date, the celebration may take place on the nearest date possible. The importance of this

HOLY PEOPLE, HOLY PLACE

celebration is further brought out when the bishop concelebrates the eucharist with the priests' council and local clergy and with the participation of as many of the people as possible.

The anniversary of a church's dedication is celebrated as a solemnity in that parish.

For directives on the observance of both anniversaries, see the General Norms for the Liturgical Year and the Calendar. Chapter 5 of this book will also offer suggestions for celebrating the anniversary of the dedication.

THE STRUCTURE OF THE RITE

The rite of dedication of a church is divided into five parts. The arrangement of these parts is familiar, since it reflects the order of other rituals that are celebrated within the eucharist.

Introductory Rites
    Entrance into the Church
        First Form: Procession
        Second Form: Solemn Entrance
        Third Form: Simple Entrance
    Blessing and Sprinkling of Water
    Hymn
    Opening Prayer
Liturgy of the Word
Prayer of Dedication and the Anointings
    Invitation to Prayer
    Litany of the Saints
    Depositing of the Relics
    Prayer of Dedication
    Anointing of the Altar and the Walls of the Church
    Incensation of the Altar and the Church
    Lighting of the Altar and the Church
Liturgy of the Eucharist
    Prayer over the Gifts
    Eucharistic Prayer
    Inauguration of the Blessed Sacrament Chapel
    Prayer after Communion
    Blessing and Dismissal

Introductory Rites

Entrance into the Church

The rich symbolism of the entrance into the new church should not be underestimated or ignored for the sake of convenience. The people assemble in a neighboring

38

church building or in another suitable place. The door of the church to be dedicated is closed. If the depositing of relics is to take place, the vessel containing the relics is in the place where the people are assembling.

The bishop and concelebrants proceed to the place where the people are. The bishop greets the assembly and offers a few words on the meaning of the rite and the nature of the church. The bishop might say something like the following:

> The new church, which is to be dedicated by the celebration of the eucharist, is where the Christian community hears the word of God, where its members are reborn in the waters of baptism and fed from the table of the Lord. They are the real temple of God, who, by word and sacraments, are to grow and become the temple of the Holy Spirit. The dedication of a church is a celebration of the people of God and of what they are and may become if they receive God's word into their hearts and nourish their lives on the body and blood of Christ.

The procession of ministers, concelebrants (with the relics and lighted candles), bishop and people to the new church is accompanied by the singing of Psalm 122 ("Let us go rejoicing to the house of the Lord"). The psalm is a pilgrimage song, as if the pilgrims had caught sight of the city and burst into song: "Jerusalem — built as a city that is bound firmly together. To it the tribes go up, the tribes of the Lord." This is appropriate, because the new church is a local realization of the new Jerusalem (see chapter 2 of this book). Another appropriate song may be sung, but whatever is chosen will likely need to be in a responsorial format, between cantor or musicians and the assembly, in order to facilitate singing and movement and to avoid dependence on a printed text.

In preparation for this part of the rite, people should be brought to an understanding of procession: Not only is it a purposeful moving from one place to another, it is a "prayer of the feet."

Handing Over the Building

When the procession arrives at the closed door of the new church, representatives of those who have been involved in the building of the church hand over the building to the bishop. The delegates may include all or some of the following people: members of the parish, parish pastoral council, contributors, building and planning committee members, architect, liturgical consultant and workers. This handing over may be represented in various ways. The delegates may hand over one or all of the following to the bishop:

1. The legal documents giving possession
2. The keys of the church
3. A model of the church

4. A record of the work showing how it developed, with the names of those who have promoted and presided over the building, as well as the names of the workers, craftspersons and artists.

One of the delegates may address the bishop and the community, perhaps pointing out what the new church signifies in its art and design.

While it is not necessary that all the above actions be part of the introductory rites, the handing over of the building by the community and those who have worked for it should certainly be included. This has much more than rubrical importance. It is an eloquent symbol of this church building as a sacramental sign of the one body made up of many parts, and of this parish as part of the larger Church.

After the ritual handing over, the bishop calls upon the priest to whom the pastoral care of the church has been entrusted to open the door of the church.

This replaces the elaborate and dramatic ritual of the former rite, although one element of it has been kept. Once the doors are open, the bishop invites the people to enter: "Go within his gates giving thanks, enter his courts with songs of praise." The hymn that follows is Psalm 24: "Lift high the ancient portals. The King of glory enters."

As in the past, this psalm has a message for the people who are the Church. If they would stand in the holy place, they must be pure of heart, they must "seek the face of the God of Jacob." Led by the crossbearer, all enter the new church.

The bishop then proceeds to the chair, without reverencing the altar, while the other ministers take their places around him and the relics are set in a suitable place in the sanctuary between lighted torches.

This is the ideal way that the *Rite of Dedication* envisions the entrance taking place. The rite provides for a variety of models based on local circumstances. If, for example, no other building is available in which to gather, the people may gather in front of the new church, with the bishop and ministers approaching the door from outside the church, and the handing over described above follows. If even a gathering outside the church is difficult or impossible, the rite takes place, with the necessary adjustments, within the church (chapter 2, 43 – 47).

Blessing and Sprinkling of Water

The next ritual element is one of renewal and purification. Ministers bring a vessel of water to the bishop, who blesses it. The bishop, with the deacon, then moves through the assembly, sprinkling the people and the walls of the church with the blessed water. During this action, the assembly joins in singing, "I saw water flowing from the right side of the temple, alleluia. It brought God's life and salvation, and the people sang in joyful praise: alleluia, alleluia." An alternate text is offered for Lent. Another appropriate song may also be sung.

The blessed water is a sign of repentance and new life. Just as at a Sunday eucharist, it replaces the penitential rite. It is also a renewal of baptism by which

Christians die with Christ, rise again with him and are made members of his body and co-heirs with him in the reign of God. The invitation to prayer and the prayer of blessing emphasize that the rite is concerned primarily with the people. The sprinkling with water is a sign of their repentance, a sign that they are being purified by God.

Several elements of this ritual action should be considered thoughtfully. Will the bishop alone sprinkle the assembly or will others (pastor, other priests and ministers) join him in sprinkling the assembly? What type of vessel will be used to hold the blessed water? Could fresh evergreen branches be used for the sprinkling? Could the blessing of water take place at the font, especially if it can be seen by the assembly? In the Episcopal Church's *Book of Common Prayer,* the "Dedication and Consecration of a Church" begins with blessing the font by celebrating baptism (if there are any to be baptized). Likewise, the Lutheran Church, in *Occasional Services: Companion to the Lutheran Book of Worship,* a dedication of the font takes place at the beginning of the "Dedication of a Church Building." Another thing to consider is how the community's catechumens and candidates might be acknowledged within this rite.

After the assembly and the walls of the church have been sprinkled, the bishop sprinkles the altar, returns to the chair and prays:

> May God, the Father of mercies,
> dwell in this house of prayer.
> May the grace of the Holy Spirit cleanse us,
> for we are the temple of his presence.

The introductory rites conclude with the sung Gloria and the opening prayer, which once again recalls the power of word and sacrament and prays that they will "strengthen the hearts of all the faithful."

Liturgy of the Word

The ambo is now dedicated by a significant action and by the word of God proclaimed from it for the first time. According to the directive (chapter 2, 53), two readers and a psalmist approach the bishop, one holding the lectionary. This is presented to the bishop, who holds it up, shows it to the people and says:

> May the word of God always be heard in this place,
> as it unfolds the mystery of Christ before you
> and achieves your salvation within the Church.

Then he hands the book to the first reader, and the readers and psalmist process to the ambo, holding up the lectionary for all to see.

This is a new and significant element in the rite. It is intended to emphasize the importance of the word, not only in the dedication of a church, but also in every eucharist and other rite that is ever celebrated in the church. God's word is the means of salvation. "Faith comes from what is heard," as Paul reminds us (Romans 10:17). The word reveals to us the mystery of Christ in his life, passion, death and resurrection. This element emphasizes in a dramatic way, the statement of the *Constitution on the Sacred Liturgy* that when the scriptures are read in church Christ is speaking to his people (7). This is consistent with a theology of the word that has been developing since before the Second Vatican Council: The proclamation of the word in the liturgy is experienced as a privileged moment when God's word is active and redemptive.

The ministry of the word follows the usual pattern, with one reading from the Old Testament, one from Acts, Revelation or the letters of the New Testament, and the gospel reading. Between these readings are the responsorial psalm and the gospel acclamation, which are to be sung. All the readings, except for the first, are to be chosen from among the passages designated in the lectionary (nos. 701–706) for the rite of dedication. The rite specifies that the first reading is always to be from the book of Nehemiah (8:1–4a, 5–6, 8–10).

In it, the people of Israel who have returned from captivity gather together and ask the scribe Ezra to take up the Book of the Law of Moses and read it to the assembly of men, women and children. When he has finished reading and the priests have finished interpreting the law, they tell the people: "This day is holy to our Lord; do not be grieved, for the joy of the Lord is your strength." Ezra tells them to go and eat, drink and give something to those in want. The passage concludes with the people going from the assembly "to make great rejoicing, because they had understood the words that were declared to them."

The general sense and appropriateness of this passage for the occasion are obvious. Biblical commentators agree that this event signified the birth of Judaism (it was at this time that the people began to be called Jews) which, in a sense, began with the rebuilding of the Temple and the city. In the reading from Nehemiah, it is solemnly inaugurated with the reading of the word of God.

So also for the new church now being dedicated. The Book of the Law was the book of teachings that laid out for the Jews the whole way of life that had come to them from God through the hands of Moses. So in the Church the scriptures give us the Christian way of life and, as the bishop said in his prayer, the word of God opens up the mystery of Christ and brings about salvation in the Church. No doubt these are the reasons the Church insists that this reading always be read. As the rite indicates in other places, the dedication of a church is, at its deepest level, a renewal of the people who receive the word of God into their hearts, like the Jews who on hearing the word cried out, "Amen, amen."

Note that in this reading, Ezra stands in a prominent place so that all may see him as he takes up the book; the day is the first day of the seventh month (that is,

New Year's day); because it is a day of renewal it is also a day of rejoicing; and finally, Ezra perhaps translated the scriptures from the Hebrew into Aramaic so that the people could understand what was read. These actions remind us of the bishop, who is the chief teacher in the diocese.

The selections for the second reading are not extensive. The readings are all concerned with the Christian people: "You are God's temple" (1 Corinthians 3:9 – 13, 16 –17); "You are members of the household of God . . . with Jesus Christ himself as the cornerstone" (Ephesians 2:19 – 22); "You have come to Mount Zion and to the city of the living God, the heavenly Jerusalem" (Hebrews 12:18 –19, 22 – 24); "Like living stones, let yourselves be built into a spiritual house" (1 Peter 2:4 – 9).

Four gospel passages are suggested: Matthew 5:23 – 24, Luke 19:1–10, John 2:13 – 22 and John 4:19 – 24. The passages from Luke 19 and John 4, in particular, underline that the rite is a celebration of Christ in his redeeming activity, for "today salvation has come to this house." The people are renewed by the saving power of the passion, death and resurrection of Christ. The passage from John 4 proclaims that true worshipers worship "in spirit and truth" and that the place of worship is of secondary importance. This recalls the teaching of Justin Martyr who said that God fills heaven and earth and the faithful worship and praise God everywhere. The passage from John 4 is a blunt reminder of the humility that is properly ours, especially when it is proclaimed in a new church building during the elaborate rite that dedicates it.

The instruction concerning the homily (chapter 2, 55) gives familiar directions: The homily should make use of the scripture texts and those of the liturgy to express the meaning of the rites. Given the length of the entire rite, a few well-chosen, heartfelt words will be enough to touch the people and lift them up.

The liturgy of the word ends with the proclamation of the Creed. There are no general intercessions, since these are included in the Litany of the Saints, which opens the prayer of dedication and anointings.

Planners need to consider several things so that the rite may be experienced in its fullness during the liturgy of the word. Since the directive (chapter 2, 54) indicates that neither incense nor lights are used at the reading of the gospel, will the gospel proclamation seem unimportant? What about the liturgical role of the deacon within this ritual element? Might a book of gospels be used in addition to the lectionary? Are both of these books dignified, well-bound and handsome?

Prayer of Dedication and the Anointings

Litany of the Saints

In the former rite, the dedication was a sort of lengthy prelude to the eucharist. The reformed rite proceeds from the ministry of the word, which illustrates all that is to follow. The Litany of the Saints is a more elaborate form of the general intercessions and serves as a bridge between the two parts of the rite.

The Litany of the Saints is prefaced with an invitation to prayer spoken by the bishop. The prayer recalls that the baptized are "faithful temples of the Spirit," and prays that all may join their voices with those of the saints.

A directive (chapter 2, 58) indicates that the litany is to be sung, with the assembly standing on Sundays and in the Easter season, and kneeling at other times. This custom preserves a practice going back to at least the second century. The deacon invites all to kneel for the litany when it is appropriate.

The text of the litany is familiar, especially if one has participated in an ordination. A variety of musical settings are available to involve the assembly actively in the responses. In the third section of the litany, there is a petition that God may "consecrate" the church, one of only two places where that word is used in the rite. (The word appears again in chapter 7 in reference to the consecration of chalices and patens. For more on this, see page 80.) The litany concludes with a prayer invoking the intercession of Mary and all the saints, asking that the church may become the home of salvation and grace and that the Christian people may worship God "in spirit and truth" and "grow together in love." The sung Litany of the Saints is an immediate prelude to the deposition of the relics (when done), in which the Church on earth invokes the Church in heaven and is in communion with it.

If a parish is named for a saint who is not usually included in the text of the litany, the name should be added. Some communities have unveiled an image of the patron saint in the church during the litany as a way of acknowledging the saint and the devotional area in the new church. Though no such practice is mentioned in the rite, this is a graceful way to include a recognition of the parish patron in the litany of the saints.

The Depositing of the Relics

The rite of the depositing of the relics is simple. The bishop approaches the altar, a deacon or priest hands the relics to him, and he puts them in the place prepared for them. He returns to the chair while the stone mason seals the aperture. Psalm 15 with its response (two are offered) is sung or another appropriate song may be sung.

Psalm 15 offers the image of the righteous person who "walks blamelessly," who acts with justice, who speaks the truth and does not slander or do wrong to others, who is faithful and honorable. This psalm has long been applied to the saints in the liturgy. It is interesting that it is used here rather than a psalm that is usually applied to martyrs. It is a song that honors a holy people, not the altar alone.

The rite indicates that the relics are to be placed beneath the altar. This would seem to require the preparation of a cavity (the directive uses the word "aperture") under the altar. Another practice is the affixing of a specially designed reliquary chest to the floor underneath an open altar. The directives offer no specifics; different interpretations are possible. The old practice of forming a "sepulcher" by cutting into the stone of the altar table is no longer to be done. Since this special reliquary or cavity must be taken into account in the planning of the altar and its space, early decisions must be made about whether this ritual will be observed.

In the former rite, the deposition of the relics and the sealing of the sepulcher were private actions, carried out by the bishop, the surrounding clergy and the mason. The reformed rite, which is based on a more ancient tradition, marks a major departure from medieval practice. Because of changing times and circumstances, it is necessary to discuss the subject of relics at some length.

Many of the first specifically Christian church buildings were *martyria,* built over the *confessio* or tomb of a martyr. The relics of the martyr were treasured as the central possession of that particular church, since they marked in a tangible way the continuity of the faithful with those who had given their lives for their faith in Christ. At the level of popular piety, relics were often believed to possess special powers—they could, for example, heal people. In twelfth-century Europe, relics were a very important in popular religious life; indeed, this might be called the century of relics. Many important churches kept lists of the relics they possessed, which they had obtained either as gifts or by exchange with other churches. These relics were not only parts of the bodies of martyrs, but also a wide variety of other objects related to martyrs, such as clothing, objects that they touched and the like. While some relics of saints and martyrs may have been genuine, it is probable that many were not.

Genuine or not, relics served as a concrete expression of the faith of past believers and as a focus for the faith of the living. The importance of relics in twelfth-century western Europe was linked to the fact that returning Crusaders brought many relics back with them from the Holy Land, ostensibly to safeguard them from unbelievers.

Relics are also significant in the Orthodox tradition. For example, a special cloth called an *antimension* (or "Greek corporal") with a relic in one corner is placed on a new altar as part of the ritual process of consecrating a church. Relics are important in Orthodox life, in some ways functioning like icons, that is, as a medium through which a saint or other sacred person may influence the living in a beneficial way.

The Second Council of Nicea in 787 established the importance of icons and pronounced an anathema, a formal curse, on anyone who denied the significance of relics. That Council made relics necessary for the consecration of a church. Today, especially in places in Europe, the preserved remains of martyrs and saints may still be seen enshrined beneath elaborate altars.

The Protestant Reformation in the sixteenth century reacted to the abuses and superstitions that often surrounded the veneration of saints and their relics. The sale of indulgences and relics (including, for example, the famous feathers from the wings of Michael the Archangel) led the reformers to reject such practices sternly, eliminating relics from liturgical and devotional practice.

Paragraphs 5 and 14 of the introduction to the *Rite of Dedication,* repeating what is found in the General Instruction of the Roman Missal (266), speaks of the meaning of the Christian altar and the relation of the relics of martyrs and other saints to it. The altar is above all "the table of the Lord" and it is in this that its dignity consists. It is not the bodies of the saints that give honor to the altar, but just the opposite. The saints are honored, first, because they are members of Christ's body and, second, because their martyrdom, which can be described as a sacrifice, points to the sacrifice of Christ, in which theirs has its origin. The association of martyrs with the sacrifice of Christ is particularly close. In the early centuries, martyrdom was regarded as the supreme expression of sanctity. This is not so much because of the sufferings the martyrs endured, or because of the witness they gave to Christ, but because they offered in their own bodies an example of the dying and rising of Jesus. For these reasons, it is appropriate that altars should be built over their tombs, or that their relics should be placed under altars.

The rite quotes Ambrose and Revelation 6:9 to support this view: "Let the triumphant victims rest in the place where Christ is victim: he, however, who suffered for all, upon the altar; they, who have been redeemed by his sufferings, beneath the altar." The Revelation text is especially significant because of the context of the heavenly liturgy: "I saw underneath the altar the souls of all people who had been killed on account of the word of God, for witnessing to it" (chapter 2, 14, n. 8).

On this principle, then, the rite builds its directives (chapter 2, 5a, b, c). The tradition of the Roman liturgy of placing relics under the altar is preserved, with these qualifications:

a. Relics intended for deposition should be of such a size that they can be recognized as parts of human bodies. Excessively small relics of one or more saints must not be placed beneath the altar.

b. Greatest care must be taken to determine whether the relics intended for deposition are authentic. It is better for an altar to be dedicated without relics than to have relics of doubtful credibility placed beneath it.

c. A reliquary must not be placed upon the altar or in the table of the altar but beneath the table of the altar, as the design of the altar may allow.

These directives are clear. Unless there are relics of considerable size (and, apart from modern martyrs and saints, such relics will be hard to come by), the altar is to be dedicated without them.

The directives in the rite regarding relics were reiterated in norms limiting the distribution of relics by the Vatican's Apostolic Sacristy. On February 15, 1994, Piero

Marini, master of papal liturgical celebrations, stated that the Apostolic Sacristy distributes small fragments of relics only for public veneration in a church, oratory or chapel, and not for private veneration by individuals; therefore, the relics are not suitable for the dedication of an altar, (see *Notitiae* 335/336 [June–July 1994]: 349–350).

While these norms govern the Vatican and the diocese of Rome, the preface indicates that these norms would serve "as a model for the elaboration of norms for distributing relics" by religious orders and other dioceses as well. This most likely means that the practice of including relics in altars will probably disappear. (See also the Bishops' Committee on the Liturgy *Newsletter* [January–February 1996]: 6.)

The *Constitution on the Sacred Liturgy* states that the "saints have been traditionally honored in the Church and their authentic relics and images held in veneration" (111). Unless it is possible to observe the directives of the rite for the deposition of relics, it would seem best to omit the relics altogether.

Even though people cherish mementos of loved ones or items used by celebrities, customs that are reminiscent of the veneration of relics, the practice of the deposition of relics, unless well understood, can be offensive in this day and age. Discussions about relics of "sufficient size" and "recognizable as parts of human bodies" tend to make people uncomfortable. We must evince in our religious practices an unmistakable reverence for the person resting in peaceful death.

The Prayer of Dedication

After the deposition of relics, or, if that does not take place, after the litany, the bishop offers the prayer of dedication. The rite places special emphasis on this prayer. No doubt this text is the one that most explicitly unfolds the meaning of the rite. The introduction to the rite states that "the celebration of the eucharist is the most important and the one necessary rite for the dedication of a church" (introduction, 15). But, continues the instruction, the common custom of both East and West is that a special prayer signifying that the church is to be dedicated to God "for all times" should be said, with "a petition for his blessing." That, according to the rite, is the principal meaning of dedication. Dedication permanently sets apart a building for the assembly of the Christian people and for the worship of God.

Since we have already discussed the prayer of dedication in Chapter 1, in this chapter we will consider the prayer of dedication of an altar, which is also included in the rite (chapter 4, 48). This would be used when it is not the whole building that is being dedicated, but a new altar.

Like the prayer of dedication of a church, the prayer for the dedication of an altar, is, in a broad sense, a eucharistic prayer, beginning with an ascription of praise and blessing to God for the fulfillment in Christ of all the sacrifices of the Old Testament. In three paragraphs it recalls the sacrifices of Noah, of Abraham "our father in faith," who offered his own son, and of Moses, who, when pouring the

The earliest rites understood the celebration of the eucharist to be the act that consecrates the altar and the building.

blood of the covenant on the altar, foreshadowed the sacrifice of the Cross. Christ brought all this to fulfillment by the paschal mystery. "As priest and victim he freely mounted the tree of the cross and gave himself to you, Father, as the one perfect oblation. In his sacrifice the new covenant is sealed, in his blood sin is engulfed" (chapter 4, 48).

Then follows the petitionary part of the prayer, asking that the altar "ever be reserved for the sacrifice of Christ" and become the table of the Lord, where God's people "will find nourishment and strength," that the altar be a "sign of Christ from whose pierced side flowed blood and water, which ushered in the sacraments of the Church." Then the prayer asks that the "friends of Christ" may approach the altar with joy, there to find consolation and help; that it may be a place of union and peace for those who share the body and blood of Christ, by which they are to grow in the love communicated by the Holy Spirit. The prayer concludes: "Make it a source of unity and friendship, where your people may gather as one to share your spirit of mutual love." Once again it is people who are in view. It is for them that the altar is dedicated.

The reformed texts for dedicating a church and an altar are greatly improved in terms of theology and pastoral application. Adolf Adam, however, offers an important criticism: The prayers lack an epiclesis or invocation of the Holy Spirit (see

Adolf Adam, *Foundations of Liturgy: An Introduction to Its History and Practice* [Collegeville: The Liturgical Press, 1992], 344).

Anointing of the Altar and the Walls of the Church

The introduction to the *Rite of Dedication of an Altar* (chapter 4) presents a treatise on the nature and dignity of the altar (paragraphs 1–4) and makes clear that the altar is, in a sense, Christ. It follows naturally that, for the completion of the symbolism, it should be anointed with chrism. Christ, chrism and anointing are correlatives. The rite of anointing makes the symbolism of the altar explicit. The anointing conforms to the pattern found everywhere in the reformed liturgy: First there is the prayer and then the ritual action.

With the anointing of the altar goes the anointing of the walls of the church. Although the instruction is not explicit on the point, the underlying sense of this action seems to be that as the altar represents Christ who is the head of the body, so the walls, standing for the whole building, represent the people who, as the rite tells us repeatedly, are the Church. In this sense the action of anointing signifies the consecration or reconsecration of the people of God, who offer the eucharist, who receive the source of divine life from the altar, and who are the praying Church (compare chapter 2, 16a, b):

> The anointing with chrism makes the altar a symbol of Christ, who, before all others, is and is called "The Anointed One;" for the Father anointed him with the Holy Spirit and constituted him the High Priest so that on the altar of his body he might "offer the sacrifice of his life for the salvation of all" (cf. Hebrews 1:9 and Psalm 44).

The instruction states that "the anointing of the church signifies that it is given over entirely and perpetually to Christian worship," and, as the rite repeats, the Church is the body of Christ. Christians are his members and it is they who, through Christ, offer acceptable sacrifices to God (see 1 Peter 2:4–9). Thus, the anointing of the walls of the church represents the anointing of the people (see Calabuig.).

The anointing of the altar and the walls forms a comprehensive concelebration by the whole community. The bishop, who represents Christ the High Priest, anoints the principal symbol, the altar; he is joined by the priests in anointing the walls; the deacons and other ministers represent Christ the Servant assisting; the people represent the body of Christ. The bishop is given the choice of inviting the priests to anoint the walls. This is fitting, and will usually be the case. The concelebration is carried through into the celebration of the eucharist, which is the climax of the dedication. It would be incongruous if the priests were excluded from taking part in the anointing.

Even in the former rite there was sharing of such tasks. Other bishops or others not in episcopal orders were invited to dedicate minor altars in the church. Frequently a priest celebrated the eucharist in lieu of the exhausted consecrating bishop, but this could hardly be called a concelebration. The current arrangements are certainly more reflective of the contemporary theology of orders and ministry.

The rite of anointing is simple (64). The bishop, standing before the altar, says: "We now anoint this altar and this building. May God in his power make them holy, visible signs of the mystery of Christ and his Church." Then he anoints the altar, in the middle of the table and at its four corners. There is no prayer text to be said while he does so, nor does he make the sign of the cross with the chrism. The directive says simply that he pours the chrism in these five places. There is no mention of crosses carved into the table of the altar, as had been customary since the Middle Ages. It should be noted, too, that the bishop is recommended to spread the chrism over the *whole* surface of the altar table. The ritual action is meant to be a generous sign. The directive also indicates that the bishop may remove his chasuble and, in a sense, roll up his sleeves for the task.

This done, the bishop hands vessels of chrism to the two or four assisting priests, who then go through the church and anoint the walls in either four or twelve places. The rite speaks of the traditional and "praiseworthy" custom of placing at the four or twelve spots on the wall that will be anointed crosses of stone, metal or another suitable material. Under the crosses are fixed sconces to hold small candles. The priests (or bishop) sign these crosses with chrism (see chapter 2, 22 and 64). Thereafter, the candles will be lit on the anniversary of dedication and other festive occasions, such as the Easter Vigil.

The symbolism of this rite is explained in the introduction (16a): The signing of four or twelve crosses signifies "that the church is an image of the holy city of Jerusalem." This symbolism is derived from the Book of Revelation (21:14 and 21:16) which describes the twelve gates of the city, guarded by twelve angels, signifying the old Israel; on the twelve gates were written the names of the twelve tribes of Israel. The Church consists of the old and the new Israel, and the foundation stones of the new Israel are the twelve apostles. In sacred numerology, twelve signified completion. If there are only four anointings, a sense of totality is still expressed. There are four cardinal points: east, west, north, south. In the Book of Revelation, twelve is the number of completion because it is made up of *three* fours; the city itself is four-square; and in some cultures "the square is the symbol of the perfection of the Absolute" (Calabuig, 28). If the church is not large, four anointings may be sufficient and the symbolism will be preserved.

During the anointing of the walls, Psalm 84 or another appropriate song may be sung. This psalm and the two antiphons provided reiterate that the whole Church is being dedicated. The first part recalls the heavenly Jerusalem: "How lovely is your dwelling place, O Lord of hosts! My soul longs for the courts of the Lord." The next verse sings of eagerness for God's altars, like a swallow seeking a home to hatch her young. Then the psalm sings of the pilgrim people who hope to see God in the heavenly Jerusalem, the "courts of the Lord," where one day is better than a thousand elsewhere.

The first response suggested gathers this up and applies it to both Church and church: "See the place where God lives among his people; there the Spirit of God will make his home among you; the temple of God is holy and you are that temple." The second response combines church and Church and emphasizes that God is the builder: "Holy is the temple of the Lord, it is God's handiwork, his dwelling place."

The text provided for the dedication of an altar (49) offers another image: "God, your God, has anointed you with the oil of gladness." The accompanying Psalm 45 is one of the great Messianic psalms that, for the Christian, sings of Christ, the Son of God, who was anointed to be the high priest. But there is another notion here as well. The psalm seems originally to have been a wedding ballad. It has been used as a bridal hymn of the Church, expressing her longing for union with Christ, her bridegroom. It might be used in the general rite of the dedication of a church during the anointing. During the Easter season, Psalm 118, with its reference to Christ the cornerstone, is used.

Those involved in the preparation for the rite should consider the vessel for the chrism for the anointings. Will it be large enough to be seen? Will it be kept in a suitable place and handled with dignity? Will there be enough chrism for the anointings? What auxiliary vessels will the priests use in anointing the walls? How and where will the bishop and priests wash their hands afterward? All these details need to be arranged thoughtfully so that the signs are not minimalized and so that the ritual action flows smoothly.

Incensation of the Altar and the Church

Just as the anointing of the altar is concerned with the living Church, the body of Christ, and the people, his members, so is this rite of incensation. Its significance is twofold.

First, "incense is burned on the altar to signify that Christ's sacrifice, which is there perpetuated in mystery, ascends to God as an odor of sweetness, and also as a sign that the prayers of the people rise up pleasing and acceptable, reaching the throne of God" (chapter 2, 16a. See also Ephesians 5:2; Revelation 8:3–4).

The second symbolism is recalled in the prayer the bishop says as he begins the rite: "Lord, may our prayer ascend as incense in your sight. As this building is filled with fragrance so may your Church fill the world with the fragrance of Christ." The same image is found in the two antiphons provided for the accompanying Psalm 138. They refer to Revelation 8:3–4: "An angel stood by the altar of the temple, holding a golden censer" or "From the hand of the angel, clouds of incense rose in the presence of the Lord." As always, another appropriate song may be sung.

The incensation rite has been simplified and has also changed in its emphasis. The former rite looked back to the sacrifices of the Old Testament. The new rite recalls the Old Testament sacrifices in the prayer of the dedication of an altar, but shifts its main emphasis to the sacrifice of Christ in the New Testament, teaching that Christ's sacrifice is sacramentally perpetuated at the sacrifice of the altar. A sacrament has nothing to do with the slaying of animals, or the sprinkling of grain, or the pouring of blood. Christ, by his sacrifice, fulfilled all the sacrifices of the old law, rendered them obsolete and, more important still, transcended them. The only sacrifice the Church has is the sacrifice of Christ, which, through his command, it is able to make present here and now. The eucharist looks back to the Last Supper, where Christ expressed the meaning of the sacrifice he was to offer. By the memorial of what he did at that supper his people can enter into his sacrifice, be joined to it and offer themselves with him. The rite has been reformed or restored in such a way as to bring out a fuller theological understanding (see Calabuig, 28 – 30).

Two ways of burning incense are indicated:

a) a brazier is placed on the altar for burning incense or aromatic gums, *or*
b) incense mixed with small wax candles is heaped up on the altar.

In the first case, the bishop puts incense into the brazier and, in the second, he lights the heap of incense with a taper. The first method would seem to be preferable because of its fuller value as a sign. The point of the rite is not so much that a "sacrifice" of incense should be burned on the altar, but that the smoke of the aromatic incense should symbolize the prayer and offering of the Church.

Then follows an incensation of the people. "The bishop puts incense into some censers" (notice the plural!) "and incenses the altar; he returns to the chair, is incensed, and then sits. Ministers, walking through the church, incense the people and the walls" (chapter 2, 67).

In an increasingly smoke-free culture, it is difficult to make full use of this symbol, especially in churches that are poorly ventilated or very small. Liturgy has always had a strong appeal to the senses (for example, with the scents of beeswax, flowers, chrism, incense). Many of these have been lost; therefore, a thoughtful consideration of this olfactory sign will be valuable to a good experience of it.

To carry out the incensation well, plan ahead. What kind of incense vessel will be placed on the altar? What kind of incense will be used? Will it truly be aromatic or will it be unpleasant? What kind of vessels will be used to incense the people and in what manner will they be incensed? Who will be the ministers that incense the assembly?

Lighting of the Altar and the Church

After the incensation, the altar table is wiped with cloths, and, if necessary, covered with waterproof linen, protecting the altar cloth from any remaining oil that might stain it. The altar is then covered with a festive cloth, most appropriately by members of the assembly. Flowers and candles may also be brought forward and placed near the altar, also by members of the assembly.

The liturgy, up to this point, has had no lights, whether candles or electrical, even at the gospel. Now the deacon goes to the bishop, who hands him a small lighted candle and says: "Light of Christ, shine forth in the Church and bring all nations to the fullness of truth." The deacon lights the candles at the altar and may be assisted in lighting the others in the church. All the candles — on the walls, near the altar — and all the lights of the church are lit. This "festive lighting" of the entire church is a sign of rejoicing (chapter 2, 71). While this is being done, the people join in singing a canticle from Tobit (13:10, 13–14ab, 14c–15, 17): "Bless the Lord, all you saints of the Lord. Rejoice and give him thanks."

The first antiphon offered in the text, from Isaiah 60, emphasizes the theme of light and sees the glory of God present in the Church, suggesting the *shekinah* of the Old Testament: "Your light will come, Jerusalem; upon you the glory of the Lord will dawn and all nations will walk in your light, alleluia." The second antiphon, for use during Lent, is also taken from the canticle: "Jerusalem, city of God, you will shine with the light of God's splendor; all people on earth will pay you homage."

A final directive says, "Another appropriate song may be sung, especially one in honor of Christ, the light of the world" (chapter 2, 71).

Light, a sign of joy, is related to Christ who is the way, the truth and the life. An implication of this is that the Church's task is to convey the truth, revealed in and by Christ, to the whole world. Jesus Christ is the light of the world who has enlightened us through his word and baptism. Christ has made us beacons of light, and since "a city built on a hill cannot be hidden" (Matthew 5:14), our light must shine before others.

In preparing for the lighting of the church, decide where the light that the bishop will give to the deacon will come from. Perhaps it could be carried in the opening procession and placed near the chrism and incense that will be used in the rite. What kind of candle will be used? What about the other lights to be lit from this candle? Will the paschal candle, the "light of lights," be lit if this is the Easter season or if it is near the font? Careful preparation will attend to the details associated with these significant symbols and ritual actions.

The Liturgy of the Eucharist

The reformed rite goes to great lengths to emphasize the unity of the dedication proper and the eucharist. The celebration of the eucharist, according to the introduction of the rite, is "the principal and the most ancient part of the whole rite." Two reasons are given for this, the second of which restates the ancient practice of dedication:

> [T]he eucharist, which sanctifies the hearts of those who receive it, in a sense consecrates the altar and the place of celebration, as the ancient Fathers of the Church assert more than once: "This altar is an object of wonder: by nature it is stone, but it is made holy when it receives the body of Christ." (17)

The quote is from John Chrysostom. This paragraph is one of only two places in the rite (the other being a petition in the Litany of the Saints) where the word "consecrate" is used. The relation between dedication and eucharist is also indicated by the provision of a proper preface for the Mass.

Once the altar has been clothed and illuminated, the ministers prepare the altar in the usual way. Although the presentation of the gifts is now done in every community eucharist, the gesture here (chapter 2, 72) is unique. The very building is a symbol of the people's work and generosity. Members of the community bring the bread and wine to the bishop who receives them while seated at the chair.

The usual collection may also be taken up, with consideration to allocating a portion of the collection to assist a local effort that helps feed the hungry or provide shelter to the homeless. Consider letting a portion of the first collection taken up in this new house of the Church go to those in need. The presentation of the gifts is accompanied by the sung antiphon provided (or another appropriate song). The antiphon is one of the few texts from the old pontifical. It says: "Lord God, in the simplicity of my heart I have joyously offered all things to you; with great joy I have looked upon your chosen people, Lord God, I have obeyed your will (alleluia)." This text, taken from 1 Chronicles 29:17–18, is part of the prayer of David for the gifts the people have given toward the building of the Temple which will be completed by his son, Solomon. Here in the rite, it can be seen as an expression of thanksgiving on the part of the people who have made their gifts, not only at the Mass but in providing the funds necessary for the building of the church.

After the presentation of the gifts the continuity of the whole rite of dedication is emphasized by a small but significant gesture (chapter 2, 73). At the beginning of the rite, when the bishop arrived at the sanctuary, he did not reverence the altar. Now, says the directive, "[W]hen all is ready, the bishop goes to the altar and kisses the altar. The Mass proceeds in the usual way; however, neither the gifts nor the altar are incensed." The prayer over the gifts sounds a note of joy, for they are "the gifts of a rejoicing Church," and the petition is for the people: By the mysteries to be celebrated "in this sacred place" may they "arrive at eternal salvation."

The preface to the eucharistic prayer is not a repetition of the prayer of dedication that was offered at the beginning of the rite, but is related to it. Clearly, the whole rite, from beginning to end, is dedicatory, and the eucharist is the culmination of it. The text of the dedication preface is a thanksgiving for the Church in all its richness and mystery.

The preface, of course, is the first part of the great prayer of thanksgiving. Through the presider, the whole community thanks God for making the whole world the temple of God's glory and at the same time allowing us to dedicate to God places that are "designed" for worship. The phrase "[t]he whole world is your temple" adds a cosmic dimension to the prayer. It reminds us that all of creation is good as God made it and that this physical place called "church" is but a fencing-off of a particular portion of a whole world made by God. The church is a symbol of the whole of created reality.

The prayer goes on to root this earthly image of the heavenly city in the concrete reality of the Incarnation: "For you made the body of your Son born of the Virgin, a temple consecrated to your glory, the dwelling place of your godhead in all its fullness" (see Colossians 2:9).

The prayer takes up the theme of the anointing: The Church is the holy city, built on the foundation of the apostles, Christ himself being the cornerstone. The Church is built of living stones, animated by the Holy Spirit, a spiritual temple bound together by love where "Christ will be its light for ever." Once again, the focus is on the Church as people, and the church building as a sacramental sign of the assembly.

The preface is a highly concentrated text, rich in scriptural and spiritual images. It expresses in condensed prayer what the Church believes it is. This prayer should be among the texts used by the building planners and for the catechesis of the rest of the community.

When the first eucharistic prayer is used there is a proper insertion (chapter 2, 76) in which the people "who with heart and hand have given and built this church as an offering to you" offer up the building. An insertion is also provided for the third eucharistic prayer (chapter 2, 77). It asks that this church may be for the people

> a place of salvation and sacrament where your gospel of peace is proclaimed and your holy mysteries celebrated. Guided by your word and secure in your peace may your chosen people now journeying through life arrive safely at their eternal home. There may all your children now scattered abroad be settled at last in your city of peace.

The Mass continues in the usual way. The communion antiphons provided (chapter 2, 78) come from Psalm 128. The antiphon provides scriptural images of church: "My house shall be called a house of prayer, says the Lord: in it all who ask shall receive, all who seek shall find, and all who knock shall have the door opened to them (alleluia)." Other appropriate communion songs may also be sung. It is appropriate that, as always, communion be offered to all present under both forms a sufficient number of communion ministers. The pattern of the communion procession in the new church should be thoughtfully worked out in advance.

Inauguration of the Blessed Sacrament Chapel

The reservation of the eucharist on the main altar of the church has been a familiar part of the devotional life of Catholics in recent centuries, even though the practice did not begin until the 16th century and became universal a hundred or so years later. Variations in the practice have appeared even up to our own day. In the great basilicas of Rome the tabernacle has never been on the main altar. All of the liturgical documents since Vatican II indicate a preference for reserving the eucharist in a separate chapel. This is not something novel, but a return to former custom. (See Archdale A. King, *Eucharist Reservation in the Western Church* [New York: Sheed and Ward, 1965] and W. H. Freestone, *The Sacrament Reserved,* Alcuin Club Collection XXI [London: A. R. Mowbray & Co., 1917].)

The General Instruction of the Roman Missal states, "Every encouragement should be given to the practice of eucharistic reservation in a chapel suited to the faithful's private adoration and prayer. If this is impossible because of the structure of the church, the sacrament should be reserved at an altar or elsewhere, in keeping with local custom, and in a part of the church that is worthy and properly adorned" (276). It is difficult to imagine that a new church could not be planned to make a separate reservation chapel possible. The U.S. bishops' document *Environment and Art in Catholic Worship* elaborates this further: "A room or chapel specifically designed and separate from the major space is important so that no confusion can take place between the celebration of the eucharist and reservation" (78). The document goes on: "Having the eucharist reserved in a place apart does not mean it has been relegated to a secondary place of no importance. Rather, a space carefully designed and appointed can give proper attention to the reserved sacrament" (78).

The *Rite of Dedication of a Church and an Altar* (chapter 4, 7) provides for the inauguration of the chapel of reservation at the close of the rite.

The ritual takes place in this manner (see introduction, 81–82). After communion, the vessel containing the blessed sacrament is left on the altar. (The instruction uses the word "pyx," although this particular vessel is normally associated with taking communion to the sick.) At the chair, the bishop invites all to pray in silence and then offers the prayer after communion. After the prayer, the bishop returns to the altar, reverences the blessed sacrament and incenses it. With a humeral veil, the bishop takes the eucharist in procession through the church to the chapel of reservation. During this time, Psalm 147 or another appropriate song is sung.

On arrival at the place of reservation, the vessel is placed in the tabernacle and incensed. There is a period of silent prayer, the tabernacle is closed and finally the lamp to burn before the tabernacle is lit. The directive says, "If the chapel where the blessed sacrament is reserved can be seen clearly by the congregation, the bishop immediately imparts the blessing of the Mass. Otherwise the procession returns to the sanctuary by the shorter route and the bishop imparts the blessing either at the altar or at the chair" (chapter 2, 82).

The blessing acknowledges those who have gathered to "dedicate this house of prayer" and asks that all be made into "the dwelling place of [the] Holy Spirit." The deacon dismisses the people in the usual way. All join in a festive closing song.

FINAL CONSIDERATIONS

The rite, when read slowly and thoughtfully, may seem complex and elaborate. Yet the signs and symbols, gestures and words, can have a strong impact on modern men and women. Several considerations will help to make the rite prayerful and ensure the participation of all the faithful.

• Be concerned about the flow and length of the rite. Admittedly, the rite can seem long and tedious, unless a well-organized and well-prepared liturgy makes clear the connections between the parts of the rite and the whole rite and the rest of life. Like the Easter Vigil, it can come across as a series of monologues rather than as an interactive and continuous drama. We begin outdoors. We walk into church. We sing a song. We watch the bishop sprinkle us and the walls (do we see the connection?) We see the building and us incensed (do we see the connection?) We see the altar and walls anointed (do we see the connection?) It should be like a symphony with a number of movements, not a stringing-together of unrelated ceremonies.

• Avoid minimalizing. It is tempting to truncate the signs and symbols of this unusual rite, but we would thereby diffuse their effects. The way such ritual elements as the sprinkling of people and walls are handled can make the difference between the action being seen and experienced as truly initiatory or as magic. Let the signs be full signs: incense rising from a massive brazier or a number of braziers; anointing of table and walls that goes further than the jingle "a little dab'll do ya!" Do we anoint the altar and then wipe it off right away — or does that falsely suggest that there is nothing "messy" about our church or the Church? What would be the effect if, in inaugurating the blessed sacrament chapel, the bishop were to give the eucharist to those who bring the sacrament to the sick? We must make a point of avoiding minimalism in the enacting of the rites.

• Use music and song fully. There is a temptation to let the choirs and music ministers sing everything at the rite of dedication, entertaining the assembly with beautiful concert pieces. There is also a danger of letting the music be tacked on as an afterthought to the rite. Because the rite is so out of the ordinary, people could be tempted to watch the unusual actions in the new church rather than participate. It is helpful to use responsorial and antiphonal music so that the assembly can sing an easily remembered text while following the ritual actions, instead of being expected to ignore the actions and keep their eyes on a printed text. Another possibility is to commission a Mass setting for the occasion. Begin using it well before the day of dedication so that the people are familiar with the music when the day comes.

• Consider thoughtfully all texts and prayers. The rite is full of beautiful texts—but a too-rich offering of words can be exhausting and hence lost. The prayer of dedication and the preface of dedication are major prayer texts and should be pondered before the day of dedication. A whole theology of Church is offered in these prayers. (Compare the texts of the 1961 rite and the 1977 rite. There is a marked difference in the Church's self-understanding.)

The community's prayers before and after the dedication should build upon these prayers. During the process of preparation, consider communal prayer that is concerned with creation, ecology, beauty, environmental protection, artists, crafts-persons, God, creatures of heaven and earth, gardens and fountains, the stars and sky, balance, harmony and so on. These are (as they should be) the concerns of our day when it comes to building. Do our prayers express that? On the day of dedication, provide well-designed participation booklets that offer only the ritual texts needed for the assembly's full, conscious and active participation. Such booklets also serve as a remembrance of the occasion that is available to everyone. A well-designed booklet with graphics, including a brief catechesis of the rite and history of the building process, will help unfold the beauty and richness of the rite. Some communities have a professionally-produced videotape made of the celebration, to be offered at a reasonable price afterward. This will help minimize the number of amateur photographers and videographers at the celebration. These details and others like them will help the rite to flow smoothly in a prayerful spirit. They need to be carefully considered during the planning process.

The dedication rite presents the Church in all its mysterious depth and extent. If simpler than in ages past, the current rite is much richer in content. It is visibly and audibly a celebration of the Church and offers a vision of Church that enables the People of God to see who they are and what they are called to be: fruitful, holy, favored and exalted.

Holy Rites, Holy Places
Other Liturgies of Blessing, Prayer and Thanksgiving

LAYING THE FOUNDATION STONE OR GROUNDBREAKING

A ritual blessing of the site of a new church and of the first stone of the building is natural and appropriate as construction begins. The practice now enshrined in the "Rite of Laying the Foundation Stone or Commencement of Work on the Building of a Church," chapter 1 of the *Rite of Dedication of a Church and an Altar,* came into existence as long ago as the high Middle Ages.

The former rite was concerned with the laying of the foundation stone. The present rite provides a blessing for the laying of a foundation stone and prayer for the commencement of work on the building of the church, or both.

Some contemporary church buildings do not use stone as a building material and thus do not have a foundation stone that helps support the building. In many cases, a plaque or tablet serves well as a tangible reminder of the inauguration of the building, installed in an appropriate place to record the event and those who took part in it. This often happens after the building itself is completed.

Two rites, which may be combined, are provided.

> In accordance with liturgical tradition, this rite consists of the blessing of the site of the new church and the blessing and laying of the foundation stone. If there is to be no foundation stone because of the particular style or plan of the building, the rite of the blessing of the site of the new church should still be celebrated in order to dedicate the beginning of the work of God. (chapter 1, 1)

This statement recognizes that the work required to bring about this building is to be dedicated to God. The rite, therefore, is a blessing of human work. This notion reflects the underlying character of the entire collection of renewed dedication rituals: People are the most important element. The building is "a visible sign of the living Church, God's building, which is formed of the people themselves" (compare 1 Corinthians 3:9; chapter 1, 1). The rite signifies the beginning of the dedication of the people, which will be completed when the eucharist is eventually celebrated in the new edifice:

Lord,
you fill the entire world with your presence
that your name may be hallowed through all the earth.

Bless all those
who have worked or contributed
to provide this site (property, land)
on which a church will be built.

Today may they rejoice in a work just begun,
soon may they celebrate the sacraments in your temple,
and in time to come may they praise you for ever in heaven.

The order of the service itself is carefully set out and, when well prepared, serves as a prayerful gathering of the Church. Two forms of approach to the construction site are offered.

• The assembly, presider and ministers meet in a place separate from the building site. The presider greets the assembly and "briefly instructs the people on their participation in the celebration and explains to them the meaning of the rite" (chapter 1, 12). He offers a prayer that recalls that the Church is built on the foundation of the apostles (Ephesians 2:20) and that Christ is the cornerstone. The prayer asks that the people gathered in Christ's name may reverence, love and follow him, so that under his guidance they may grow into a temple of his glory and come at the end to the heavenly city. A deacon may announce, "Let us go forth in peace" as a procession forms. Psalm 84, with the antiphon, "My soul is yearning for the courts of the Lord," or another appropriate song is sung during the procession to the construction site. Every effort should be made to help all experience the procession as a prayerful movement and pilgrimage.

• If a procession to the site cannot take place, or for some reason is inappropriate, the people, presider, and ministers meet at the building site. The rest of the rite continues as below.

A reading of the word of God takes place, with selections from the Common for the Dedication of a Church. The rite also offers selections which, it says, are particularly appropriate when a stone is to be blessed. However, there are no special readings for the blessing of the site of a new church or the laying of a first stone. Those indicated in the rite all refer to stones and the greater number refer to Christ as the cornerstone: Isaiah 28:16–17, the source of all the New Testament texts on the subject; Acts 4:8–12; Mark 12:1–2, and so on.

The first suggested Old Testament reading, 1 Kings 5:2–18, is about the preparation for the building of Solomon's Temple. If the new church is to be built of stone, either wholly or in part, this reading might be used. Of the gospel passages,

Matthew 7:21–29 and Luke 6:46–49 are parallel and offer suitable material for the homily. Matthew 16:13–18, also provided, is often associated with the ministry of Peter. The Lutheran *Occasional Services: Companion to the Lutheran Book of Worship* offers several additional scriptural texts for their ritual of groundbreaking: Exodus 3:1–6, about Moses' encounter with God and being on "holy ground;" 1 Corinthians 3:10–14, about building on the foundation which is Jesus Christ; Ephesians 2:19–22, about the household of God built on the foundation of the apostles; and Hebrews 11:8–10, about Abraham looking forward to a city whose architect and builder is God.

Of the psalms provided, several are appropriate even if there is no actual stone: Psalm 24, with the response, "I have chosen and sanctified this place" (from 2 Chronicles 7:16a); Psalm 42, with its response from Psalm 43, "Lord, may your truth lead me to your holy mountain;" and Psalm 100, with its response from Ezekiel 37:27, "I will make my dwelling place among the people." Psalm 118, with its response from 1 Corinthians 3:11, "There is no other foundation than Christ Jesus," is particularly appropriate when there *is* a stone to be laid. It sums up much of the Old Testament material on the imagery of the cornerstone.

After the scriptural readings, there is a homily. The rite suggests some themes: "Christ is the cornerstone of the Church, and the temple that is going to be built by the living Church of the community of believers will be at once the house of God and the house of God's people" (chapter 1, 22).

There may follow the reading of the document that records the laying of the stone and the beginning of the building of the church. This is to be signed by the presider and by representatives of those responsible for the project. It is to be inserted into the foundation with the stone. A "time capsule" sometimes contains this document, along with mementos or materials with local significance. If there is no foundation or cornerstone, these items could be placed in the walls that are beginning to rise or in another appropriate place, with a plaque or tablet commemorating the event.

The rite for the blessing of the construction site of the church consists of a prayer said by the presider, and a sprinkling with holy water. The sprinkling may take place by standing at the middle of the area or by going in procession around the foundations. When a procession is made, it is accompanied by the singing of Psalm 48 with the response, "The walls of Jerusalem will be made of precious stones, and its towers built with gems" (taken from the former office of the dedication of a church). Or another appropriate song may be sung.

Once the sprinkling has been done, the laying of the first stone follows. After a prayer, the presider blesses the stone with holy water and lays it in the place provided, either in silence or offering another prayer (chapter 1, 28).

The prayer before the blessing of the stone (in its Latin version) refers to "the Son of Mary" who the prophet Daniel foretold would be the stone broken from the mountain, now the stone "firmly founded" as the foundation of the Church. It asks that Christ, who is "the beginning and end of all things" may help "this work begin, continue, and be brought to fulfillment." This prayer blends references and images of Daniel 2:34; 1 Corinthians 3:11 and Revelation 1:8 and 21:6. The second, optional prayer during the laying of a cornerstone asks that the church that is to rise "be a place of sacrament and a source of grace."

After the stone has been set in place and cemented by a stone mason, general intercessions are offered, including a unique petition that "those who are prevented from building places of worship may bear witness to the Lord by conducting themselves as living temples of glory and faith." Thus the rite acknowledges Christians in nations whose governments prevent the building of new churches. Other intercessions may also be added. The rite concludes with the Lord's Prayer, a concluding prayer, a blessing and dismissal. The concluding prayer focuses on the people, asking God to "enable them to grow into the temple of your glory, until shaped anew by your grace, they are gathered by your hand into your heavenly city."

A number of directives are provided at the beginning of this rite (chapter 1, 2 – 8). The rite may be celebrated on any day except during the Easter Triduum. Whatever day and time are chosen should make possible the participation of a large number of the people.

It is appropriate, when possible, that the bishop of the diocese preside over the rite, though another bishop or priest (vicar, dean, pastor) may be delegated. As with all rites of dedication when a bishop presides, directives for the celebration are found in the *Ceremonial of Bishops*.

As before the other rites, the people are to be instructed in the meaning of the rite and "the reverence to be shown toward the church that is to be built for them" (chapter 1, 4). The people are to be encouraged "to give their generous and willing support in the building of the church."

Finally, if possible, the area of the new church is to be clearly marked out, and arranged so that it is possible for the presider and ministers to move around it without difficulty. As in the former rite, a wooden cross is to be set up on the place where the future altar will be located. And finally, "speaking equipment should be so arranged that the assembly may clearly hear the readings, prayers and instructions" (chapter 1, 7).

The rite for the commencement of work makes no mention of a groundbreaking in the form of turning over the first shovelful of ground at the site, but some communities have devised creative expressions for "breaking the soil" before the work on the building commences, with the participation of presider and ministers, building planners and workers and members of the community young and old.

The ritual prayer at the beginning of the work to provide a house for the Church will remind the community that "unless the Lord builds the house, those who build it labor in vain" (Psalm 127:1).

RITUALS FOR RENOVATED CHURCHES

What kind of liturgical celebration is appropriate when a church building is being renovated or restored? Unless the building is a renovated secular building or a church building that had been used by another religious community, the building most likely has already been dedicated or blessed according to the Roman rite. This should be researched through parish and diocesan archives.

Chapter 3 of the rite, "Dedication of a Church Already in General Use for Sacred Celebrations," and Chapter 4, "Dedication of an Altar," provide direction when the issues are not so obvious. The reformed rite clearly states: "Care should be taken that, as far as possible, Mass is not celebrated in a new church before it is dedicated" (chapter 3, 1; see also chapter 2, 8, 15, 17). Recently built churches are to be dedicated according to chapter 2 of the rite.

In order for a church that has been standing for a time to be dedicated, two conditions must be met: (1) the altar of that church was never dedicated; or (2) "that there is something new or greatly changed in it which affects the building, for example, the church has been completely restored or its juridical status, for example, has been raised to the rank of a parish church" (chapter 3, 1).

The first criterion is difficult to assess. If a "temporary altar of sacrifice" was placed without being dedicated in front of the "high altar" soon after Vatican II, surely one would not dedicate the whole building again if it did not meet the second criterion. But would one dedicate the altar, using chapter 4? What about the tradition that the first celebration of the eucharist on a altar is what in fact dedicates it? The rite is silent on these questions.

By requiring a dedication (according to chapter 2) of a church that has been thoroughly renovated, the rite also does not take into account the fact that although it has been renovated, the building has its history. The rite treats the building as if it were new, making no recognition of the work of past generations that has been restored or replaced. Nor can the dedication rite in chapter 2 address the community's experiences of change in the church's interior, experiences of both pain and promise. Future adaptations of the rite, perhaps with American additions (as in, for example, the *Book of Blessings*), will need to address more specifically some of these questions.

Another commentary (*The Code of Canon Law: A Text and Commentary* [New York: Paulist Press, 1985], 847) states:

> If a sacred place is to undergo extensive restoration, the question to be asked is whether the restored place is a new place and therefore to be dedicated or blessed anew, or whether it is the former place restored. If

the latter is true, it would not be dedicated or blessed anew (for it never ceased to be sacred) and the completion of the work would be marked by some other celebration of gratitude and praise. Important in this decision would be whether or not the exercise of cult continued in the place during the renovation.

Any adaptation of the rite will need to make provision for a form of service "in gratitude and praise" for restored spaces.

It was common in the history of founding parishes in the United States that a school, convent and rectory would be built first, while the church itself would be housed in a temporary space, often the school gymnasium. These temporary arrangements were meant to be replaced at a later time by a permanent structure; however, that did not always happen. These spaces then were often renovated for the reformed liturgy after Vatican II.

In some worship spaces, either the old altar turned out to be inadequate for the needs of the reformed liturgy and therefore substantially refashioned, or the altar was removed from the reredos and brought forward to be closer to the assembly and approachable from all four sides. This usually meant a radical reshaping of the altar and, in such circumstances, the dedication of the altar only would be appropriate.

In some cases, even though the altar had been dedicated by rite, the church was not dedicated at the time. Later, the church itself would be dedicated with the full rite, much like the practice of emergency infant baptism, where the rest of the rites were "supplied" later. This practice is now forbidden (a word rarely found in any liturgical text today): "It is rightly forbidden both by custom and by liturgical law to dedicate a church without dedicating the altar, for the dedication of the altar is a principal part of the whole rite" (chapter 3, 1). In some cases, the original building may never have been formally dedicated by rite, but by use.

If the building is a restoration of a church that had been ruined or abandoned, a church in one way or another that had been alienated, or a church that required extensive rebuilding and a reordering of the interior, then, according to the terms of the rite, it may be dedicated with the full rite of chapter 2.

Sometimes a new church is built in an area where the population has grown significantly and the need for the church building is urgent. Such churches are used after a blessing, before being solemnly dedicated. The rite makes provision for such a blessing in chapter 3. Dedication should follow as soon as possible.

The introduction to chapter 3 observes that certain features of the full rite of dedication are not appropriate for a dedication of a new church that has been blessed and has been in general use. Fundamentally, the rite is an adaptation of the full ritual. The following are the main adaptations:

1. Since the church has already been used, the solemn entrance rite and the opening of the doors are appropriately omitted. The people gather in the church and the bishop and ministers enter in procession in the usual way. The psalm provided in the dedication rite may be sung during the procession.

2. The rite of handing over the church may be retained, omitted or adapted according to circumstances. It may be retained in the case of a recently built church. It is to be omitted if there has been no structural change. It is adapted in the case of a radically restored building.

The underlying principle here is that which is found everywhere in the reformed rite; namely, we should not say one thing and do another, or, in this case, we should not pretend that the building is new if indeed it is not. The handing over of the church, if retained, takes place after the bishop goes to the chair and offers the greeting.

3. If relics are to be interred, they may be carried in the procession or, "for a just cause, before the celebration begins, the relics may be placed between lighted torches in a suitable part of the sanctuary" (chapter 3, 4). If they are reserved in a chapel overnight, a vigil with the Liturgy of the Hours is to be observed.

4. There follows a penitential rite consisting of a blessing of water and the sprinkling of the people while all sing the antiphon "I saw water" or another appropriate song. A prayer said by the bishop concludes the rite. The Gloria is sung, followed by the opening prayer. The invitation to the blessing of water underlines the fact that the rite is a reminder of baptism and penance. The prayer asks that the people be made "the temple of your Spirit." The walls of the church are not sprinkled but the altar is, if it is "completely new" (chapter 3, 9).

5. The readings are chosen from those given for the dedication of a church. The reading from Nehemiah, since it is not appropriate to this occasion, is not used.

6. After the homily, the creed is said. The general intercessions are replaced by the sung Litany of the Saints.

7. The depositing of relics, if it is to take place, follows.

8. The bishop offers the prayer of dedication, followed by the anointing of the altar and the walls of the church. The anointing of the walls is retained because it is a dedicatory action. The sprinkling of the walls (omitted, as noted above) is a purificatory action, and is clearly inappropriate if a church has been in use for some time.

9. The incensing and lighting of the altar and the church are retained. Appropriate antiphons accompany these actions.

10. A special preface for this rite is provided. It speaks of the visible church (building), which God's power, assisting the people, has made possible. The building is an image of God's communion with his pilgrim people and a means of "shaping us here as your temple." The building is likewise an image of the Church spread throughout the world, growing into the body of Christ and destined to achieve completion "in the vision of your peace, the heavenly city of Jerusalem."

11. If the chapel of eucharistic reservation is already in use, its inauguration is omitted.

Chapter 5 of the rite gives an order for the "Blessing of a Church." What is the difference between dedication and blessing? The rite itself gives no definition of either, any more than it defines "consecration." However, liturgical practice and canonical legislation make a distinction between *consecrare* ("consecrate" or "dedicate") and *benedicere* ("bless"). The Code of Canon Law says: "As soon as its construction is properly completed, a new church is to be dedicated or at least blessed as soon as possible, observing the laws of the sacred liturgy. Churches, especially cathedral and parochial churches, are to be dedicated with a solemn rite" (canon 1217).

According to the General Instruction of the Roman Missal (265) and the texts of the rites themselves, the difference between dedication and blessing is in the degree of solemnity of prayers and rites. "Dedication" implies permanence—a building is set apart in perpetuity for the worship of God. "Blessing" assumes that the building is to be used for worship only for a time, or, as the rite says (chapter 5, 1), the building is "set aside" for the worship of God temporarily, however long "temporary" may become.

The idea can be discerned from the categories of buildings to which blessing is appropriate: oratories, chapels or "other sacred edifices." There are private chapels that have been converted to secular uses after a change of ownership. Sometimes temporary "chapels" are set up to meet a particular need, for instance, in a migrant workers' camp, or in vacation or tourist areas. These chapels accommodate a population for the time being and may eventually give way to a more permanent parish church. Other places of worship, such as those on military bases, that will be used for some time and then no longer used if the base or area is abandoned, may be blessed with the form in the rite.

Another feature distinguishing "dedication" from "blessing" is that symbols that signify a permanent setting (apart from the building itself) are omitted in a blessing; that is, the depositing of relics, the anointing, incensing and illuminating rituals are omitted.

Finally, the placement of the rite of blessing in the liturgy is significant. It takes place after the entrance rite and after the liturgy of the word. This seems to indicate that it is a rite of purification, though, like other purificatory rites in the renewed liturgy, it is intended to be first a purification of the people and only secondarily of the building. We see the spirit of this intent in the invitatory of the bishop before the blessing of water. The bishop prays that the water which will be blessed by God's power will recall to the people their baptism and their need for repentance. Before sprinkling the people and then the walls, the bishop says, "[F]irst let us call to mind that we ourselves, who are bound here in faith and love, are the living Church, set in the world, as a sign and witness of God's love for all" (chapter 5, 10). This is just one more example of many where the people are in the forefront of the thought in the rite.

Since the rite of blessing is less solemn than the rite of dedication, the directives concerning its celebration are less demanding. The bishop or a priest delegated for the purpose may preside. It may take place on any day except during the Easter Triduum. The texts of the Mass will be those of the day or the Mass of the titular of the church. During the introductory rites, the assembly, the walls of the church and the altar (if not yet blessed or dedicated) are sprinkled with holy water. After the general intercessions the altar (if necessary) is blessed with a short prayer of blessing and then incensed, as are the assembly and the main body of the church. The eucharistic celebration concludes with a solemn blessing and dismissal.

If the building is not to be blessed, the blessing of an altar (chapter 6) takes place during the Mass of the day. After the intercessions and a suitable song, the presider recites the prayer of blessing. The altar is sprinkled with holy water and incensed. It is then made ready, and the eucharist is celebrated. Because this is an important pastoral occasion, the people should be prepared as they would be for the dedication of a church.

LEAVE-TAKING BEFORE A RENOVATION

When a church will be closed for a period of time for renovation or restoration, the community may benefit from ritualizing its leave-taking from the space. There is no official rite for such an occasion, but a brief ritual could certainly be planned to take place at the conclusion of the last eucharist in the place. For example, following the prayer after communion, the presider may say these or similar words:

> Brothers and sisters, today we take leave of our church building during the time it will be renovated (or renewed or restored). We are God's pilgrim people, never fully at home in this world, until we reach our lasting home in heaven. In the liturgy, we have a foretaste of the heavenly banquet and our places of worship remind us that one day we will be citizens of the new and eternal Jerusalem.

Members of the parish community may bring forward any of the following, which will be carried in procession out of the building:
- a beautiful vessel filled with water taken from the baptismal font
- the paschal candle
- the book of the gospels or the lectionary
- the holy oils
- an icon or image of Mary or the parish patron
- the altar cloth removed from the altar table
- the reserved sacrament (carried by the presider) and the sanctuary lamp (carried by a server)

When the people carrying these objects have assembled, the presider says:
Let us go forth in peace as we look forward to returning to our holy place.

The assembly joins in singing a processional or antiphonal song. The cross and candle bearers are led by a minister carrying a censer or brazier with burning incense. Following them are those carrying the items mentioned above and the assembly. All process to the place that will be used for the community's worship during the interim. The items are appropriately placed in the new space and all depart quietly.

In place of carrying certain items out of the church, the assembly could be invited to reverence various symbols in the church before they depart the space that is to be renovated or restored. All could be invited, for example, to kiss the altar or venerate a saint's image.

Thought should be given to a ritual to introduce these items back into the space when the renovation or restoration is completed. If a particular item is not to be returned to the worship space, another suitable space on the parish site should be found for it.

CELEBRATING THE ANNIVERSARY OF DEDICATION

The celebration of the anniversary of the dedication of the parish church building is an often-forgotten opportunity to celebrate the life of the local church and re-emphasize to the people the importance of the gathering place for God's holy people. It is an occasion in which sacred identity and local history become tangible. The continuity of the faith from generation to generation is celebrated.

In an article entitled "To Celebrate the Local Church" (*Liturgy 90* [April 1990]: 8–11, 13), G. Thomas Ryan points out that Pius Parsch, a repected scholar of the liturgy in the decades preceding the Second Vatican Council, began the last chapter of his final volume of *The Church's Year of Grace* with this challenge:

> Annually the church celebrates in a solemn manner the day commemo-rating the dedication of her churches in order to recall to the minds of the faithful the high dignity and sanctity and also the deep symbolism of the material edifice. She celebrates the dedication of the parish church, the cathedral church, and the four principal churches of Rome, the mother churches, we may call them, of Christendom. Every parish church, then, celebrates two feast days of its own each year, a name day feast (patron saint) and a baptism feast (dedication). These two days should again be solemnized, using the means and inspiration provided in the liturgy. (Pius Parsch, *The Church's Year of Grace,* vol. 5, [Collegeville: The Liturgical Press, 1958], 429)

The anniversaries of dedication are high on the list of solemnities in the Table of Liturgical Days in the General Norms for the Liturgical Year and Calendar:

4. Proper solemnities, namely:

    a) Solemnity of the principal patron of the place, that is, the city or state.

    b) Solemnity of the dedication of a particular church and the anniversary.

    c) Solemnity of the title of a particular church.

    d) Solemnity of the title, or of the founder, or of the principal patron

of a religious order or congregation.

Items (b) and (c) occur every year in every parish of the United States, yet both local days are frequently ignored. Celebrating the *dies natalis* of the parish church can be richly rewarding. It is an occasion for the local community to remember that this place, built by our own flesh, blood and sacrifice, is sacred; to recall that the place where we pray each Sunday is the threshold of the gate of heaven.

It is important that each parish community know and celebrate its own specific identity in the midst of celebrating our universal identity. Local dedication anniversaries help situate the congregation in the full mystery of universality. Just as we celebrate and develop local traditions of the days of the universal church, we need to celebrate and develop local traditions of the days of our local church. Salvation is taking place here and now in *this* place.

The parish's day of anniversary stands in the tradition of several other days mentioned by Parsch. Each year on August 5, all parishes have the option of observing a memorial of the anniversary of St. Mary Major in Rome. On November 9, we celebrate as a feast of the Lord the dedication anniversary of Rome's cathedral, St. John Lateran. This observance has fallen on Sunday a few times since the calendar's reform, reminding us of our union with the bishop of Rome. Like all churches, the Lateran basilica is both a building and a symbol. As a feast of the Lord on the universal calendar, it takes precedence over November's Sundays and recognizes the priorities of our ecclesial life and spirituality. The other two major basilicas in Rome, St. Peter and St. Paul, are commemorated in an optional memorial on November 18. Finally, there is a fourth dedication day — this one different in each diocese — the feast of the cathedral's dedication, which is to be observed in every parish.

As a solemnity, the parish's dedication anniversary rises above these other four days as the preeminent day for celebrating locally the biblical images of living stones, of temple and of new Jerusalem. We should immerse ourselves in these images. We need to spend some time, energy and resources fostering this day that is our own. The high ranking of this day, as a solemnity, is no accident. It is a gift of our tradition and of the other churches with whom we are in communion. It sets off an observation of time. This local day has always been a cornerstone of the universal observances.

At the dedication anniversary, the assembly sings of the joy of its temple (and itself as that temple). The assembly finds comfort and communion in the references to people of every age dedicating their own liturgical houses, and to their parents and grandparents who built this very place. Newcomers are drawn into the spiritual bonds that gave shape to this place. History becomes palpable. Parents and elders have a sense of handing on the work of their hands and finances to future generations. Faith has a geography and we are standing in it!

In our modern rational approach to life, this may seem like hearkening to the past. Indeed, this might be the reason why the observance is so rare. Perhaps we have let our perception of sacred buildings become utilitarian. We are reluctant to admit the power of architecture over us. In the age of the global village, some are hesitant to do anything that is too specific local. In an age of advanced communication technology, we sometimes know people in faraway places better than we know our next-door neighbors. But celebrating *this* holy people is an important part of the whole picture.

If the date of dedication is unknown, research the archives in the parish, diocese or perhaps even the local civic center or historical society to discover the actual date. Once the date is known, three options are possible (see the Vatican's semi-official liturgical journal *Notitiae* 8 [1972], 103; reprinted in *Liturgy Documentary Series 6: Norms Governing Liturgical Calendars* [Washington: United States Catholic Conference, 1984], 161):

a) The actual anniversary date when the community can really keep this day as a holy day or holiday; monastic communities are cited as examples;

b) The Sunday nearest the anniversary date if it is a Sunday in Ordinary Time (except for Trinity Sunday, the Body and Blood of Christ, and Christ the King) or a Sunday in the Christmas season (except for Epiphany);

c) The Sunday before November 1 (All Saints' Day), "in order to focus on the bond between the church on earth and the church in heaven."

Since the actual anniversary date is rarely convenient for a full-scale celebration, most parishes will want to move the celebration to the nearest Sunday in Ordinary Time. Parishes whose buildings were dedicated in late November, December, February, March, April, May and early June — that is, during Advent, Lent or Eastertime — should use the third option.

Thus, about half the parishes in a diocese may observe their anniversary on the last Sunday of October. This is the usual day when we change our clocks and say a clear farewell to summertime. The time of darkness arrives. The transition to late fall and to the eschatological focus of November can be marked by local festivals of the new Jerusalem.

The Vatican-issued commentary mentioned above notes that those who cannot find the date of dedication have a choice for their observance: They may choose October 25 if the community will always be free on this day to make a true solemnity, or they may choose the Sunday before All Saints.

Most people can readily understand the value of keeping the parish dedication anniversary. Other anniversaries in life are important, like the anniversaries of birth and marriage. Once pastoral leaders are willing to reclaim this local festival, catechesis and preparation for the parish can draw from several sources: local histories, oral traditions regarding the church, images in the liturgy of dedication, awareness of the ethnic groups that formed the parish when the church was built, and the rite of dedication itself. If a parish history has never been written, discussion of this festival might motivate leaders to commission someone to pull the stories and facts together in a readable format — a gift to all the faithful and to future generations, immediately useful in homilies, catechetical sessions and bulletin articles.

Imbued with the liturgical images and local histories, pastoral leaders can use the Sunday bulletin to prepare the community. Parish newsletters and invitations to the dedication anniversary can use the concept of "homecoming," particularly if the ethnic composition of the parish has shifted and new peoples are inviting other groups for a truly ecclesial event. Other materials can be prepared that provide reflective reading and prayers for every household. Religious education classes, Catholic school assemblies, family groups and members of adult education programs can be given tours of the parish church by pastors, original members, local historians, guides — whoever can tell about font and table, images and architectural design as well as about the people who helped to make this place.

The anniversary observance should permeate all aspects of parish life on that solemnity. Gather the whole parish for a single eucharistic celebration, if this is physically possible, especially if this is in contrast to a more usual schedule of several Masses. If circumstances of space, climate and budget suggest that the central celebration take place outdoors or in a tent near the church, the disappointment about not celebrating in the place being honored can be relieved by a benefit: The assembly will be able to see the entire building. A procession around the building, accompanied by singing the Litany of the Saints from the rite of dedication, could begin or end the eucharist.

Taking a cue from the rite of dedication, the assembly might gather in a separate place and then go together in procession to the church. With little modification, the blessing and sprinkling with water from the rite of dedication could form part of the introductory rites as well. If the font is accessible to everyone in the assembly, the entire assembly might be invited to process there after the blessing prayer to sign themselves with the water. The Gloria, assigned to such a solemnity, could be sung during the sprinkling with water. The three presidential prayers, the preface and the solemn blessing are all propers in the sacramentary. Their rich images of Church can provide guidance for introductions, children's liturgy of the word, homily, intercessions and the selection of the eucharistic prayer (the inserts for eucharistic prayers I and III given in the rite of dedication and in appendix VIII of the sacramentary are appropriate for anniversary Masses).

Three readings, a psalm and gospel verse are to be chosen from the Common for the Dedication of a Church, 701. The citations for these readings might be included in an anniversary booklet or participation aid for the occasion. This booklet may also include pictures of the church, historical facts and anecdotes, music for the liturgy and prayers for use at home. These criteria will aid in selecting from among the readings available:

• harmony with the time of year (if, for example, the observance is just before All Saints, consider the Hebrews passage, which relates the church on earth and the assembly of the first-born);

• harmony with the surrounding Sundays and the semi-continuous lectionary (do any of the readings fit with what is currently being read?);

• compelling images for the parish at this time.

The homily could be based not just on the scriptures and liturgy of the solemnity but on the sacred place itself. The dismissal of the catechumens might include a word expressing the faithful's prayer for their full membership in the Church.

The selection of music is equally important. Musicians will need to search for appropriate hymns and psalm settings. Hymns in the *Liturgy of the Hours* for the Common of the Dedication of a Church are known to many. Complete hymnals usually have at least one or two other hymns appropriate for dedications. Look in the index.

The church's environment on this occasion should serve the events that will unfold on the day. For example, attention could be given to the place and signs of baptism. Decorations might even echo the tone of the season or the span of Ordinary Time during which the celebration is held. They should be designed with an awareness of the day's ecclesial and eschatological images.

Specifically, decorations might call attention to the doorways by which the assembly enters; banners and festive hangings might be installed on bell towers; flowers and greenery might be thoughtfully arranged throughout the building and among the assembly. In order to highlight the holiness of the space and enliven the senses of the gathering, consider the following:

• decorate the places where the walls were anointed. Light the dedication candles at those places and ornament them with flowers and greenery;

• find ways for seasonal flowers, branches and candles to accent different features of the building, including cross, ambo, altar, font, oil repository, eucharistic chapel, devotional shrines; if you have pew candles, this would be a good occasion to use them;

• bring out the parish's finest vesture, vessels and paraments.

As the Mass ends, eucharistic ministers could be sent, as on Sunday, to bring communion to the homebound. The day's visit might include sharing copies of the commemorative booklet about the occasion. Homebound parish members are living stones too, and sharing the liturgical events with them can lift them up in their vital role within the parish.

The eucharistic liturgy concludes with the solemn blessing found at 19 in the sacramentary.

Videos of the anniversary festivities might be made available after the date. How might the anniversary also be celebrated at the nursing homes or other institutions that the parish serves?

Other liturgical celebrations can also become part of the dedication anniversary. The Common of the Dedication of a Church from the *Liturgy of the Hours* is particularly rich. The evening before might be marked by a vigil service as outlined in appendix I of the *Liturgy of the Hours.* The same appendix contains canticles to add to the Office of Readings to form an extended vigil service. Such a vigil could include a reading from the decree establishing the parish, a selection from the homily on dedication day, an account of the liturgy from the local press or an excerpt from another document important to the parish's history. The climax of the vigil, the singing of the Te Deum, may become a treasured annual feature.

A celebration of Morning Prayer may be followed by a breakfast or, in good weather, a parish picnic. Evening Prayer might precede an annual parish supper. Weddings or other events that ordinarily involve less than the whole parish should not be scheduled on this day. The anniversary is a day for the parish to spend together, for the parish to become parish.

Attention to the observance of the solemnity of the dedication will help remove it from the endangered liturgies list. As Thomas Ryan points out, "Pastoral ministers will finish the day and go to bed with the tiredness born of satisfaction. It is the sleep of Christmas and Easter nights" ("To Celebrate the Local Church," *Liturgy 90* [April 1990]: 13). Once this anniversary is established, energy can be found to look at the other rewarding local festivals — the feast of the local titular, the feast of the diocesan patron and the anniversary of the cathedral's dedication.

CELEBRATING THE TITULAR OF THE COMMUNITY

Every church has a title. The title may refer to the Trinity. It may be one of a variety of titles of Christ (Christ the King, Holy Redeemer, St. Savior and so on), or refer to the Holy Spirit. Many parishes are named after one of Mary's titles, or for angels or saints. From the earliest centuries, Christians have celebrated their local identity on the feast day of the titular or saint. Such a celebration helps a parish claim its identity and reaffirm its mission.

If the titular solemnity falls during Ordinary Time, it may be moved to the preceding Sunday, if this will help the community to participate more fully. When the celebration falls in Advent, Christmastime, Lent or Eastertime, it should be kept in the style of that season (for example, Immaculate Conception festivities should be in keeping with the season of Advent, or St. Patrick festivities should be appropriate for Lent).

Titles such as Ascension or Transfiguration are celebrated on the day specified in the universal calendar, or, if the day is not on the current calendar, on the day assigned to it on older calendars. If the title is on neither list and it relates to Jesus, tradition suggests that it be celebrated on August 6, the Feast of the Transfiguration.

With Marian titles, the local solemnity is observed on the day on which the title is celebrated in the universal calendar (Visitation, Immaculate Conception, Holy Rosary, and so on). If the title is not in the calendar, then it can be celebrated on a day on which the title had traditionally been celebrated in older calendars. If the title still cannot be found, tradition suggests August 15, the Feast of the Assumption.

If the titular is one of the saints, observe the solemnity on the date listed in the universal calendar. If the saint is without a place on the current universal calendar, then celebrate on the date given by tradition, moving it to the nearest available date if it now conflicts with a universal feast or solemnity.

Traditional dates for saints can be discovered in one of the following ways, listed in order of priority:

• the date given in the old calendar and now left to local observances (listed in "Variations in the Roman Calendar," *Liturgy Documentary Series 6: Norms Governing Liturgical Calendars* [Washington: Bishops' Committee on the Liturgy, 1984] 115 ff., or in the index of older missals);

• the date in the martyrology; since the old edition is rarely available and the new one may not yet be available, see the *Companion to the Calendar* by Mary Ellen Hynes (Chicago: Liturgy Training Publications, 1993) or *Butler's Lives of the Saints* (Collegeville: The Liturgical Press, 1996);

• the day of death of the saint, if known;

• another date traditionally associated with the saint.

Parish leaders can provide educational and inspirational stories about the saint or titular for school and religious education programs, for parish mailings and for Sunday bulletins. Such materials should focus on the meaning of the mystery being celebrated or on the ways that the patron saint exemplifies the living-out of the paschal mystery. Always include any "local angle" to the title: why the parish was given this name, what the bishop or pastor said about it at the founding of the parish, what this name suggests for our living of the gospel today.

Prepare one major liturgy on the solemnity to gather the community together. Texts for the eucharistic liturgy can be found in the sacramentary. Texts for saints who are without specific readings in the current sacramentary and lectionary are to be taken from the "commons" of their type – Mary, apostle, martyr, pastor, doctor, virgin, holy men and holy women.

Musicians will want to search for music appropriate to the mystery being celebrated or texts that include praise of apostles, saints, prophets and martyrs, as well as general hymn texts for patrons in any of these categories. If no hymns in honor of the saint or titular can be found, the parish could commission one, seeking a competent composer with proven experience in liturgical music. Texts or themes for the music can be found in the works or writings of the saint, in the antiphons assigned to the saint or in the commons in the sacramentary and in the *Liturgy of the Hours.* In lieu of commissioning new music, researchers might find existing texts or music in the motherhouses of congregations founded by the saint, the basilica where the saint is buried or diocese where the saint lived. Litanies center around other titulars such as the Sacred Heart, St. Joseph and the Blessed Virgin Mary, for example. The general intercessions might take the form of a litany.

The environment for the celebration should be thoughtfully considered. No images are required in a church, apart from the image of Christ's cross, but our tradition gives an image of the titular patron pride of place. A rediscovery of the patronal or titular day can motivate a parish to review its art and images. Does the name of the parish find expression in a suitable image? Might a new one be commissioned? Can an existing image be brought out for this occasion? If so, is the image in good condition? Is the image properly located to attract veneration but not to interfere with the celebration of the sacred mysteries?

Some parishes, especially those with strong ties to old-world heritages, schedule a procession on the patronal day, carrying their patronal image through the streets. If the procession is organized by an independent association, negotiations may result in an agreement allowing the parish once again to celebrate its patron in a more ecclesial and liturgical manner. This may include beginning or ending the procession with a liturgy for the whole community. Any practices that are inappropriate or that may be misunderstood should be carefully avoided. If the parish alone is responsible for the procession, then it should be scheduled on or near the actual date of the liturgical solemnity, with the image in a place of honor in the church. There should be only one titular image, to focus devotion and avoid overshadowing other liturgical elements.

Seasonal flowers and greenery can be placed near the image for the celebration along with votive candles and lights. Festive hangings and banners should decorate the church, both indoors and outdoors. Luminarias (farolitos) might be placed on the ground surrounding an outdoor image. Special lighting might highlight an image high on the church building if it is not normally illuminated. Once again, the parish's finest vesture, vessels and linens should be brought out for this celebration.

See also the practices encouraged by the *Book of Blessings,* chapter 59 ("Order for Blessing of Food or Drink or Other Elements Connected with Devotion: Order of Blessing within Mass on a Feast Day").

A collection could be taken up for a local, national or international effort that is somehow related to the mystery or life of the titular being celebrated (for example, a parish named for the Blessed Sacrament could contribute to the Bread for the World organization, collect food for the local food bank or soup kitchen and so on). Be sure to remember the sick, homebound and elderly members of the parish in this celebration. Communion should be brought to all of them directly from the Mass. Materials and prayers connected to the parish's titular can be brought to them also.

Other liturgical celebrations on the occasion of the titular feast could include evening prayer on the vigil or day of the celebration. An extended vigil service including the Office of Readings or Morning Prayer are also possibilities. One of these liturgies might include veneration of the relics if relics of the titular are present. This ancient custom should be handled with great reverence and care and be accompanied by liturgical prayer and readings about the life of the saint. Sound catechetical preparation will prevent the possibility of pietistic superstition unduly exaggerating the practice.

ANNIVERSARY OF THE DEDICATION OF THE CATHEDRAL

The mother church of all the churches in a diocese is the cathedral. It houses the bishop's *cathedra* (seat), from which it receives its name. The cathedral, the sign of diocesan unity, is the place where that unity can be given concrete expression. For all these reasons, it should be a model of liturgical life, both in architecture and in celebration (see the *Ceremonial of Bishops* [Collegeville: The Liturgical Press, 1989], 42 ff.)

Esteem and reverence for the cathedral are supported by the ancient practice of remembering the cathedral in every parish every year (see *Dedication of a Church and an Altar,* chapter 2, 26). Observance of the cathedral's anniversary of dedication helps link the individual parishes as a communion of communities around their bishop.

The date of this celebration may be found in the diocesan calendar (the ordo) or by asking the diocesan office of worship or liturgical commission. The anniversary is celebrated as a solemnity in the cathedral itself, but has the rank of feast in the other churches of the diocese. If the date is always impeded, the celebration may be assigned to the nearest open date. It is not normally moved to Sunday.

Many of the features of the local solemnity of the dedication of the parish church may be included here as well. The rite of dedication notes that the bishop should preside at the eucharist at the cathedral on that day with as many priests and people as possible. A time should be scheduled that will allow the gathering of a large congregation. Evening Prayer could also be the main celebration, if this is more convenient. If so, use the texts in the Common of a Dedication of a Church from the *Liturgy of the Hours.*

If there is one central event in the cathedral itself, parish observances should not conflict with that gathering. Parish delegates should be sent to the celebration to represent the parish. When the anniversary of the cathedral's dedication is observed in the eucharistic liturgy at the parish on that day, Mass texts are chosen from the sacramentary selections for "outside the dedicated church." Intercessions should pray for the bishop, for the bishops who occupied the *cathedra* before him, for the unity of the diocese and for the cathedral parish.

A SERVICE FOR BURNING THE MORTGAGE

Paying off the debt on a church building is a significant event in the life of a community. It is an occasion for giving thanks and praise. In many places, for homes as well as community buildings, a piece of paper representing the mortgage is ceremoniously burned when the debt is paid. A solemn celebration of Morning or Evening Prayer would be appropriate on such an occasion, and could include a burning of the mortgage document. The following prayer service may serve as a model.

Gathering Rite
When all have gathered, a hymn of praise is sung.

Call to Prayer
Presider: Come, let us worship the Lord.
Assembly: The Lord has done great things for us and we rejoice!
Presider: Let us pray. (pause)

> Almighty and gracious God, we offer this unencumbered building for your divine worship. We pray that we may always worship in spirit and in truth in this place and that our prayer may give you praise and thanks. We ask this through Christ, our Lord. Amen.

Liturgy of the Word
1 Chronicles 29:10–18 or Romans 12:1–21
Psalm 105 or another appropriate psalm
Gospel: Matthew 5:23–24, Luke 19:1–10, John 2:13–22 or John 4:19–24
Homily and testimonials of thanks from community members

Mortgage Burning
The assembly and presider go to a place where a brazier has been prepared. When all have gathered, the presider may say these or similar words:

> We cannot fully offer to God what is not ours. We have now completed payment on the debt on this house for God's Church. It is unencumbered and completely ours. Therefore, to God we now offer it, with gratitude and joy.

> The presider or another person representing the community places the mortgage document in the brazier. A period of silence follows as the document is burned. Applause may follow.

Prayers of Thanksgiving
Presider: Let us now give thanks to God for this accomplishment.

Reader: For this assembly and all God's holy people,
Assembly: Lord, we give you thanks.

Reader: For generous hearts and hardworking hands,
Assembly: Lord, we give you thanks.

Reader: For successful sacrifices and patient saving,
Assembly: Lord, we give you thanks.

Reader: For faith and hope and love,
Assembly: Lord, we give you thanks.

Reader: For those who dared to dream and to build, for founders and for ancestors, for all who have gone before us,
Assembly: Lord, we give you thanks.

Presider:

Receive, God, the heartfelt prayers and thanks of your people who are mindful of the ultimate gift of your Son on the cross. May our worship in this place unite us always with the one, true sacrifice of Christ, now and forever.

Assembly: Amen.

Presider: Gathering our prayers and thanks into one, we pray as Jesus taught us.

Assembly: Our Father . . .

Presider: Let us offer each other a sign of Christ's peace.

Blessing
Presider:

May God, the loving Father, bless us who gather here in worship; may Jesus, the Son, unite us always in heart and soul; may the Spirit animate us and send us forth in loving service. And may we be blessed now and all days.

Assembly: Amen.

All join in a concluding song.

BLESSINGS FOR PARTICULAR SPACES AND FURNISHINGS

Just as the rite of dedication is the essential liturgy for the setting apart of buildings for the worship of God, other ritual blessings are used to recognize the value of places and objects within the church building that are used in worship.

In the Roman pontifical, before its recent reform, many blessings of the church building itself or of liturgical accoutrements were reserved to the bishop. Bells, for example, which call the faithful to worship and which mark periods of prayer throughout the day, were not only blessed with holy water and incense but also consecrated with chrism in an elaborate ritual. Likewise, chalices and patens were consecrated with chrism prior to use. There were also blessings for antimensions (a corporal-like linen with relics sewn into it that took the place of an altar stone), eucharistic vessels (such as tabernacle, ciborium, monstrance, pyx), church appointments (candlestick, oil stock), altar cloths and linens (corporal, pall, purificator), and vestments. (Amice, alb, cincture, maniple, stole and chasuble, according to the rubric of the time, *had* to be blessed, whereas dalmatic, tunic, cope, humeral veil, surplice, burse and chalice veil *could* be blessed.) There were also blessings for a new cross, for an image of the Blessed Virgin Mary, with a separate order for the crowning of an image of Mary, for images of saints, for reliquaries. The pontifical also contained a special blessing for the incense to be burned on an altar to be consecrated! Everything related to divine worship was set apart by ritual prayer.

Some of these occasions, for instance, the consecration of a bell, involved various ministers and the presence of the faithful. Other blessings were carried out by the bishop, or a delegated priest, more privately. Many of these practices came from a period of liturgical history where there was felt a need to sacralize or purify everything against the effects of a profane world. (For a more complete treatment of this subject see Thomas G. Simons, *Blessings: A Reappraisal* [San Jose, CA: Resource Publications, 1981]).

Likewise, before the Second Vatican Council's reform of the section of the Roman ritual that concerned blessings, there were many blessings related to the church edifice or divine worship that could be delegated to or used by a priest. These included a blessing for the laying of a church cornerstone, for a private or domestic oratory, for a baptismal font, for a church organ, and for a church bell. (A priest could bless the church bell; the bishop consecrated it.) Priests could also bless eucharistic vessels, church linens and vestments (see *Practical Handbook of Rites, Blessings and Prayers* [St. Paul: North Central Publishing Company, 1961]). The blessing for the Stations of the Cross, historically reserved to the Franciscans, could also be delegated to a diocesan or other religious priest.

The *Rite of Dedication of a Church and an Altar,* perhaps as a carryover from the former rite, retains one of the many auxiliary blessings that were part of the former pontifical. Chapter 7 contains a "Rite of Blessing a Chalice and Paten." The chalice (cup) and paten (communion bowl or plate) are the principal vessels necessary for the celebration of the eucharist. These should be made of worthy materials, valued in the region or place they come from, suitably designed and fashioned for the liturgy. They should be treated with respect and are to be devoted solely and permanently for divine worship. For these reasons, says the introduction (chapter 7, 1–2), they should be blessed.

What is the meaning of this blessing? The use of the word "consecrate" in the introduction indicates that the vessels are being "set apart" exclusively for use at the eucharist. As the prayer of blessing shows, the vessels are blessed by being put to use. In other words, they are blessed by the body and blood of Christ that they hold: "May they be sanctified, for in them the body and blood of Christ will be offered, consecrated, and received." There is no longer any anointing of the vessels with chrism, nor any sprinkling with holy water. This is a return to the more ancient concept that things are blessed by use.

The rite may be celebrated either within or outside of Mass, following the liturgy of the word. Within Mass it takes place before the presentation of the gifts, with the vessels being presented by members of the assembly. The vessels are placed on the altar, clearly relating them to the eucharistic action that is to follow. During the presentation of the vessels an antiphon is sung ("I will take the cup of salvation and call on the name of the Lord") or another appropriate song. During the preparation of the gifts Psalm 116 with an antiphon ("I will take the cup of salvation and offer a sacrifice of praise") or another song may be sung.

Special texts for readings and psalms are suggested, all referring to the chalice. The gospel reading may be either Matthew 20:20–28 ("You shall indeed drink from my cup") or Mark 14:12–16, 22–26 ("This is my body. . . . This is my blood").

The form for the blessing outside Mass offers general intercessions that culminate in the Lord's Prayer. While the meaning of the chalice is very clear in the rite, the vessel for the eucharistic bread is hardly mentioned. This might be interpreted as emphasizing that communion of all present from the cup is to be normal practice.

Part III of the 1989 *Book of Blessings* is entitled "Blessings of objects that are designed or erected for use in churches, either in the liturgy or in popular devotions." When a church building is to be dedicated or blessed by the *Rite of Dedication,* "everything in the church, except the altar, is regarded as blessed and erected in virtue of the rite of dedication or blessing, so that no further rite is needed" (*Book of Blessings,* 1078). However, "certain blessings . . . have a particular significance and importance in the life of the ecclesial community: for example, the blessing of a crucifix or image that is to be offered for public veneration, the blessing of bells, an organ, church doors, the erection of stations of the cross" (1079). Another use of these blessings might be in the case of a partial renovation of a church: the installation of a new baptistry or shrine, for example.

Either the bishop, the priest assigned to the church or a priest who is delegated may preside at the celebration of these blessings. If no priest is available, these blessings may also be assigned to a deacon.

Most of the blessings in this section offer a form of the blessing for use within as well as outside of Mass. When the blessing takes place within Mass it follows the homily, with the usual pattern of general intercessions concluding in the prayer of blessing. If the blessing takes place outside of Mass, the celebration usually consists of an introductory rite of song, liturgical greeting and brief words by the presider to prepare those present for the blessing. This is followed by a reading of the word of God, with various scriptural texts and psalm responses offered, followed by a homily. Intercessions follow, concluding with the Lord's Prayer and the blessing prayer. The service concludes with a prayer over the people, blessing and an appropriate closing song. A gesture of blessing is usually indicated, such as the sign of the cross. At times, a blessing with holy water or incense is indicated.

Attention should be given to the place or object to be blessed and to its environment. For example, when a new repository for the holy oils is blessed, the repository should be decorated with flowers and lights, expressions of the life and joy that these oils bring sacramentally. The introductions to each chapter offer references to scriptural texts and church documents on the subject of blessing and the Church's intent in these blessings. Examine the texts ands documents of catechetical concepts.

In Part III of the *Book of Blessings*, chapter 31 contains an "Order for the blessing of a baptistry or of a new baptismal font." This may take place within a celebration of baptism or outside of baptism. The introduction recognizes that the baptistry or font "is rightly considered to be one of the most important parts of a church" (1080) and that "every cathedral and parish church ought to have its own baptistry or a special place where the baptismal font flows or is situated" (1081). The order contains guidance on the choice of day for the blessing, pastoral preparation and liturgical requisites. While the font is considered to have been inaugurated or blessed as part of the rite of dedication (the blessing of water and the sprinkling of church building and people could begin there), a parish community might consider celebrating this blessing when a new font has been installed as part of a church renovation.

Chapter 32 contains an "Order for the blessing of a repository for the holy oils." "The oils used for the celebration of the sacraments of initiation, holy orders, and the anointing of the sick according to ancient tradition are reverently reserved in a special place in the church" (1125). The form provided may be used for blessing either a repository for the holy oils or for blessing the vessels in which the oils are stored. In the past, the place where the holy oils — in metal "stocks" — were kept was either in the sacristy or on a wall in the sanctuary. In recent times, more impressive repositories in which the oils are visible in sizable glass containers, often near the font, have become common. The blessing of the repository could take place during the Easter season, after newly blessed oils have been received in the parish, or within a sacramental celebration in which one or more of the oils has been used.

Chapter 33 contains an "Order for a blessing on the occasion of the installation of a new episcopal or presidential chair, a new lectern, a new tabernacle, or a new confessional." In a sense, a presidential chair is "inaugurated" when the bishop presides from it for the first time in the dedication of a new church. It is another case of blessing by use. However, if a new chair is obtained after the church is dedicated, such a blessing may be a significant time to reflect on liturgical and pastoral leadership and the teaching role that is symbolized by the chair. There is considerable discussion today about the placement of the presider's chair within the assembly. The design and the placement of the chair should reflect the presider's role of "guiding the prayer of the people of God" (1154).

The blessing for a new ambo or lectern likewise takes place at the rite of dedication when the bishop commissions the readers to proclaim the scriptures in this place. Again, it is blessing by use. However, as the introduction to the *Book of Blessings* states, "the lectern or ambo must be worthy to serve as the place from which the word of God is proclaimed and must be a striking reminder to the faithful that the table of God's word is always prepared for them" (1173). The blessing is intended for an ambo that is "fixed and of a design worthy of its function" (ibid.). However, a less permanent ambo may be blessed "if it is truly becoming, worthy of its function, and designed with beauty" (ibid.). Once merely a part of the altar (recall the epistle and gospel sides of the altar), the ambo has become prominent once again as the other table in the eucharistic assembly — the table of God's word. The blessing may be joined to the celebration of Mass or joined to a celebration of the word of God.

A tabernacle is blessed when the bishop takes the eucharist in procession to the eucharistic chapel and inaugurates it (as the rite calls it) at the conclusion of the rite of dedication. The blessing provided recalls the purpose of the tabernacle: It is to be a place of prayer and of eucharistic reservation "for the sake of the sick and the dying" (1192). Particularly where a separate chapel for eucharistic reservation has been provided in a building that has already been dedicated, it would be appropriate to have this blessing after a eucharistic liturgy, much like the inauguration of a new chapel in a new church, as found at the end of the rite of dedication.

The blessing for a new confessional or reconciliation chapel recognizes the practice "of reserving a special place in churches for the celebration of the sacrament of reconciliation" (1203). The document *Environment and Art in Catholic Worship*, taking up the recommendation of the *Rite of Penance*, suggests that this room or rooms "may be located near the baptismal area (when that is at the entrance) or in another convenient place" (81). As the introduction to the *Book of Blessings* indicates, the blessing is not to be joined to a celebration of Mass. However, it may be opportune to join the blessing to a penitential service (1204).

Chapter 34 provides an "Order for the blessing of new church doors." The introduction to this rite states:

> In the liturgical celebrations of baptism, marriage, and funerals, provision is made for a rite of reception at the doors of the church. On certain days of the liturgical year, the faithful pass through these doors in procession into the body of the church. It is proper, then, that in construction, design, and decoration church doors should stand as a symbol of Christ, who said: 'I am the door, whoever enters through me will be safe,' and of those who have followed the path of holiness that leads to the dwelling place of God. (1216)

We tend to think of doors in a more utilitarian manner and do not often recognize them as liturgical symbols or church furnishings. Doors can be considered inaugurated or blessed at the rite of dedication when we either gather at them or pass through them at the beginning of the dedication liturgy. The blessing of new doors, apart from the dedication rite, can be seen as "an occasion for offering special prayers to God and for gathering together the faithful to hear the word of God and to give voice to their petitions" (1217).

Just as we decorate the doors of our homes at special times and seasons, so should the doors of our churches be highlighted at various times. The church once had a minor order of "porter" or doorkeeper, whose work is now part of the ministry of ushers and greeters who welcome us when we come through the church's doors to gather for prayer and worship.

Chapter 35 provides an "Order for the blessing of a new cross for public veneration." This blessing was found in the former pontifical and ritual. "The cross is the image most cherished by the Christian people and the most ancient; it represents Christ's suffering and victory and at the same time, as the fathers of the Church have taught, it points to his Second Coming" (1233). The cross is a sign that we recognize when we gather for worship. It also has a place of honor in Christian homes.

The introduction to this rite notes that "the image of the cross should preferably be a crucifix, that is, have the corpus attached, especially in the case of a cross that is erected in a place of honor inside a church" (1235).

In Chapter 36, an "Order for the blessing of images for public veneration by the faithful" is provided. "The Church encourages the devout veneration of sacred images by the faithful, in order that they may see more deeply into the mystery of God's glory" (1258). The order provides a blessing for an image of our Lord, an image of the blessed Virgin Mary, and an image of a saint or of saints.

The blessing of images of Christ, Mary or the saints is not celebrated within Mass but within a service of the Word or within Evening Prayer. The introduction offers a format for such a celebration.

Chapter 37 offers the "Order for the blessing of bells." In the former rite, bells were consecrated by the bishop with an elaborate ritual. (See Aimé Georges Martimort, "Bells," *The Church at Prayer,* vol. 1, *Principles of the Liturgy,* [Collegeville: The Liturgical Press, 1987], 214–215; also Harold Collins, "Church Bells," *The Church Edifice and Its Appointments* [Westminster: The Newman Bookstore, 1946], 14–16.) The reformed rite recognizes "the longstanding custom of blessing bells before they are hung in the belfry or campanile" (1306). The bells may be blessed either within or outside of Mass. "The bells should be hung or set up in the place chosen for the blessing in such a way that it will be easy to walk around the bells or ring them, if this suits the occasion" (1307) and "depending on the place and the individual circumstances, the bells are blessed either outside or inside the church" (1308).

Chapter 38 contains the "Order for the blessing of an organ." The *Constitution on the Sacred Liturgy* states, "in the Latin Church the pipe organ is to be held in high esteem" (120). Whether as an accompaniment for singing or as a solo instrument, says the order, it adds splendor to sacred celebrations, offers praise to God, fosters a sense of prayer in the faithful and raises their spirits to God (1325). The introduction states, "because of its close connection with the music and song for liturgical services and popular devotions, an organ should be blessed before being played for the first time in a liturgical celebration" (ibid.). The order indicates that the blessing "may be celebrated on any day, except in those seasons when liturgical law limits the use of the organ" (1327). The blessing would likely be celebrated in a service outside of Mass, such as either at Evening Prayer or the blessing service of the word itself. A concert of sacred music could follow such a blessing celebration.

Chapter 39 provides an "Order for the blessing of articles for liturgical use." This blessing brings together a variety of separate blessings that were found in the former pontifical and ritual. The introduction says, "Certain objects that are used in divine worship are deserving of special respect and therefore should be blessed before being used" (1341). Such liturgical objects would include communion vessels (apart from the chalice and paten, which have their own blessing), and eucharistic vessels such as the pyx or monstrance. This blessing would also be appropriate for vesture worn by ordained ministers, linens and altar cloths, as well as hymnals and service books, such as a new copy of the sacramentary, lectionary or book of the gospels. The "blessing of hymnals and service books" is an American addition to the *Book of Blessings.* It was combined with this collective blessing for articles for liturgical use. As the introduction indicates, "it is preferable that several such items be blessed in the one rite, either within Mass or in a separate celebration" (1345).

Chapter 40 reprints the "Order for the blessing of a chalice and paten" found in the *Rite of Dedication of a Church and an Altar* (chapter 7). Formerly reserved to the bishop, this blessing may also be celebrated by a priest. The introduction states that "if it is a chalice or paten alone that is to be blessed, the text should be suitably adapted" (1363).

Chapter 42 offers the "Order for the blessing of stations of the cross." The introduction indicates that "stations of the cross that have been installed in a church that is to be dedicated or blessed do not require a distinct celebration of their erection" (1400). The stations themselves can consist of crosses with images (formerly, the crosses were required to be made of wood) or simply of crosses alone. The placement of these stations should be carefully considered, whether they are set up in the church or in a place of their own, so that private devotion will not conflict with the public prayer of the Church. When stations of the cross have been erected in a church or oratory, the blessing found in this chapter may be celebrated and "should immediately precede the devotion of the Way of the Cross" (ibid.).

There has been much development of this devotion within recent times. In addition to the familiar fourteen stations of the cross, a fifteenth station commemorating the resurrection has sometimes been added. Other alternative sets of stations have been popularized, such as that used by Pope John Paul II on Good Friday evening in Rome. The cathedral in Bristol, England, received approval from Rome to erect and bless this alternative version of the stations. Likewise, the Salesians of St. Don Bosco have promoted another set of stations, the "stations of light," which focus on fourteen biblical events between the resurrection and Pentecost. Since many devotional booklets exist today with images and reflections on various versions of the stations, some contend that it is no longer necessary to place permanent images in the church. Others approach the devotion in much the same way as the Christmas crèche, placing images of the stations in the church or chapel during the Lenten season. It is certainly acceptable to use movable and seasonal devotional art that need not become permanent in the church building.

It is interesting to note that services for the "dedication of church furnishings and ornaments" are also provided among other Christian traditions, such as in the Episcopal Church (see *The Book of Occasional Services* [New York: The Church Hymnal Corporation, 1995], 196 – 211). In addition to the kinds of blessings found in the Roman Catholic *Book of Blessings,* dedications are provided for candlesticks and lamps, a repository for the scriptures, chairs, benches and prayer desks, a stained glass window, an organ or other musical instrument and a funeral pall.

PUBLIC PRAYER AFTER THE DESECRATION OF A CHURCH

Since the Middle Ages, the church's liturgical books have contained rituals for the reconciliation of sacred places that have been violated. Until recently, the pontifical and the ritual contained orders for the reconciliation of a desecrated church, a desecrated cemetery and the consecration of altars that have been desecrated. The services themselves are an expression of public prayer asking forgiveness for wrongful human acts and seeking to return the sacred place, particularly if it is a church building, to cultic purity.

The pontifical contained a more solemn form of the rite, for a consecrated church, which was to be celebrated by a bishop. The ritual contained a simpler form of the rite, usually for a church that was only blessed, to be used by a priest. A priest could reconcile a consecrated church only if he had the permission of the bishop, in which case he was to use the solemn rite in the pontifical. In real and urgent necessity, if the bishop could not be reached, the pastor of a church that had been consecrated could reconcile it without delay, and later inform the bishop of the fact. On September 26, 1964, the Sacred Congregation of Rites revoked canon 1176 of the 1917 Code of Canon Law, and ruled that any priest can reconcile a church that had been violated, whether the church had been consecrated or only blessed.

Previously, canon law recognized four situations that resulted in the desecration or violation of a church:

1. Criminal homicide, which, according to common interpretation, included suicide. Causing the death of another in self-defense or under the influence of grave fear did not come under this rule.

2. The shedding of blood under grave and unjust circumstances, and in such a manner as to do serious injustice to the victim and to constitute a real irreverence to the edifice.

3. The impious and sordid use of the church, such as the exercise of heretical or superstitious worship or acts repugnant to the sacred character of the house of God, such as the execution of a capital sentence. (The Sacred Congregation of Rites once ordered the reconciliation of a church that been used as a barracks and stable for horses and mules).

4. Burial or entombment of an infidel or of a person excommunicated by declaratory or condemnatory sentence.

Acts of defilement, in order to constitute a legal desecration, had to be certain, notorious and committed in the church itself. (See Collins, *op cit.,* 31–35.)

The former rite began with a gathering at the doors of the desecrated church. When the bishop presided Psalm 68 was prayed: "Let God rise up, let his enemies be scattered; let those who hate him flee before him." When a priest presided, Psalm 51 was prayed: "Have mercy on me, O God, according to your steadfast love; according to your abundant mercy blot out my transgressions." During this psalmody, the bishop or priest would circle the exterior of the church, sprinkling the walls of the building. The bishop used Gregorian water, a mixture of salt, water, ashes and wine. The priest made use of blessed water. All entered the church while the ministers proceeded to the altar. The bishop sprinkled the altar and offered an invocation. Afterward, a deacon invited all to kneel. There followed a period of silence, after which the deacon invited all to stand. The bishop then offered a prayer followed by a sung preface. The deacon then said, "Let us bless the Lord," and all responded, "Thanks be to God." Mass then followed, if opportune, either celebrated by the bishop or another priest.

When a priest presided, the litany of the saints was sung as the assembly entered the church, followed by a prayer offered by the priest. Then he sprinkled the interior of the church, particularly the place where defilement took place, while Psalm 68 was sung. Upon returning to the altar, the priest offered a prayer asking that this place "may remain inviolably sanctified, and that the body of faithful who invoke thee may be the recipients of thy liberality" ("Reconciliation of a Profaned Church [which previously was only blessed]," *The Roman Ritual in Latin and English, Volume III, The Blessings,* translated and edited by Philip T. Weller, [Milwaukee: The Bruce Publishing Company, 1946, second revised edition, 1952]).

The current 1983 Code of Canon Law stipulates that "sacred places are violated through serious harmful actions posited in them which scandalize the faithful and are so serious and contrary to the holiness of the place, in the judgment of the local ordinary, that it is not licit to perform acts of worship in them until the harm is repaired through a penitential rite in accord with the norm of the liturgical books" (canon 1211). This thought of the scandal to the faithful is a shift in emphasis from the 1917 Code. The previous code focused more on the act that violated the holiness of a sacred place, rather than the scandal. There is no question of a sacred place losing its dedication or blessing (formerly referred to as "execration"). Canon 1212 is concerned with actions contrary to the nature of the sacred place, in which the faithful who worship there would see a need for public penance before the place could be used again for worship.

In March of 1983 a draft edition of the *Book of Blessings* was distributed by the Congregation for Divine Worship to the national bishops' conferences. This draft contained an appendix with "forms of public prayer," including "public prayer in the case of desecration of a church building." However, this appendix, which was translated by the International Committee on English in the Liturgy and included in the English-language draft of the *Book of Blessings,* was not included in the final text of the Roman edition in May of 1984. The English-language *Ceremonial of Bishops,* published in 1989, does contain a chapter (20) on "public prayer after the desecration of a church." It notes that the Latin edition of this rite has not been completed or issued by the Holy See, and that this rite may be published in the future as a supplementary part of the *Book of Blessings.*

The introduction to this chapter of the *Ceremonial* contains directives and guidance for such situations, as follows.

1070. Crimes committed in a church affect and do injury to the entire Christian community, which the church building in a sense symbolizes and represents.

The crimes in question are those that do grave dishonor to sacred mysteries, especially to the eucharistic species, and are committed to show contempt for the Church, or are crimes that are serious offenses against the dignity of the person and of society.

A church, therefore, is desecrated by actions that are gravely injurious in themselves and a cause of scandal to the faithful. In the judgment of the local Ordinary, they are so serious and so offensive to the sanctity of the church building that divine worship may be celebrated in the church only after penitential reparation for the wrong done.

1071. Reparation for the desecration of a church is to be carried out with a penitential rite celebrated as soon as possible. Until that time neither the eucharist nor any other sacrament or rite is to be celebrated in the church. But through preaching and devotional exercises the faithful should be prepared for the penitential rite of reparation, and for their own inner conversion they should celebrate the sacrament of penance.

To symbolize the theme of penance, the altar of the church should be stripped bare, and all customary signs of joy and gladness should be put away, for example, lights, flowers, and other such articles.

1072. It is fitting that the bishop of the diocese preside at the rite of reparation. This will demonstrate that not only the immediate community but the entire diocesan Church joins in the rite and is ready for repentance and conversion.

As circumstances suggest, the bishop together with the rector of the church of the local community will decide whether the rite should be carried out with a celebration of the eucharistic sacrifice or with a celebration of the word of God.

1073. The penitential rite may be celebrated on any day except the Easter Triduum, Sundays, or solemnities. But nothing precludes celebration of this rite on the vigil of a Sunday or solemnity; rather, such an arrangement has the advantage of avoiding spiritual harm to the faithful.

1075. The rite most suitable for use in reparation for the desecration of a church is one in which the penitential service is aptly joined to the celebration of the eucharist. A new church is most properly dedicated through a celebration of the eucharist, and a desecrated church should be restored to divine service in the same way.

1077. The proper texts required for the celebration of the Mass are all indicated in their place in The Roman Ritual. But the Mass celebrated may also be one that is best suited to the reparation of the wrong done, for example, one of the votive Masses of the holy eucharist in a case of profanation of the blessed sacrament (Roman Missal, Votive Masses, Holy Eucharist) or the Mass for promoting harmony in a case of a violent clash in the church building between members of the community (Roman Missal, Masses and Prayers for Various Needs and Occasions, IV. For Particular Needs, 42. For Promoting Harmony).

The following is an outline of each form of the penitential rite along with the prayer texts. (The translation is by the International Commission for English in the Liturgy, Inc., Washington, DC, 1983, but has not been officially promulgated. It is quoted here with permission for purposes of study and research only, and is not to be used in public worship.)

I) Penitential Rite within Mass
The rite provides two forms of entrance into the church. The first form, with a procession, begins at a nearby church. All (bishop, concelebrants, deacons and other ministers) go to the place where the people have gathered. The bishop greets the people and gives a brief instruction to prepare the faithful for the celebration of the rite.

(English translation of Latin text)	(ICEL alternative)
My dear brothers and sisters, we have all come together to celebrate this penitential rite. But beforehand we should implore God to give us his gift of genuine repentance. Forgetting his goodness, we have all dishonored his name and disregarded his commandments. Let this rite be for us an effective lesson that we must never disfigure the Church, God's dwelling place among us, by our sins. Let this rite be the occasion for our solemn affirmation that we will keep our own hearts as true temples of God.	*Brothers and sisters in Christ, we begin this service of penance by turning to God our Father and asking him for the spirit of true repentance. We have failed to remember his goodness, we have refused to obey his commands, we have dishonored his name. We must take care never to allow sin to defile the Church of Christ, which is the dwelling place of God on earth, and the temple of the Holy Spirit.*

He invites them to pray and, after a brief pause for silent prayer, says:

O God, the author and restorer of human nature, look with pity on your people, whom in baptism you have marked with your own name and whom you sustain in the other sacraments. Grant that those who are gathered here to make reparation to your wronged majesty may offer you truly contrite hearts, genuine repentance, and the resolve to avoid all sin in the future. Grant that they may by your grace persevere in living holy lives. We ask this through Christ our Lord. Amen.

Lord, you have chosen us, you have marked us with your name, and you renew us by your sacraments. We are gathered here to manifest our sorrow and regret at the dishonor shown to your name. Look with kindness on your children as we repent of our sins. Forgive us and send your Holy Spirit to renew within us the holiness that we gained in the waters of baptism. We ask this through Christ our Lord. Amen.

The deacon may invite all to go forth, and the procession to the desecrated church is formed (crossbearer, servers with lighted candles, concelebrating priests, bishop, deacons and the faithful). During the procession the Litany of the Saints is sung, with invocations of the patron of the place or the titular of the church added to the litany in the appropriate place. Before the invocation, "Jesus, Son of the living God," an invocation related to the rite of reparation is added (e.g. "Restore this house of prayer to its former dignity") as well as other invocations pertinent to the needs of the community.

Upon entering the church, the bishop proceeds to the chair (without reverencing the altar), with the other ministers going to their places. The bishop blesses water and sprinkles the people (as a reminder of their baptism) and altar and walls (as a sign of purification) of the desecrated church.

The second form, the simple entrance, takes place when a procession is not feasible or possible. All gather in the church. The bishop and ministers process into church while Psalm 130 (with the antiphon: "If you, O Lord, should mark our guilt, Lord who would survive. Because with you there is mercy, God of Israel") or another appropriate song is sung. The rite continues with the blessing and sprinkling of water.

Ministers bring water to the bishop at the chair. He invites all to pray and, after a period of silence, he says:

Brothers and sisters, let us pray to God, the Father of mercies, through Jesus Christ in the Holy Spirit. Let us ask his blessing on this creation, water, which will be sprinkled on us as a gesture of repentance and on the altar and walls of this church

Brothers and sisters in Christ, let us ask the Father of mercies, through Jesus Christ in the Holy Spirit, to bless this gift of water. It is a sign of our repentance, a reminder of our baptism, and a symbol of the cleansing of these walls and this

as a sign of cleansing. We deplore the vile deeds committed in this house of the Church and we confess our own sinfulness. As we do so, may God's grace come to our aid to change us by a conversion of heart and to give us the power to praise his name by the holiness of our lives.

altar. May the grace of God strengthen us, for we both acknowledge our own sinfulness and deplore the defiling of this church. May he touch our hearts and turn us to him again to praise and bless his goodness by the holiness of our lives.

The bishop then says the invocation over the water:

O God, through whom every creature comes into the light of life, you shower us with an immense love. Not only do you sustain us with your fatherly care, but you also mercifully cleanse us from our sins by the outpouring of your love and again and again bring us back to Christ our Head. Your merciful plan has determined that those who go down into the waters of baptism as sinners die together with Christ and rise again in innocence as his members and as coheirs of eternal life. By our sins we turn away from you daily, yet each time in your mercy you knock at the door of our hearts, you gently purge us, and you are pleased to take us back into your friendship. By your blessing + make holy this creature, water, so that it will be a reminder of our baptism, a sign of conversion and repentance, and a new pledge of heavenly graces. Grant the final attainment of the heavenly Jerusalem to us and to all our brothers and sisters who will celebrate the sacred mysteries in this house of your Church. We ask this through Christ our Lord. Amen.

Lord, you call every creature to the light of life, and surround us with such great love that you not only safeguard our every action but lovingly forgive us when we stray and continually lead us back to Christ our Head. For you have established an inheritance of such mercy that those sinners who pass through water made sacred die with Christ to rise restored as members of his Body and heirs of his eternal covenant. When we turn away from you by sin, your kindness follows us, your goodness cleanses us, and your holiness restores us to your friendship. Bless + the gift of this water that it may be a reminder of our baptism, a sign of our contrite return and a fresh promise of the outpouring of your grace. May all here today and all those in days to come who celebrate your mysteries in this church be united at last in the city of your peace.

The altar, people, and walls of the church are sprinkled while an appropriate song is sung, with several appropriate antiphons being offered:

O wash me more and more from my guilt, O Lord, and cleanse me from my sin.

or

Cleanse us, O Lord, from all our sins, wash us and we shall be whiter than snow.

or

I will pour water over you and wash away all your defilement. A new heart will I give you, says the Lord.

After the sprinkling, the bishop says the opening prayer:

O God, in your unfailing care you purify your Church and enrich it with your grace. Hear us as we ask for your mercy. Cleanse this your family, already consecrated to you through baptism. May this place of worship take on again the splendor of its restored dignity and may your people as well, restored by salutary penance, stand before the world as a shining sign of your presence. We ask this through Christ our Lord. Amen.

Lord, with a Father's love you constantly renew your Church in holiness and surround it with your enriching grace. Hear our prayer, and cleanse your people, once made holy in the waters of baptism. As this church has been restored to its former glory so may your people, restored by penance, become a clearer sign of your presence in the world. We ask this through Christ our Lord. Amen.

For the liturgy of the word, the scriptural readings and responses are taken from the Lectionary (Masses for Various Occasions, IV: "For Particular Needs: For Forgiveness of Sins," nos. 886-890). Other readings may also be chosen in view of the particular circumstances. The bishop gives a homily which centers around the biblical readings, the restored dignity of the church's house, and the need for all to grow in holiness.

If the Litany of the Saints has been sung, the general intercessions are omitted. If not, the general intercessions should be prepared in such a way that besides the usual intentions, petition(s) are added for conversion and pardon. The following are examples:

Brothers and sisters, let us raise our petitions to God, the giver of pardon and grace, so that as he hears the earnest pleas in our voices, he may find in our hearts the sorrow of true penitents.

1. For the faithful who will come to this restored church to celebrate the liturgy, that they may listen to God's word attentively, be refreshed by the sacraments, filled with God's praises, and strengthened for their life and apostolate, we pray to the Lord.
(Response: Hear us, O Lord)

2. For this assembly, that the Holy Spirit may dwell in us when we have been renewed by penance, we pray to the Lord. (Response)

3. For the Church, that by grace the Holy Spirit may purify it, strengthen it, and make it grow in holiness, we pray to the Lord. (Response)

4. For those who serve in public office, that freed from the lust for power and motivated only by the will to serve, they may protect the rights of citizens, eliminate the causes of strife, and promote harmony in the community, we pray to the Lord. (Response)

5. For those who in desecrating this church have offended the divine majesty, that delivered from their ignorance and malice they may experience the effects of forgiveness and return to the path of salvation with us, who are also sinners, we pray to the Lord. (Response)

6. For all people, that with open hearts they will receive Christ's admonition: "Reform your lives and believe in the Gospel," we pray to the Lord. (Response)

The bishop concludes the general intercession in these words:

O God, you show your almighty power above all by your compassion and forgiveness. Pour forth your mercy on us and turn your people back to you with all their hearts as they offer you the signs of genuine repentance. What they ask with suppliant voices may they receive with hearts gladdened by your mercy. We ask this through Christ our Lord. Amen.

After the general intercessions, the altar is prepared and suitably decorated for the eucharistic celebration. The gifts are brought forward and received. During the procession with gifts the following antiphon may be sung or another appropriate song:

If you bring your gift to the altar and there recall that your brother or sister has anything against you, leave your gift at the altar, go first and be reconciled with your brother or sister, and then come and offer your gift.

When the bishop goes to the altar, he kisses it and offers the gifts. The altar and the gifts are then incensed by the bishop. He then prays the prayer over the gifts:

Lord, trusting in your fatherly care, we come bringing these gift to your altar. May the mysteries we are about to celebrate cleanse us by the purifying power of your grace. We ask this through Christ our Lord. Amen.

Lord, as we bring these gifts to your altar, we remain confident of your goodness. May we be cleansed by your grace and transformed by the mysteries we celebrate. We ask this through Christ our Lord. Amen.

At communion one of the following antiphons, with Psalm 69, or another appropriate song may be sung:

> My house shall be called a house of prayer, says the Lord; ask here and you shall receive; seek and you shall find; knock and the door will open.

or

> I burn with zeal for your house.

In the case of desecration of the eucharistic species, the concluding rites of the Mass are replaced by exposition and benediction of the blessed sacrament, or the bishop prays the prayer after communion:

Lord, may the reception of the divine sacrament fill us with your grace and by its power may it make us pass from old ways to newness of life. We ask this through Christ our Lord. Amen.

Lord, may the sacrament we have received fill our hearts with your grace. Cleansed by its power, may we abandon our lives of sin and walk in a new way of holiness. We ask this through Christ our Lord. Amen.

The bishop offers the final blessing, using one of the forms for a solemn blessing found in the sacramentary. The deacon dismisses the faithful and all join in a concluding song.

II) Penitential Rite within a Celebration of the Word

Depending on the circumstances, the special penitential rite may be combined with a celebration of the word of God rather than of the eucharist. The bishop, or a priest charged with the pastoral care of the church, presides. Generally, the rite and its prayers, as shown above, are followed. During the sprinkling with holy water, Psalm 51 is sung with one of the antiphons previously indicated. After the homily, penitential intercessions and the preparation of the altar takes place. The intercessions are prayer for God's mercy. This may take the form of the intercessions given here, some of which may be changed or omitted. The presider says:

> Dear brothers and sisters, the words of Saint Paul today have a pointed application to us: "We implore you in Christ's name: be reconciled to God." Therefore let us confess our sins to the Lord and he will take pity on us, for he is generous in forgiving.

Another minister leads the intentions:

> That we who have departed from your love through our sins may be welcomed back into your company through your mercy. (Response: We have sinned, O Lord, have mercy on us.)

> That those who have done injury to this house of prayer by their crimes may receive pardon and the lightening of their guilt. (Response)

> That by the settlement of quarrels and disputes quiet peace may return to your house. (Response)

> That we who by offending others have offended you may reach out to them with renewed love and so receive pardon. (Response)

> That in your mercy you will bring those who have gone astray back to the way of your commandments. (Response)

> That sin, which brings ruin, may be vanquished and that your mercy which brings redemption, may triumph. (Response)

Some of the ministers or members of the assembly cover the altar with an altar cloth and adorn it with flowers. During this time the church is illumined as on feast days. The presider reverences the altar with a kiss and incenses it. After this he stands at the altar and says:

> The Lord's Prayer is the perfect prayer of penitents, since it is a petition that we may sanctify the name of the Lord and obtain pardon for our offenses.

All join in praying the Lord's Prayer to which the presider adds at the end:

> Look with kindness, O Lord, on these your children, whose repentance has reconciled them to yourself and whose humility has brought them closer to you. When they gather around the table of this altar, refresh them with the sacraments of life, so that they may enter more deeply into the mystery of redemption. We ask this through Christ our Lord. Amen.

The presider blesses and dismisses the people. All join in a concluding song.

Not only are there ritual parallels to the rite of dedication of a church and an altar, but the corresponding emphasis in that rite on people is maintained in this ritual as well. Elements of this rite flow from the former rites found in the pontifical and ritual, but their language and orientation show it to clearly be a post-conciliar reform of an ancient rite.

RITUALS FOR THE CLOSING OF A CHURCH

In the past several years, cultural changes in city neighborhoods, suburban growth, shrinking urban and rural populations, the financial strain on parishes with large, aging church buildings and many other factors have all contributed to the closing or consolidation of churches. This is not a new phenomenon. Parish churches have closed throughout history.

What is new perhaps is an awareness of the need to give this event ritual expression. Today we sense more strongly the need to provide a ritual experience for "remembering, grieving, and above all, giving thanks" (see Rita Fisher, "The Grace of this Place: Closing a Church," *Liturgy 90* [February/March 1996]: 9–11).

Canon 1212 of the Code of Canon Law states that "sacred places lose their dedication or blessing if they suffer major destruction or if they have been permanently given over to profane uses, de facto or through a decree of the competent authority." Canon 1205 describes how a place is ascribed sacred status while canon 1212 states how a place loses that status. According to *The Code of Canon Law: A Text and Commentary,* commissioned by the Canon Law Society of America, the words "desecration" and "secularization" are no longer used by the Code. "Major destruction" means that the place no longer functions according to the definition of "sacred place," namely, a place for divine worship or for the burial of the faithful. If, after destruction, a place is restored to use for worship, it would be dedicated or blessed, using the appropriate rites, once again.

Canon 1212 recognizes that it is the diocesan bishop who has authority to determine that a place once used exclusively for divine worship can be given over to another use. A diocesan bishop could issue a decree allowing a parish to build a new church and use the former church for a parish hall. This decree would be sufficient to recognize the change in status of the place and no other ritual is needed.

Canon 1212 states:

[I]f a church can in no way be employed for divine worship and it is impossible to repair it, it can be relegated to profane but not sordid use by the diocesan bishop.

Where other serious reasons suggest that a church no longer be used for divine worship, the diocesan bishop, after hearing the presbyteral council, can relegate it to profane but not sordid use with the consent of

The sharing of communion reveals the sacred purpose to which this building is dedicated: God's house is the house of God's people.

those who legitimately claim rights regarding the church and as long as the good of souls is not thereby impaired.

The decision to close a church is almost always a heart-wrenching experience for a community. The Roman rite has no official rituals in the liturgical books that provide for prayer or thanksgiving when a church is no longer to be used by a Catholic community. The Episcopal Church, in its *Book of Occasional Services,* has a service for "Secularizing a Consecrated Building" (223–225).

Because of the significance a community attaches to the place where it has gathered and celebrated sacramental life, it is appropriate that some form of ritual prayer take place. Some diocesan offices of worship have provided such rituals. The liturgy office of the diocese of Columbus, Ohio, provided a concluding rite to be used after communion at the last Mass, preferably on a Sunday, celebrated in the church building that will be closed (Rita Fisher, "The Grace of this Place: Closing a Church," *Liturgy 90* [February/March 1996]: 9–11).

Rita Fisher writes, "If the decision to close the church has caused great pain and anger, it might be advisable before celebrating this rite to have a listening session or town hall meeting to allow people to speak about their anger or hurt. The services of a professional therapist or facilitator also might be helpful."

The rite proposed by the Columbus diocese consists of a procession to the major stations in the church: the font, the reconciliation chapel, shrine areas, the ambo and altar. It is presumed that the tabernacle has been emptied in preparation for the closing, so no ritual recognition is provided. The tone and character of the entire rite should be one of thanksgiving for this place that has served to gather God's people together in sacramental encounter with God.

Several representatives of the assembly accept ritual objects that will be transferred to a new place of worship. These objects, such as a sacred vessel, an image or icon, a book of the gospels, and so forth, should be thoughtfully determined beforehand. The objects may be received during the procession as it makes its way through the church or they may be placed near the final station or the altar. It is important to arrange in advance with the new parish's leadership that whatever accompanies the people to the new parish will be received with respect and put to use there.

One adaptation of the rite is to provide some form of sharing of memories at each station. People can be invited to say the names or tell the stories of those who were baptized, reconciled, married or buried from this place. Some spontaneous sharing might also be provided for. The feasibility of this will depend on the size and nature of the assembly. The presider must carefully and sensitively coordinate the flow of these remembrances and gracefully bring them to closure so that the service is not unduly prolonged, especially when it is within the eucharistic celebration. The presider might add the invocation "And so we say, Blessed be God for ever!" after each remembrance, long or short. All would respond, "Blessed be God for ever!"

For the Closing of a Church
After the people have gathered, the introductory rites begin in the usual way. Following the greeting, the presider says these or similar words:

> As we celebrate the eucharist here today for the last time, let us enter with full hearts into thanksgiving for the gifts of God and the grace of this place.

The rite of blessing and sprinkling of the people with holy water may take place as a renewal of baptism and as a reminder of the sprinkling of the church at its dedication. During the preparation of gifts, both the gifts and the people are incensed, reminiscent of the dedication liturgy.

Following the prayer after communion, the presider says these or similar words:

> Blessed are you, Emmanuel, God with us. In this place we have come to know and celebrate your love for us, your people. We trust in your providential care for us and your guidance to our true and lasting home. Be with us now and always and so we say, "Blessed be God for ever!"

All respond: Blessed be God for ever!

The presider then says:

As we leave this place of worship, we give thanks to God for all the blessings we have received here.

If possible, all join in a procession for remembering. Adapt the route according to the layout of the building, but the procession should end at the altar. Sing during the procession, using Psalm 90 ("You have been our haven, Lord, from generation to generation"), another psalm of thanksgiving or a well-known hymn of thanks or praise. If it is not possible for all to join the procession, invite all to turn in the direction of the prayer and sing between each thanksgiving. Candle bearers lead the procession to the various areas.

At the font the presider says:

Let us remember the baptisms celebrated here (pause for silence). We thank you and we praise you for the life of faith to all who have passed through the waters of new life at this font. Blessed be God for ever!

All respond: Blessed be God for ever!

At the confessional or reconciliation chapel, the presider says:

Let us remember the times when we have been forgiven, comforted, consoled in the sacrament of penance (pause for silence). We thank you and we praise you for the healing and reconciling love that has been given through the sacrament of penance in this church. Blessed be God for ever!

All respond: Blessed be God for ever!

At a station of the cross, at a significant statue or icon, or at a shrine (repeat as desired), the presider says:

Let us remember the generations of prayer and devotion that this sacred image has inspired (pause for silence). We thank you for inspiring in us here true devotion to (the way of the cross; Blessed Mother Mary, Saint . . .) Blessed be God for ever!

All respond: Blessed be God for ever!

At the ambo, the presider says:

Let us remember the power of God's word proclaimed here in scripture and in preaching (pause for silence). We thank you and we praise you for your holy word proclaimed here in faith and preached here in sincerity. May it echo always in our hearts. Blessed be God for ever!

All respond: Blessed be God for ever!

Finally, at the altar, the presider says:

Let us remember the times we have gathered for the sacred banquet: the Triduum kept each year, the Sundays on which we worshiped faithfully, the first communion celebrations, the feast days of saints and martyrs, the marriages witnessed here, the funerals held here in hope. Let us pray (pause for silence). God our refuge, our home is in you. You are greater than any temple, church or cathedral that can be built by human hands, yet in this place we have met your divine presence. This church building has been a place of blessing for us. Protect us on our way. Lead us to a new assembly of your faithful people. We ask this through Christ our Lord.

All respond: Amen.

If the entire community is being transferred to another church, delegate one or more members (for example, the president of the pastoral council, the eldest member of the parish or the youngest) to carry an object (or objects) that will be used in the new place (such as a sacred vessel, an icon or the book of the gospels). If there are relics that have been removed from the altar, these may also be carried out. The presider presents the delegated persons with the objects they will carry, and says:

The life of this community will continue in another place. (Name), receive this (name of item) that will be used at (name of the new church). Take it (directly) from this place to (name of the new pastor/pastoral administrator) as a sign that our journey of faith will continue there.

The final blessing may be taken from among the solemn blessings found in the sacramentary at 12, 13 or 14.

During the singing of the final hymn, all may be invited to come forward and kiss the altar or offer a profound bow as a final gesture of leave-taking. The final hymn could be "Now thank we all our God," "Holy God we praise thy Name," a hymn in honor of the parish titular, or something familiar. All process out of the building.

A similar ritual was developed by the parish of St. Paschal Baylon in Oakland, California, when their church was closed for renovation ("Rite of farewell for a church," *Modern Liturgy Magazine,* September 1995). This ritual could also be adapted to local circumstances.

The presider, at the beginning of the liturgy, addresses the assembly:

My sisters and brothers, we gather together today in this space that has formed us as church and in which we have celebrated the mysteries of our faith. We begin the liturgy remembering that we are on a journey, a pilgrimage that leads us one day to the banquet table of heaven.

In addition to remembering and giving thanks for some of the specific symbols and spaces mentioned above, the sick who were anointed in this church were also recognized with prayer:

> We hear the prayers for healing and remember those sick who have come here for comfort, who with the oil of strength have been anointed in this place.

At the altar the presider says:

> And most especially, we remember our celebration of the Lord's Supper. We hear music and see gestures. We recall breaking open the Word, eating the Bread, drinking the Cup. God has indeed offered God's self to us and we have offered ourselves to God and one another in this place. Let us bless the Lord.

All respond: Thanks be to God.

After the final blessing, the presider says:

> Let us now take a few moments within the silence of our own hearts to thank God for our worship here and to say "farewell" to this sacred space as we have known it.

After a few moments of silence, the musicians begin the accompaniment to "What is this place?" A procession is formed with members of the assembly gathering symbols and various liturgical artifacts to be carried out of the building. As the procession moves forward all join in singing, "What is this place?"

Sometimes a ritual or service of closure may more appropriately take place within a service of prayer apart from Mass. Such was the occasion when the Cathedral of St. Francis de Sales in Oakland, California, was closed in 1993 (see Thomas G. Simons, "Requiem for a Church: Closing St. Francis de Sales Cathedral," *Environment and Art Letter,* April 1994). The building was heavily damaged by an earthquake in 1989. Costly repairs proved unfeasible.

The assembly gathered in front of the church. A large wooden cross used during the Triduum was at the center of the environment, along with banners and bells. A sound system was provided along with musical instruments to lead the assembly with music.

After the assembly sang the Taizé version of "Veni Sancte Spiritus," Bishop John Cummins greeted the assembly and prayed:

> Most merciful God, whose wisdom is beyond our understanding, surround our family of St. Francis de Sales with your love, so that we may not be overwhelmed by our loss. Let us find comfort in our sadness, certainty in

our doubt, courage to live through this hour, and strength to meet the days to come.

Among the readings chosen was a passage from the Book of Revelation (21:1–5, 6 –7) which speaks of God's dwelling place among people, a God who comforts and makes all things new, a God who is the beginning and end of all things. Following the homily and a period of silent reflection, the bishop said:

> Here we and those who have gone before us have celebrated our joys and sorrows. In this church we have encountered Jesus Christ in word, sacraments and one another. But now, after 100 years of faith, it is my sad duty to close the Cathedral of St. Francis de Sales this day. In Christ's name I now do so.

The bishop closed the church's open doors and locked them. The doors that had opened wide for years in welcome were closed for the last time. Intercessions followed, sung between choir and people. There followed several brief, eulogy-like reflections, offered by representative members of the parish. At times the comments brought forth applause, laughter and tears from the assembly.

The bishop concluded by saying:

> With thanks for the good accomplished here, I declare this Cathedral of St. Francis de Sales now closed.

He offered the blessing and all sang, "O God our help in ages past."

Everyone received a memento of the occasion: a picture of the cathedral with historical dates and the date of closure. In other places a videotape of the last liturgy in the church was made available or a special booklet of the parish's history with photographs. All these serve as ongoing remembrances of the community that gathered in these places.

Likewise, the diocese of Harrisburg developed "Rituals of Transition" when faced with the closure and merging of a large number of parishes in 1995. The format they offered suggests a last week of events in the church being closed.

At the Sunday liturgy inaugurating the final week of prayer in the church, after the blessing and dismissal, the assembly comes forward with tapers or candles and receives light from the paschal candle, held by the presider. The litany of the saints, including the name of the parish patron, is sung by the assembly as all process out of the building with the presider leading them with the paschal candle.

During the week between the closing liturgy of the former parish and the first liturgy in the new parish, a vigil celebration or celebrations take place. These may either take the form of evening prayer from the Liturgy of the Hours or a liturgy of the word. At each service, the presider enters the assembly carrying the paschal candle. After the reading, the priest or deacon gives a homily, focusing with hope on the future. During the singing of the gospel canticle of evening prayer, the altar, paschal candle and people are incensed. Before the final blessing, a member or members of the community may be invited to offer remembrances about the parish. The paschal candle remains in its place throughout the week, and is lighted during other liturgies that take place. The sung litany of the saints accompanies the recession at each service.

One of the vigil celebrations during that last week might employ a telling of the parish history. After a liturgy of the word, names of members of the parish could be read from the baptismal register, perhaps those who were baptized during the first year of the parish's existence and those who were baptized during the final year, along with some anecdotes by pastor or parishioners. After a group of names is recited, an acclamation (such as the Taizé "Jesus, remember me, when you come into your Kingdom") could be sung. A reflection on the sacrament of baptism could be given, perhaps by a parishioner who helps with baptismal preparation. The same could be done with other sacramental registers.

This type of celebration requires careful preparation but would be a way of telling the parish story and allowing good memories to accompany the parishioners during this time of closure, transition and merger.

Other recommended celebrations during the final week include exposition and benediction of the blessed sacrament, a celebration in honor of the Blessed Virgin Mary or of the patron saint of the closing parish. It is recommended that the church be made available to parishioners for visitation as much as possible during the week of closing. They should be afforded the opportunity to savor its beauty, images, atmosphere.

On the day of the opening of the newly combined parish, all gather outside the new parish church, if circumstances permit. The liturgy may begin outside the worship space with a gathering hymn. Representatives from each of the former parishes should be involved in the opening procession and ministries of the liturgy. Name tags should be made available and worn by all. The paschal candle is used in place of the processional cross. Vessels of water, one from each of the former parishes, are carried in.

After the gathering hymn, the bishop's decree establishing the new parish is read by the pastor. The litany of the saints, using the names of the former patrons and the new patron, is sung as the procession into the church or to the altar begins. During the procession, symbols and liturgical artifacts that will be used in the new parish may be carried into the church and placed in appropriate settings.

After the greeting, water from each former parish community is called forth, combined into one vessel, blessed and sprinkled. The litany of the saints may continue during the sprinkling, or another familiar acclamation may be sung. The Gloria is also sung. In the homily, the presider expresses the hope of going forward together with gratitude for the past.

After communion, the blessed sacrament chapel is inaugurated.

During the preparation of gifts, the gifts and the assembly are incensed. Following the prayer after communion, the new pastor expresses thanks to those who assisted in the process of transition. A solemn blessing from the sacramentary (such as no. 11) is recommended. A festive hymn accompanies the recessional, with the new pastor and pastoral leaders leading the assembly from the tables of word and sacrament to tables of fellowship at a reception.

When St. Sebastian church on Chicago's near north side burned in 1990, parishioners gathered for a church closing ceremony to terminate their 78-year-old parish (see Bishop William McManus, "A Funeral for a Parish," *Liturgy 90,* February/March 1991). They assembled outside the church building and were greeted by auxiliary bishop Timothy Lyne, representing Chicago's archbishop, Cardinal Joseph Bernardin. He said:

> Here you and those who have gone before you have celebrated your joys and sorrows. In this church you have encountered Jesus Christ in word, sacraments and one another. But now, after 78 years of faith, circumstances require this damaged church to be closed. It is Cardinal Bernardin's sad duty to close these church doors. In his name I now do so.

The doors were closed and two parishioners then sealed the church doors with a purple ribbon.

A procession formed that led to the parish school's auditorium next door. At the end of the procession the pastor carried a simple cross that for years had been mounted over the church entrance. Its only ornamentation for this liturgy was a crown of thorns.

In the penitential rite at the beginning of the Mass, the parishioners asked God's healing for their bitterness and frustration during the meetings, marches and demonstrations they held in hopes of saving their parish despite the necessity of a large-scale reordering of the archdiocese. A Gloria, led by the choir, helped the congregation shift its mood from sorrow and regret to joy and hope.

The homily radiated hope and optimism about the future. Rather than being a recital of the parish's history, it was a message encouraging trust in God's providence. After the homily, the pastor led the assembly in a recommitment to Christian life. He blessed water in the parish's baptismal font (saved from the burned building) and invited the parishioners to dip their hands into the water, bless themselves and profess their continued faith in Jesus Christ and his gospel.

At the preparation of the altar and gifts, in addition to the bread and wine, the holy oils used for the sacraments of baptism, confirmation and anointing of the sick were presented, as well as the parish sacramental register holding the names of all who had received the sacraments of initiation and all whose funerals were celebrated in the parish church. The sign of peace was a farewell for many who no longer would be together in this community. During the liturgy's concluding rites, the following litany was offered:

Leader: Whenever we eat this eucharistic bread and wine we proclaim the Lord's death until he comes.

Pastor: Whatever table we gather around may we be reminded of the love we have shared around this one.

Leader: The grass withers, the flower fades, but the word of our God will stand forever.

Pastor: May we always be open to God's word; it challenges us to justice and comforts us with hope.

Leader: (holding the paschal candle) Jesus said: "I am the light of the world."

Pastor: May we share the light of our faith with our new parishes. You are a chosen race, a royal priesthood, a holy nation, God's own people.

The bishop then approved the official proclamation by the deacon: "With thanks to God for the good accomplished here, this parish of St. Sebastian is now closed." The congregation concluded with singing.

Places hold special meaning for human beings. Churches in particular are places where conversion is celebrated and redemption is actively encountered. Church buildings become a locus of human community, a treasury for stories and lives. It is fitting, then, that if we initiate a building before we use it, that we also offer a thanksgiving or funeral liturgy for a place that will no longer be used. Given the mobility of society, Christians will need to learn how to ritualize the closing of a church building. Such rituals are instrumental in helping all to give thanks and remember.

Selected Bibliography

PRIMARY SOURCES

Book of Blessings. English translation prepared by the International Commission on English in the Liturgy and published by the National Conference of Catholic Bishops. New York: Catholic Book Publishing Company, 1989.

Book of Common Prayer (The Episcopal Church). New York: The Church Hymnal Corporation, 1977.

The Book of Occasional Services 1994 (The Episcopal Church). New York: The Church Hymnal Corporation, 1995.

Ceremonial of Bishops. English translation prepared by the International Commission on English in the Liturgy. Collegeville: The Liturgical Press, 1989.

Dedication of a Church and an Altar. English translation prepared by the International Commission on English in the Liturgy. Included in *The Rites: Volume Two.* New York: Pueblo, 1980.

Dedication of a Church and an Altar (provisional text). English translation prepared by the International Commission on English in the Liturgy. Washington: Bishops' Committee on the Liturgy, National Conference of Catholic Bishops, 1989 (revised edition).

Documents on the Liturgy: 1963–1979, Conciliar, Papal and Curial Texts. Collegeville: The Liturgical Press, 1982.

Flannery, Austin, OP, ed. *Vatican II: The Conciliar and Post-Conciliar Documents.* Collegeville: The Liturgical Press, 1987.

General Instruction of the Roman Missal. Liturgy Documentary Series 2. Washington: Office of Publishing Services, United States Catholic Conference, 1982.

Occasional Services: Companion to Lutheran Book of Worship. Minneapolis: Augsburg Publishing House, 1982.

Ordo Dedicationis Ecclesiae et Altaris. Vatican City: Vatican Polyglot Press, 1977.

Pontificale Romanum. Rome: Marietti, 1962.

Rituale Romanum. New York: Benziger Brothers, Inc., 1953.

The Roman Ritual. Volume III, "The Blessings." Translated and edited by Philip T. Weller. Milwaukee: The Bruce Publishing Company, 1946.

ARTICLES

Field, James. "The Rite of Dedication: History, Theology and Celebration." *Environment and Art Letter,* March 1994. Chicago: Liturgy Training Publications.

Ford, Paul. "How a Church Becomes Catholic." *Liturgical Life* 8 (1995): 5 & 6. Los Angeles: Office for Worship.

Melloh, John. "The Rite of Dedication." *Assembly* 10 (November 1983): 2. Notre Dame: Center for Pastoral Liturgy.

Ryan, G. Thomas, et al., "The Local Church: Dedication and Anniversary." *Sourcebook for Sundays and Seasons* (1995). Chicago: Liturgy Training Publications.

Searle, Mark. "Sacred Places." *Assembly* 10 (November 1983): 2. Notre Dame: Center for Pastoral Liturgy.

ART AND ARCHITECTURE

Adam, Adolf. *Foundations of Liturgy: An Introduction to Its History and Practice.* Collegeville: The Liturgical Press, 1992.

Bouyer, Louis. *Liturgy and Architecture.* Notre Dame: University of Notre Dame Press, 1967.

Boyer, Mark. *The Liturgical Environment: What the Documents Say.* Collegeville: The Liturgical Press, 1990.

Bruening Lewis, Elizabeth. *The Power of Sacred Images: A Guide to the Treasures of Early Christian Art.* Allen, Texas: Christian Classics, 1997.

Bugnini, Annibale. *The Reform of the Liturgy, 1948–1975.* Translated by Matthew J. O'Connell. Collegeville: The Liturgical Press, 1990.

Calabuig, Ignazio, OSM. *The Dedication of a Church and an Altar: A Theological Commentary.* Washington: United States Catholic Conference, 1980.

Chengalikavil, Luke, OSB. "The Rite of Dedication of a Church and Altar," *Anamnesis 7: Sacramentals and Blessings* (in Italian). Genoa: Marietti Publishing House, 1989.

Collins, Harold. *The Church Edifice and Its Appointments.* Westminster: The Newman Bookshop, 1935 (completely revised 1940; reprinted 1946).

Coriden, James, Thomas Green, Donald Heintschel, eds. *The Code of Canon Law: A Text and Commentary.* New Jersey: Paulist Press, 1985.

Crichton, J. D. *The Dedication of a Church: A Commentary.* Dublin: Veritas Publications, 1980.

DeBuyst, Frederic. *Modern Architecture and Christian Celebration.* Ecumenical Studies in Worship, no. 18. Richmond: John Knox Press, 1968.

DeSanctis, Michael. *Renewing the City of God.* Meeting House Essays, no. 5. Chicago: Liturgy Training Publications, 1993.

Dillenberger, John. *The Visual Arts and Christianity in America: From the Colonial Period to the Present.* New York: Crossroad Publishing Company, 1988.

Doherty, Richard, ed. *Practical Handbook of Rites, Blessings and Prayers.* St. Paul: The North Central Publishing Company, 1961.

Environment and Art in Catholic Worship. Bishops' Committee on the Liturgy, National Conference of Catholic Bishops. Washington: United States Catholic Conference, 1978.

The Environment for Worship: A Reader. Edited by the Secretariat, Bishops' Committee on the Liturgy, National Conference of Catholic Bishops, and the Center for Pastoral Liturgy, Catholic University of America. Washington: United States Catholic Conference, 1980.

Giles, Richard. *Re-Pitching the Tent: Re-ordering the Church Building for Worship and Mission in the New Millennium.* Norwich: The Canterbury Press Norwich, 1996.

Holm, Jean, ed., with John Bowker. Themes in Religious Studies Series: *Sacred Place.* New York: St. Martin's Press, 1994.

Hoppe, Leslie, OFM. *The Synagogues and Churches of Ancient Palestine.* Collegeville: The Liturgical Press, 1994.

Huels, John. "Eucharistic Reservation," in *More Disputed Questions in the Liturgy.* Chicago: Liturgy Training Publications, 1996.

Kuehn, Regina. *A Place for Baptism.* Chicago: Liturgy Training Publications, 1992.

Martimort, A. G., I. H. Dalmais, OP, P. M. Gy, OP, and P. Jounel. *The Church at Prayer.* Vol. 1, Principles of the Liturgy. Collegeville: The Liturgical Press, 1987.

Mauck, Marchita. *Shaping a House for the Church.* Chicago: Liturgy Training Publications, 1990.

Milburn, Robert. *Early Christian Art and Architecture.* Berkeley: University of California Press, 1988.

Navone, John. *Toward a Theology of Beauty.* Collegeville: The Liturgical Press, 1996.

Newton, Eric, and William Neil. *2000 Years of Christian Art.* New York: Harper and Row, 1966.

Nichols, Aiden, OP. *The Art of God Incarnate: Theology and Symbol from Genesis to the Twentieth Century.* New York: Paulist Press, 1980.

The Place of Worship: Pastoral Directory on the Building and Reordering of Churches, 3rd edition. Irish Institute of Pastoral Liturgy: Veritas Publications, 1991.

Prayers for the Dedication of a Church. Chicago: Liturgy Training Publications, 1997.

Rouet, Albert. *Liturgy and the Arts* (originally published under the title *Art et Liturgie,* Desclee de Brouwer, 1992; translated by Paul Philibert, OP). Collegeville: The Liturgical Press, 1997.

Seasoltz, Kevin, OSB. *New Liturgy, New Laws.* Collegeville, The Liturgical Press, 1980.

Simons, Thomas G. *Blessings: A Reappraisal of their Nature, Purpose and Celebration.* Saratoga: Resource Publications, 1981.

Vosko, Richard. *Designing Future Worship Spaces.* Meeting House Essays, no. 8. Chicago: Liturgy Training Publications, 1996.

Vosko, Richard. *Through the Eye of a Rose Window: A Perspective on Environment for Worship.* Saratoga: Resource Publications, Inc., 1981.

Walton, Janet. *Art and Worship: A Vital Connection.* Wilmington: Michael Glazier, Inc., 1988.

ECCLESIOLOGY

Cenkner, William, ed. *The Multicultural Church.* New Jersey: Paulist Press, 1995.

Dulles, Avery. *Models of the Church.* New York: Image Books, 1987.

Garijo-Guembe, Miguel. *Communion of the Saints: Foundation, Nature, and Structure of the Church.* Translated by Patrick Madigan, SJ. Collegeville: The Liturgical Press, 1994.

Lawler, Michael, and Thomas Shanahan, SJ. *Church: A Spirited Communion.* Collegeville: The Liturgical Press, 1995.

O'Donnell, Christopher, OCARM. *Ecclesia: A Theological Encyclopedia of the Church.* Collegeville: The Liturgical Press, 1996.

Tavard, George. *The Church, Community of Salvation: An Ecumenical Ecclesiology.* Collegeville: The Liturgical Press, 1992.

UNPUBLISHED SOURCES

Chengalikavil, Luke, OSB. *The Mystery of Christ and the Church in the Dedication of a Church: A Historical and Theological Study on the Rite of Dedication in the Roman liturgy.* Doctoral dissertation, Pontifical Liturgical Institute, Pontificium Athenaeum Anselmianum, Rome, 1984.

Trudu, Fabio. *Symbolic Images of the Church in the Order for the Dedication of a Church.* Thesis (in Italian), Pontifical Liturgical Institute, Pontificium Athenaeum Anselmianum, Rome, 1992.

The Roman Pontifical
Revised by Decree of the Second Vatican Ecumenical Council
and Published by the Authority of Pope Paul VI

Dedication of a Church and an Altar
Provisional Text

Copublished by Catholic Truth Society, London; Veritas Publications, Dublin;
United States Catholic Conference, Washington, D.C.

Revised 1989

English Translation Prepared by
The International Commission on English in the Liturgy
A Joint Commission of Catholic Bishops' Conferences

Bishops' Committee for the Liturgy
National Conference of Catholic Bishops
Washington, D.C.

The English translation of liturgical texts in this publication has been approved for use in the dioceses of the United States by the Bishops' Committee on the Liturgy and the Executive Committee of the National Conference of Catholic Bishops and has been confirmed *ad interim* by the Apostolic See, the Congregation for the Sacraments and Divine Worship (Prot. CD 1016/78, September 25, 1978).

+ Joseph P. Delaney
Bishop of Fort Worth
Chairman
Bishops' Committee on the Liturgy
August 15, 1989

Concordat cum originali:
Reverend Ronald F. Krisman
Executive Director
Secretariat for the Liturgy
National Conference of Catholic Bishops
August 15, 1989

The English translation of the liturgical texts in this publication has been approved for the continued *ad interim* use by the Bishops of England and Wales.

+ Mervyn
Bishop of Clifton
February 2, 1990

This text was typeset and printed in the United States of America and, therefore, has adopted American spelling throughout.

Contents

117   *Decree*

119   *Chapter One*   Laying of a Foundation Stone or Commencement
           of Work on the Building of a Church
119   Introduction
121   Rite of Blessing

129   *Chapter Two*   Dedication of a Church
129   Introduction
138   Rite of Dedication

157   *Chapter Three* Dedication of a Church Already in General Use
           for Sacred Celebrations
157   Introduction
159   Rite of Dedication

173   *Chapter Four*   Dedication of an Altar
173   Introduction
182   Rite of Dedication

195   *Chapter Five*   Blessing of a Church
195   Introduction
197   Rite of Blessing

205   *Chapter Six*   Blessing of an Altar
205   Introduction
207   Rite of Blessing

209   *Chapter Seven*   Blessing of a Chalice and Paten
209   Introduction
210   Rite of Blessing within Mass
212   Rite of Blessing outside Mass

215   *Appendix*   Litany of the Saints

Sacred Congregation for the Sacraments and Divine Worship
Prot. no. CD 300/77

DECREE

The rite for the dedication of a church and an altar is rightly considered among the most solemn liturgical services. A church is the place where the Christian community is gathered to hear the word of God, to offer intercessions and praise to him, and above all to celebrate the holy mysteries, and it is the place where the holy sacrament of the eucharist is kept. Thus it stands as a special kind of image of the Church itself, which is God's temple built from living stones. And the altar of a church, around which the holy people of God gather to take part in the Lord's sacrifice and to be refreshed at the heavenly meal, stands as a sign of Christ himself, who is the priest, the victim, and the altar of his own sacrifice.

These rites, found in the second book of the Roman Pontifical, were revised and simplified in 1961. Nevertheless it was judged necessary to revise the rites again and to adapt them to contemporary conditions in view of the purpose and the norms of the liturgical reform that Vatican II set in motion and fostered.

Pope Paul VI by his authority has approved the new *Ordo dedicationis ecclesiae et altaris* prepared by the Congregation for the Sacraments and Divine Worship. He has ordered it to be published and prescribed that it replace the rites now in the second book of the Roman Pontifical.

This Congregation, by mandate of the Pope, therefore publishes this *Ordo dedicationis ecclesiae et altaris*. In the Latin text it will be in effect as soon as it appears; in the vernacular, it will take effect, after the translations have been confirmed and approved by the Apostolic See, on the day determined by the conferences of bishops.

Anything to the contrary notwithstanding.

From the office of the Congregation for the Sacraments and Divine Worship, May 29, 1977, Pentecost.

+ James R. Cardinal Knox
Prefect
+ Antonio Innocenti
Titular Archbishop of Eclano
Secretary

Chapter One

Rite of Laying the Foundation Stone or Beginning Work on the Building of a Church

Introduction

1. When the building of a new church begins, it is desirable to celebrate a rite to ask God's blessing for the success of the work and to remind the people that the structure built of stone will be a visible sign of the living Church, God's building that is formed of the people themselves.[1]

In accordance with liturgical tradition, this rite consists of the blessing of the site of a new church and the blessing and laying of the foundation stone. When there is to be no foundation stone because of the particular architecture of the building, the rite of the blessing of the site of the new church should still be celebrated in order to dedicate the beginning of the work of God.

2. The rite for the laying of a foundation stone or for beginning a new church may be celebrated on any day except during the Easter triduum. But the preference should be for a day when the people can be present in large numbers.

3. The bishop of the diocese is rightly the one to celebrate the rite. If he cannot do so himself, he shall entrust the function to another bishop or priest, especially to one who is his associate and assistant in the pastoral care of the diocese or of the community for which the new church is to be built.

4. Notice of the date and hour of the celebration should be given to the people in good time. The pastor or others concerned should instruct them in the meaning of the rite and the reverence to be shown toward the church that is to be built for them.

It is also desirable that the people be asked to give their generous and willing support in the building of the church.

5. Insofar as possible, the area for the erection of the church should be marked out clearly. It should be possible to walk about without difficulty.

6. In the place where the altar will be located, a wooden cross of suitable height is fixed in the ground.

HOLY PEOPLE, HOLY PLACE

7. For the celebration of the rite the following should be prepared:
— The Roman Pontifical and Lectionary;
— chair for the bishop;
— depending on the circumstances, the foundation stone, which by tradition is a rectangular cornerstone, together with cement and the tools for setting the stone in the foundation;
— container of holy water with sprinkler;
— censer, incense boat and spoon;
— processional cross and torches for the servers.

Sound equipment should be set up so that the assembly can clearly hear the readings, prayers, and instructions.

8. For the celebration of the rites the vestments are white or of some festive color. The following should be prepared:
— for the bishop: alb, stole, cope, miter and pastoral staff;
— for the priest, when one presides over the celebration: alb, stole and cope;
— for the deacons: albs, stoles, and if opportune, dalmatics;
— for other ministers: albs or other lawfully approved dress.

OUTLINE OF THE RITE

APPROACH TO THE CONSTRUCTION SITE
A. First Form: Procession
  Greeting
  Brief Introduction
  Prayer
  Procession
B. Second Form: Station at the Construction Site of the New Church
  Acclamation or Song
  Greeting
  Brief Instruction
  Prayer

READING OF THE WORD OF GOD
  Reading(s)
  [Responsorial Psalm]
  Homily
  Placing of the Document(s) in the Foundation Stone

BLESSING OF THE SITE OF THE NEW CHURCH
  Prayer of Blessing
  Laying of the Foundation Stone

CONCLUDING RITE
  General Intercessions
  Lord's Prayer
  Concluding Prayer
  Blessing and Dismissal

Rite of Blessing

Part I
Approach to the Construction Site

9. The assembly of the people and the approach to the construction site take place, according to the circumstances of time and place, in one of the two ways described below.

A. First Form: Procession

10. At a convenient hour the people assemble in a suitable place, from which they will go in procession to the site.

11. The bishop, in his vestments and with the miter and pastoral staff, proceeds with the ministers to the place where the people are assembled. Putting aside the pastoral staff and miter he greets the people, saying:

> *The grace of our Lord Jesus Christ*
> *and the love of God*
> *and the fellowship of the Holy Spirit*
> *be with you all.*
> *R. And also with you.*

> Other suitable words taken preferably from sacred Scripture may be used.

12. Then the bishop briefly instructs the people on their participation in the celebration and explains to them the meaning of the rite.

13. When the bishop has finished the instruction he says:

> *Let us pray.*

All pray in silence for a brief period. The bishop then continues:

> *Lord,*
> *you built a holy Church,*
> *founded upon the apostles*
> *with Jesus Christ its cornerstone.*
>
> *Grant that your people, gathered in your name,*
> *may fear and love you*
> *and grow as the temple of your glory.*

May they always follow you,
until, with you at their head,
they arrive at last in your heavenly city.

We ask this through Christ our Lord.
R. Amen.

14. When the bishop has finished the prayer, he receives the miter and pastoral staff, and, should the occasion demand, the deacon says:

Let us go forth in peace.

The procession takes place in the usual way: the crossbearer leads between two servers with lighted torches; the clergy follow, then the bishop with the assisting deacons and other ministers, and lastly, the congregation. As the procession proceeds the following antiphon is sung with Psalm 84.

My soul is yearning for the courts of the Lord (alleluia).

Another appropriate song may be sung.
Then the reading of the word of God takes place as described below in nos. 18–22.

B. Second Form: Station at the Construction Site of the New Church

15. If the procession cannot take place or seems inappropriate, the people assemble at the construction site of the new church. When the people are assembled the following acclamation is sung.

Eternal peace be yours.
Let the Father's peace unite you in his love.

Abiding peace be yours.
Let the word be peace to those who bear his name.

Lasting peace be yours.
Let the Spirit's peace comfort all the world.

Another appropriate song may be sung.
Meanwhile, the bishop, in his vestments and with his miter and pastoral staff, approaches the people. Putting aside the pastoral staff and miter, he greets the people, saying:

The grace of our Lord Jesus Christ
and the love of God
and the fellowship of the Holy Spirit

be with you all.
R. And also with you.

Other suitable words taken preferably from sacred Scripture may be used.

16. Then the bishop briefly instructs the people on their participation in the celebration and explains to them the meaning of the rite.

17. When the bishop has finished the instruction, he says:

Let us pray.

All pray in silence for a brief period. The bishop then continues:

Lord,
you built a holy Church,
founded upon the apostles
with Jesus Christ its cornerstone.

Grant that your people,
gathered in your name,
may fear and love you,
and grow as the temple of your glory.

May they always follow you,
until, with you at their head,
they arrive at last in your heavenly city.

We ask this through Christ our Lord.
R. Amen.

Part II

Reading of the Word of God

18. Then one or more relevant passages of sacred Scripture are read, chosen especially from those in *The Lectionary* (nos. 704 and 706) for the rite of the dedication of a church, with an appropriate intervening responsorial psalm or other appropriate song. However, it is in keeping with the occasion, especially if a foundation stone is used in the rite, to read one of the following passages.

Readings from Sacred Scripture

19.   1. 1 Kings 5:2 – 18 "At the king's orders they quarried huge stones, special stones, for the laying of the temple foundations."

2. Isaiah 28:16 – 17 "See how I lay in Zion a stone of witness, a precious cornerstone, a foundation stone."

3. Acts 4:8 – 12 "Jesus, the one you crucified, has proved to be the keystone."

4. 1 Corinthians 10:1 – 6 "And that rock was Christ."

Responsorial Psalms

20. 1. Psalm 24:1 – 2, 3 – 4ab, 5 – 6
    R. (2 Chronicles 7:16a) I have chosen and sanctified this place.
    2. Psalm 42:3, 5bcd; Psalm 43:3 – 4
    R. (See Psalm 43:3) Lord, may your truth lead me to your holy mountain.
    3. Psalm 87:1 – 3, 4 – 6, 6 – 7
    R. (See 1) The city of God is founded on the holy mountains.
    4. Psalm 100:2, 3, 5
    R. (See Ezekiel 37:27) I will make my dwelling place among the people.
    5. Psalm 118:1 – 2, 16ab – 17, 22 – 23
    R. (See 1 Corinthians 3:11) There is no other foundation than Christ Jesus.

Gospel

21. 1. Matthew 7:21 – 29 "A house built on rock and a house built on sand."
    2. Matthew 16:13 – 18 "On this rock I will build my Church."
    3. Mark 12:1 – 12 "It was the stone rejected by the builders that became the keystone."
    4. Luke 6:46 – 49 "He laid the foundation on rock."

22. When the readings are finished the homily is given, in which the biblical readings are elucidated and the significance of the rite explained: Christ is the cornerstone of the Church, and the temple that is going to be built by the living Church of the community of believers will be at once the house of God and the house of God's people.

23. After the homily, according to the custom of the place, the document of the blessing of the foundation stone and of the beginning of the building of the church may be read: it is signed by the bishop and by representatives of those who are going to work on the building of the church, and together with the stone, is enclosed in the foundations.

Part III

Blessing of the Site of the New Church

24. When the homily is finished, the bishop takes off the miter, rises, and blesses the site of the new church, saying:

> *Let us pray.*
>
> *Lord,*
> *You fill the entire world with your presence*
> *that your name may be hallowed through all the earth.*
>
> *Bless all those*
> *who have worked or contributed*
> *to provide this site (property, land)*
> *on which a church will be built.*
>
> *Today may they rejoice in a work just begun,*
> *soon may they celebrate the sacraments in your temple,*
> *and in time to come may they praise you for ever in heaven.*
>
> *We ask this through Christ our Lord.*
> *R. Amen.*

25. Then the bishop puts on the miter and sprinkles the site of the new church with holy water. To do this he may stand in the middle of the site or go in procession around the foundations with the ministers; in the latter case the following antiphon is sung with Psalm 48.

> *The walls of Jerusalem will be made with precious stones, and its towers built with gems (alleluia).*

Another appropriate song may be sung.

Part IV

Blessing and Laying of the Foundation Stone

26. When the site has been blessed, if a foundation stone is to be laid, it is blessed and placed in position as described in nos. 27–29; otherwise the conclusion of the rite takes place immediately as indicated in nos. 30–31.

27. The bishop goes to the place where the foundation stone is to be laid and, taking off the miter, blesses the stone, saying:

> *Let us pray.*

Father,
the prophet Daniel spoke of your Son,
as a stone woundrously hewn from a mountain.

The apostle Paul spoke of him,
as a stone firmly founded.

Bless + this foundation stone
to be laid in Christ's name.

You appointed him
the beginning and end of all things.

May this work begin, continue,
and be brought to fulfillment in him,
for he is Lord for ever and ever.
R. Amen.

Then the bishop may sprinkle the stone with holy water and incense it. Afterward he receives the miter again.

28. When he has finished, the bishop lays the stone on the foundation in silence or, if he wishes, saying these or similar words:

With faith in Jesus Christ
we lay this stone
on which a church will rise.

May it be a place of sacrament
and a source of grace
to the glory of the Father
who with the Son and the Holy Spirit
lives and reigns for ever and ever.
R. Amen.

29. A stone mason then fixes the stone in the mortar. Meanwhile, if the occasion demands, the following antiphon is sung.

The house of the Lord is firmly built on solid rock (alleluia).

Another appropriate song may be sung.

Concluding Rite

30. When the singing is finished, the bishop takes off the miter, and invites the people to pray the general intercessions, in these or similar words:

Brothers and sisters, now that we have laid the cornerstone of our new church, let us pray to God, our Father.

All pray in silence for a brief period.

That he may transform into a living temple of his glory all whom he has gathered here and who look upon Christ as the cornerstone of their faith, let us pray to the Lord:

R. Bless and watch over your Church, O Lord.

That God in his power may overcome the division and sin which separate his people so that they may ultimately worship as one, let us pray to the Lord: R.

That he may ground upon the bedrock of his Church the faith of all those who have undertaken to work on this building, let us pray to the Lord: R.

That those who are prevented from building places of worship may bear witness to the Lord by conducting themselves as living temples of glory and faith, let us pray to the Lord: R.

That all here present may be cleansed by his divine power and come to share in the celebration of his holy mysteries, let us pray to the Lord: R.

Then the bishop may introduce the Lord's Prayer in these or similar words:

Let us join the voice of the Church with that of Christ in praying to the Father using those words which the Son has given us. And so, with one voice, let us say:

Our Father . . .

The bishop continues immediately:

God of love,
we praise your holy name,
for you have made us your temple by baptism
and inspire us to build on earth
churches dedicated to your worship.

Look favorably upon your children,
for they have come with joy
to begin work on this new church.

Enable them to grow into the temple of your glory,
until, shaped anew by your grace,
they are gathered by your hand into your heavenly city.

We ask this through Christ our Lord.
R. Amen.

31. When the bishop has received the miter and pastoral staff, he blesses the people in the usual way.

The deacon dismisses them, saying:

Go in peace.
R. Thanks be to God.

Chapter Two

Dedication of a Church

Introduction

I. Nature and Dignity of Churches

1. Through his death and resurrection, Christ became the true and perfect temple[1] of the New Covenant and gathered together a people to be his own.

This holy people, made one as the Father, Son and Holy Spirit are one, is the Church,[2] that is, the temple of God built of living stones, where the Father is worshiped in spirit and in truth.[3]

Rightly then, from early times "church" has also been the name given to the building in which the Christian community gathers to hear the word of God, to pray together, to receive the sacraments, and to celebrate the eucharist.

2. Because the church is a visible building, it stands as a special sign of the pilgrim Church on earth and reflects the Church dwelling in heaven.

When a church is erected as a building destined solely and permanently for assembling the people of God and for carrying out sacred functions, it is fitting that it be dedicated to God with a solemn rite, in accordance with the ancient custom of the Church.

3. The very nature of a church demands that it be suited to sacred celebrations, dignified, evincing a noble beauty, not mere costly display, and it should stand as a sign and symbol of heavenly realities. "The general plan of the sacred edifice should be such that in some way it conveys the image of the gathered assembly. It should also allow the participants to take the place most appropriate to them and assist all to carry out their individual functions properly." Moreover, in what concerns the sanctuary, the altar, the chair, the lectern, and the place for the reservation of the blessed sacrament, the Norms of the General Instruction of the Roman Missal are to be followed.[4]

Also, the norms must be observed that concern things and places destined for the celebration of other sacraments, especially baptism and penance.[5]

II. Titular of a Church and the Relics of the Saints to be Placed in It

4. Every church to be dedicated must have a titular. This may be: the Blessed Trinity; our Lord Jesus Christ invoked according to a mystery of his life or a title already accepted in the liturgy; the Holy Spirit; the Blessed Virgin Mary, likewise

invoked according to some appellation already accepted in the liturgy; one of the angels; or, finally, a saint inscribed in the Roman Martyrology or in a duly approved Appendix. A blessed may not be the titular without an indult of the Apostolic See. A church should have one titular only, unless it is a question of saints who are listed together in the Calendar.

5. The tradition in the Roman liturgy of placing relics of martyrs or other saints beneath the altar should be preserved, if possible.[6] But the following should be noted:

a) Such relics should be of a size sufficient for them to be recognized as parts of human bodies. Hence excessively small relics of one or more saints must not be placed beneath the altar.

b) The greatest care must be taken to determine whether the relics in question are authentic. It is better for an altar to be dedicated without relics than to have relics of doubtful authenticity placed beneath it.

c) A reliquary must not be placed upon the altar or set into the table of the altar; it must be placed beneath the table of the altar, as the design of the altar permits.

III. Celebration of the Dedication

Minister of the Rite

6. Since the bishop has been entrusted with the care of the particular Church, it is his responsibility to dedicate to God the new churches built in his diocese.

If he cannot himself preside at the rite, he shall entrust his function to another bishop, especially to one who is his associate and assistant in the pastoral care of the community for which the church has been built or, in altogether special circumstances, to a priest, to whom he shall give a special mandate.

Choice of Day

7. A day should be chosen for the dedication of the new church when the people can be present in large numbers, especially a Sunday. Since the theme of the dedication pervades this entire rite, the dedication of a new church may not take place on days on which it is altogether improper to disregard the mystery then being commemorated: the Easter triduum, Christmas, Epiphany, Ascension, Pentecost, Ash Wednesday, the weekdays of Holy Week, and All Souls.

Mass of the Dedication

8. The celebration of the eucharist is inseparably bound up with the rite of the dedication of a church; when a church is dedicated therefore the liturgical texts of the day are omitted and texts proper to the rite are used for both the liturgy of the word and the liturgy of the eucharist.

9. It is fitting that the bishop concelebrate the Mass with the priests who take part with him in the rite of dedication and those who have been given charge over the parish or the community for which the church has been built.

Office of the Dedication

10. The day on which a church is dedicated is kept as a solemnity in that church.

The office of the dedication of a church is celebrated, beginning with Evening Prayer I. When the rite of depositing relics takes place, it is highly recommended to keep a vigil at the relics of the martyr or saint that are to be placed beneath the altar; the best way of doing this is to have the office of readings, taken from the respective common or proper. This vigil should be properly adapted to accommodate the people's participation, but the requirements of the law are respected.[7]

Parts of the Rite

A. Entrance into the Church

11. The rite of the dedication begins with the entrance into the church; this may take place in one of the three following ways; the one best suited to the circumstances of time and place is to be used.

— Procession to the church to be dedicated: all assemble in a nearby church or other suitable place, from which the bishop, the ministers, and the congregation proceed to the church to be dedicated, praying and singing.

— Solemn entrance: if the procession cannot take place or seems inopportune, the community gathers at the entrance of the church.

— Simple entrance: the congregation assembles in the church itself; the bishop, the concelebrants, and the ministers enter from the sacristy in the usual way.

Two rituals are most significant in the entrance into a new church:

a) the handing over of the church: representatives of those who have been involved in the building of the church hand it over to the bishop.

b) the sprinkling of the church: the bishop blesses water and with it sprinkles the people, who are the spiritual temple, then the walls of the church, and finally, the altar.

B. Liturgy of the Word

12. Three readings are used in the liturgy of the word. The texts are chosen from those in the Lectionary (nos. 704 and 706) for the rite of the dedication of a church.

The first reading is always, even during the Easter season, the passage of Nehemiah that tells of the people of Jerusalem gathered in the presence of the scribe Ezra to hear the proclamation of the law of God (Nehemiah 8:1 – 4a, 5 – 6, 8 – 10).

13. After the readings the bishop gives the homily, in which he explains the biblical readings and the meaning of the dedication of a church.

The profession of faith is always said. The general intercessions are omitted, since the Litany of the Saints is sung in their place.

C. Prayer of Dedication and the Anointing of the Church and the Altar

Depositing the Relics of the Saints

14. If it is to take place, the relics of a martyr are deposited after the singing of the Litany of the Saints, to signify that the sacrifice of the members has its source in the sacrifice of the Head.[8] When relics of a martyr are not available, relics of another saint may be deposited in the altar.

Prayer of Dedication

15. The celebration of the eucharist is the most important and the one necessary rite for the dedication of a church.

Nevertheless, in accordance with the tradition in both East and West, a special prayer of dedication is also said. This prayer is a sign of the intention to dedicate the church to the Lord for all times and a petition for his blessing.

Rites of Anointing, Incensing, Covering and Lighting the Altar

16. The rites of anointing, incensing, covering and lighting the altar express in visible signs several aspects of the invisible work that the Lord accomplishes through the Church in its celebration of the divine mysteries, especially the eucharist.

a) *Anointing* of the altar and the walls of the church:

— The anointing with chrism makes the altar a symbol of Christ, who, before all others, is and is called "The Anointed One"; for the Father anointed him with the Holy Spirit and constituted him the High Priest so that on the altar of his body he might offer the sacrifice of his life for the salvation of all.

— The anointing of the church signifies that it is given over entirely and perpetually to Christian worship. In keeping with liturgical tradition, there are twelve anointings, or, where it is more convenient, four, as a symbol that the church is an image of the holy city of Jerusalem.

b) *Incense* is burned on the altar to signify that Christ's sacrifice, there perpetuated in mystery, ascends to God as an odor of sweetness and also to signify that the people's prayers rise up pleasing and acceptable, reaching the throne of God.[9]

The incensation of the nave of the church indicates that the dedication makes it a house of prayer, but the people of God are incensed first, because they are the living temple in which each faithful member is a spiritual altar.[10]

c) *The covering of the altar* indicates that the Christian altar is the altar of the eucharistic sacrifice and the table of the Lord; around it priests and people, by one and the same rite but with a difference of function, celebrate the memorial of Christ's death and resurrection and partake of his supper. For this reason the altar is prepared as the table of the sacrificial banquet and adorned as for a feast. Thus the dressing of the altar clearly signifies that it is the Lord's table at which all God's people joyously meet to be refreshed with divine food, namely, the body and blood of Christ sacrificed.

d) *The lighting of the altar,* which is followed by the lighting of the church, reminds us that Christ is "a light to enlighten the nations";[11] his brightness shines out in the Church and through it in the whole human family.

D. Celebration of the Eucharist

17. After the altar has been prepared, the bishop celebrates the eucharist, the principal and the most ancient part of the whole rite,[12] because the celebration of the eucharist is in the closest harmony with the rite of the dedication of a church:

— For the celebration of the eucharistic sacrifice achieves the end for which the church was built and the altar erected and expresses this end by particularly clear signs.

— Furthermore, the eucharist, which sanctifies the hearts of those who receive it, in a sense consecrates the altar and the place of celebration, as the ancient Fathers of the Church often assert: "This altar should be an object of awe: by nature it is stone, but it is made holy when it receives the body of Christ."[13]

— Finally, the bond closely connecting the dedication of a church with the celebration of the eucharist is likewise evident from the fact that the Mass for the dedication has its own preface, which is a central part of the rite itself.

IV. Adaptation of the Rite

Adaptations within the Competence of the Conferences of Bishops

18. The conferences of bishops may adapt this rite, as required, to the character of each region, but in such a way that nothing of its dignity and solemnity is lost.

However, the following are to be respected:

a) The celebration of Mass with the proper preface and prayer for a dedication must never be omitted.

b) Rites that have a special meaning and force from liturgical tradition (see no. 16) must be retained, unless weighty reasons stand in the way, but the wording may be suitably adapted if necessary.

With regard to adaptations, the competent ecclesiastical authority is to consult the Holy See and introduce adaptations with its consent.[14]

Adaptations within the Competence of the Ministers

19. It is for the bishop and for those in charge of the celebration of the rite:
   — to decide the manner of entrance into the church (see no. 11);
   — to determine the manner of handing over the new church to the bishop (no. 11);
   — to decide whether to have the depositing of relics of saints. The decisive consideration is the spiritual good of the community; the prescriptions in no. 5 must be followed.

It is for the rector of the church to be dedicated, helped by those who assist him in the pastoral work, to decide and prepare everything concerning the readings, singing, and other pastoral aids to foster the fruitful participation of the people and to ensure a dignified celebration.

V. Pastoral Preparation

20. In order that the people may take part fully in the rite of dedication, the rector of the church to be dedicated and others experienced in the pastoral ministry are to instruct them on the import of the celebration and its spiritual, ecclesial, and evangelizing power.

Accordingly, the people are to be instructed about the various parts of the church and their use, the rite of dedication, and the chief liturgical symbols employed in it. Thus led by suitable pastoral resources to a full understanding of the meaning of the dedication of a church through its rites and prayers, they will take an active, intelligent, and devout part in the sacred service.

VI. Requisites for the Dedication of a Church

21. For the celebration of the rite the following should be prepared:
a) *In the place of assembly:*
   — The Roman Pontifical;
   — processional cross;
   — if relics of the saints are to be carried in procession, the items in no. 24a.
b) *In the sacristy or in the sanctuary or in the body of the church to be dedicated,* as each situation requires:
   — The Roman Missal;
   — The Lectionary;
   — container of water to be blessed and sprinkler;
   — container with the chrism;
   — towels for wiping the table of the altar;
   — if needed, a waxed linen cloth or waterproof covering of the same size as the altar;

— basin and jug of water, towels, and all that is needed for washing the bishop's hands and those of the priests after they have anointed the walls of the church;

— linen gremial;

— brazier for burning incense or aromatic spices; or grains of incense and small candles to burn on the altar;

— censer, incense boat and spoon;

— chalice, corporal, purificators, and hand towel;

— bread, wine, and water for the celebration of Mass;

— altar cross, unless there is already a cross in the sanctuary or the cross that is carried in the entrance procession is to be placed near the altar;

— altar cloth, candles, and candlesticks;

— flowers, if opportune.

22. It is praiseworthy to keep the ancient custom of hanging on the walls of the church crosses made of stone, brass, or other suitable material or of having the crosses carved on the walls. Thus twelve or four crosses should be provided, depending on the number of anointings (see no. 16), and fixed here and there at a suitable height on the walls of the church. Beneath each cross a small bracket should be fitted and in it a small candlestick is placed, with a candle to be lighted.

23. For the Mass of the dedication the vestments are white or of some festive color. The following should be prepared:

— for the bishop: alb, stole, chasuble, miter, pastoral staff, and pallium, if the bishop has the right to wear one;

— or the concelebrating priests: the vestments for concelebrating Mass;

— for the deacons: albs, stoles, and dalmatics;

— for other ministers: albs or other lawfully approved dress.

24. If relics of the saints are to be placed beneath the altar, the following should be prepared:

a) *In the place of assembly:*

— reliquary containing the relics, placed between flowers and lights. When the simple entrance is used, the reliquary must be placed in a suitable part of the sanctuary before the rite begins;

— for the deacons who will carry the relics to be deposited: albs, red stoles, if the relics are those of a martyr, or white in other cases, and, if available, dalmatics. If the relics are carried by priests, then in place of dalmatics chasubles should be prepared.

The relics may also be carried by other ministers, vested in albs or other lawfully approved dress.

b) *In the sanctuary:*
— a small table on which the reliquary is placed during the first part of the dedication rite.

c) *In the sacristy:*
— a sealant or cement to close the cover of the aperture. In addition, a stonemason should be on hand to close the depository of the relics at the proper time.

25. The record of a dedication of a church should be drawn up in duplicate, signed by the bishop, the rector of the church, and representatives of the local community; one copy is to be kept in the diocesan archives, the other in the archives of the church. Where the depositing of relics takes place, a third copy of the record should be made, to be placed at the proper time in the reliquary.

In this record mention should be made of the day, month, and year of the church's dedication, the name of the bishop who celebrated the rite, also the titular of the church and, where applicable, the names of the martyrs or saints whose relics have been deposited beneath the altar.

Moreover, in a suitable place in the church, an inscription should be placed stating the day, month, and year when the dedication took place, the titular of the church, and the name of the bishop who celebrated the rite.

VII. Anniversary of the Dedication

A. Anniversary of the Dedication of the Cathedral Church

26. In order that the importance and dignity of the local Church may stand out with greater clarity, the anniversary of the dedication of its cathedral is to be celebrated, with the rank of a solemnity in the cathedral itself, with the rank of a feast in the other churches of the diocese, on the date on which the dedication of the church recurs.[15] If this date is always impeded, the celebration is assigned to the nearest date open. It is desirable that in the cathedral church on the anniversary the bishop concelebrate the eucharist with the chapter of canons or the priests' senate and with the participation of as many of the people as possible.

B. Anniversary of the Dedication of a Particular Church

27. The anniversary of a church's dedication is celebrated with the rank of a solemnity.[16]

OUTLINE OF THE RITE

INTRODUCTORY RITES
    A. First Form: Procession
        Greeting
        Brief Address
        Procession
        Handing Over the Building
        Entrance into the Church

    B. Second Form: Solemn Entrance
        Greeting
        Brief Address
        Handing Over the Building
        Entrance into the Church

    C. Third Form: Simple Entrance
        Entrance Procession
        Greeting
        Handing Over the Building

        Blessing and Sprinkling of Water
        Hymn: Gloria
        Opening Prayer

LITURGY OF THE WORD
    Presentation of the Lectionary
    First Reading
    Responsorial Psalm
    Second Reading
    Gospel Acclamation
    Gospel
    Homily
    Profession of Faith

PRAYER OF DEDICATION AND THE ANOINTINGS
    Invitation to Prayer
    Litany of the Saints
    Concluding Prayer
    [Depositing of the Relics]
    Prayer of Dedication
    Anointing of the Altar and the Walls of the Church
    Incensation of the Altar and the Church
    Lighting of the Altar and the Church

LITURGY OF THE EUCHARIST
    Preparation of the Altar and the Gifts
    Prayer over the Gifts
    Eucharistic Prayer

    Communion
    [Inauguration of the Blessed Sacrament Chapel
        Prayer after Communion
        Procession to the Chapel
        Incensation of the Eucharist]
    Prayer after Communion

CONCLUDING RITE
    Blessing and Dismissal

Rite of Dedication

Part I

Introductory Rites

Entrance into the Church

28. The entry into the church to be dedicated is made, according to the circumstances of time and place, in one of the three ways described below.

A. First Form: Procession

29. The door of the church to be dedicated should be closed. At a convenient hour the people assemble in a neighboring church or other suitable place from which the procession may proceed to the church. The relics of the martyrs or saints, if they are to be placed beneath the altar, are prepared in the place where the people assemble.

30. The bishop, the concelebrating priests, the deacons, and ministers, each in appropriate vestments, proceed to the place where the people are assembled. Putting aside the pastoral staff and miter, the bishop greets the people, saying:

> *The grace and peace of God*
> *be with all of you*
> *in his holy Church.*
> *R. And also with you.*

Other suitable words taken preferably from sacred Scripture may be used. Then the bishop addresses the people in these or similar words:

> *Brothers and sisters in Christ, this is a day of rejoicing: we have come together to dedicate this church by offering within it the sacrifice of Christ.*
> *May we open our hearts and minds to receive his word with faith; may our fellowship born in the one font of baptism and sustained at the one table of the Lord, become the one temple of his Spirit, as we gather round his altar in love.*

31. When he has finished addressing the people, the bishop receives the miter and pastoral staff and the procession to the church to be dedicated begins. No lights are used apart from those which surround the relics of the saints, nor is incense used either in the procession or in the Mass before the rite of the incensation and the lighting of the altar and the church (see below, nos. 66–71). The crossbearer leads

the procession; the ministers follow; then the deacons or priests with the relics of the saints, ministers or the faithful acompanying them on either side with lighted torches; then the concclebrating priests; then the bishop with two deacons; and lastly, the congregation.

32. As the procession proceeds, the following antiphon is sung with Psalm 122.

Let us go rejoicing to the house of the Lord.

Another appropriate song may be sung.

33. At the threshold of the church the procession comes to a halt. Representatives of those who have been involved in the building of the church (members of the parish or of the diocese, contributors, architects, workers) hand over the building to the bishop, offering him according to place and circumstances either the legal documents for possession of the building, or the keys, or the plan of the building, or the book in which the progress of the work is described and the names of those in charge of it and the names of the workers recorded. One of the representatives addresses the bishop and the community in a few words, pointing out, if need be, what the new church expresses in its art and in its own special design.

If the door is closed, the bishop then calls upon the priest to whom the pastoral care of the church has been entrusted to open the door.

34. When the door is unlocked, the bishop invites the people to enter the church in these or similar words.

Go within his gates giving thanks, enter his courts with songs of praise.

Then, preceded by the crossbearer, the bishop and the assembly enter the church. As the procession enters, the following antiphon is sung with Psalm 24.

Lift high the ancient portals. The King of glory enters.

Another appropriate song may be sung.

35. The bishop, without kissing the altar, goes to the chair; the concelebrants, deacons, and ministers go to the places assigned to them in the sanctuary. The relics of the saints are placed in a suitable part of the sanctuary between lighted torches. Water is then blessed with the rite described below, nos. 48–50.

B. Second Form: Solemn Entrance

36. If the procession cannot take place or seems inappropriate, the people assemble at the door of the church to be dedicated, where the relics of the saints have been placed beforehand.

37. Preceded by the crossbearer, the bishop and the concelebrating priests, the deacons, and the ministers, each in appropriate vestments, approach the church door, where the people are assembled. The door of the church should be closed, and the bishop, concelebrants, deacons, and ministers should approach it from outside.

38. Putting aside the pastoral staff and miter, the bishop greets the people, saying:

> *The grace and peace of God*
> *be with all of you*
> *in his holy Church.*
> *R. And also with you.*

Other suitable words taken preferably from sacred Scripture may be used. Then the bishop addresses the people in these or similar words:

> *Brothers and sisters in Christ, this is a day of rejoicing: we have come together to dedicate this church by offering within it the sacrifice of Christ.*

> *May we open our hearts and minds to receive his word with faith; may our fellowship born in the one font of baptism and sustained at the one table of the Lord, become the one temple of his Spirit, as we gather round his altar in love.*

39. When the bishop has finished addressing the people, he puts on the miter, and, if it seems appropriate, the following antiphon is sung with Psalm 122.

> *Let us go rejoicing to the house of the Lord.*

Another appropriate song may be sung.

40. Then representatives of those who have been involved in the building of the church (members of the parish or of the diocese, contributors, architects, workers) hand over the building to the bishop, offering him according to place and circumstances either the legal documents for possession of the building, or the keys, or the plan of the building, or the book in which the progress of the work is described and the names of those in charge of it and the names of the workers recorded. One of the representatives addresses the bishop and the community in a few words, pointing out, if need be, what the new church expresses in its art and in its own special design.

If the door is closed, the bishop then calls upon the priest to whom the pastoral care of the church has been entrusted to open the door.

41. The bishop takes the pastoral staff and invites the people to enter the church in these or similar words:

> *Go within his gates giving thanks, enter his courts with songs of praise.*

Then, preceded by the crossbearer, the bishop and the assembly enter the church. As the procession enters, the following antiphon is sung with Psalm 24.

Lift high the ancient portals. The King of glory enters.

Another appropriate song may be sung.

42. The bishop, without kissing the altar, goes to the chair; the concelebrants, deacons, and ministers go to the places assigned to them in the sanctuary. The relics of the saints are placed in a suitable part of the sanctuary between lighted torches. Water is then blessed with the rite described below, in nos. 48–50.

C. Third Form: Simple Entrance

43. If the solemn entrance cannot take place, the simple entrance is used. When the people are assembled, the bishop and the concelebrating priests, the deacons, and the ministers, each in appropriate vestments, preceded by the crossbearer, go from the sacristy through the main body of the church to the sanctuary.

44. If there are relics of the saints to be placed beneath the altar, these are brought in the entrance procession to the sanctuary from the sacristy or the chapel where since the vigil they have been exposed for the veneration of the people. For a just cause, before the celebration begins, the relics may be placed between lighted torches in a suitable part of the sanctuary.

45. As the procession proceeds, the entrance antiphon is sung with Psalm 122.

God in his holy dwelling, God who has gathered us together in his house: he will strengthen and console his people.

Or:

Let us go rejoicing to the house of the Lord.

Another appropriate song may be sung.

46. When the procession reaches the sanctuary, the relics of the saints are placed between lighted torches in a suitable place. The concelebrating priests, the deacons, and the ministers go to the places assigned to them; the bishop, without kissing the altar, goes to the chair. Then, putting aside the pastoral staff and miter, he greets the people, saying:

The grace and peace of God
be with all of you
in his holy Church.
R. And also with you.

Other suitable words taken preferably from sacred Scripture may be used.

47. Then representatives of those who have been involved in the building of the church (members of the parish or of the diocese, contributors, architects, workers) hand over the building to the bishop, offering him according to place and circumstances either the legal documents for possession of the building, or the keys, or the plan of the building, or the book in which the progress of the work is described and the names of those in charge of it and the names of the workers recorded. One of the representatives addresses the bishop and the community in a few words, pointing out, if need be, what the new church expresses in its art and in its own special design.

Blessing and Sprinkling of Water

48. When the entrance rite is completed, the bishop blesses water with which to sprinkle the people as a sign of repentance and as a reminder of their baptism, and to purify the walls and the altar of the new church. The ministers bring the vessel with the water to the bishop who stands at the chair. The bishop invites all to pray, in these or similar words:

> Brothers and sisters in Christ, in this solemn rite of dedication, let us ask the Lord our God to bless this water created by his hand.
> It is a sign of our repentance, a reminder of our baptism, and a symbol of the cleansing of these walls and this altar.
> May the grace of God help us to remain faithful members of his Church, open to the Spirit we have received.

All pray in silence for a brief period. The bishop then continues:

> God of mercy,
> you call every creature to the light of life,
> and surround us with such great love
> that when we stray
> you continually lead us back to Christ our head.
>
> For you have established an inheritance of such mercy,
> that those sinners, who pass through water made sacred,
> die with Christ and rise restored
> as members of his body
> and heirs of his eternal covenant.
>
> Bless + this water;
> sanctify it.

As it is sprinkled upon us and throughout this church
make it a sign of the saving waters of baptism,
by which we become one in Christ, the temple of your Spirit.

May all here today,
and all those in days to come,
who will celebrate your mysteries in this church,
be united at last in the holy city of your peace.

We ask this in the name of Jesus the Lord.
R. Amen.

49. The bishop, accompanied by the deacons, passes through the main body of the church, sprinkling the people and the walls with the holy water; then, when he has returned to the sanctuary, he sprinkles the altar. Meanwhile the following antiphon is sung.

I saw water flowing from the right side of the temple, alleluia. It brought God's life and his salvation, and the people sang in joyful praise: alleluia, alleluia.

Or, during Lent:

I will pour clean water over you and wash away all your defilement. A new heart will I give you, says the Lord.

Another appropriate song may be sung.

50. After the sprinkling the bishop returns to the chair and, when the singing is finished, standing with hands joined, says:

May God, the Father of mercies,
dwell in this house of prayer.
May the grace of the Holy Spirit cleanse us,
for we are the temple of his presence.
R. Amen.

Hymn

51. Then the Gloria is sung.

Opening Prayer

52. When the hymn is finished, the bishop, with hands joined, says:

Let us pray.

All pray in silence for a brief period. Then the bishop, with hands extended, says:

Lord,

fill this place with your presence,
and extend your hand
to all those who call upon you.

May your word here proclaimed
and your sacraments here celebrated
strengthen the hearts of all the faithful.

We ask this through our Lord Jesus Christ, your Son,
who lives and reigns with you and the Holy Spirit,
one God, for ever and ever.
R. Amen.

Part II

Liturgy of the Word

53. The proclamation of the word of God is fittingly carried out in this way: two readers, one of whom carries *The Lectionary,* and the psalmist come to the bishop. The bishop, standing with miter on, takes *The Lectionary,* shows it to the people, and says:

May the word of God always be heard in this place,
as it unfolds the mystery of Christ before you
and achieves your salvation within the Church.
R. Amen.

Then the bishop hands *The Lectionary* to the first reader. The readers and the psalmist proceed to the lectern, carrying *The Lectionary* for all to see.

54. The readings are arranged in this way:
   a) The first reading is always taken from the Book of Nehemiah 8:1 – 4a, 5 – 6, 8 – 10, followed by the singing of Psalm 19B:8 – 9, 10, 15, with the response:

R. Your words, Lord, are spirit and life.

   b) The second reading and the gospel are taken from the texts in *The Lectionary* (nos. 701 – 706) for the rite of the dedication of a church. Neither lights nor incense are carried at the gospel.

55. After the gospel the bishop gives the homily, in which he explains the biblical readings and the meaning of the rite.

56. The profession of faith is said. The general intercessions are omitted since in their place the litany of the saints is sung.

Part III
Prayer of Dedication and the Anointings

Invitation to Prayer

57. Then all stand, and the bishop, without his miter, invites the people to pray in these or similar words:

> Let us ask the saints to support our prayers to God the Father almighty,
> who has made the hearts of his people faithful temples of his Spirit.

Deacon (except on Sundays and during the Easter season):

> Let us kneel.

Litany of the Saints

58. Then the litany of the saints is sung, with all responding. On Sundays and also during the Easter season, all stand; on other days, all kneel.

59. The cantors begin the litany (appendix, p. 215); they add, at the proper place, names of other saints (the titular of the church, the patron saint of the place, and the saints whose relics are to be deposited, if this is to take place) and petitions suitable to the occasion.

60. When the litany is finished, the bishop, standing with hands extended, says:

> Lord,
> may the prayers of the Blessed Virgin Mary
> and of all the saints
> make our prayers acceptable to you.
>
> May this building,
> which we dedicate to your name,
> be a house of salvation and grace
> where Christians gathered in fellowship
> may worship you in spirit and truth
> and grow together in love.
>
> Grant this through Christ our Lord.
> R. Amen.

If it is applicable, the deacon says:

Let us stand.

All rise. The bishop receives the miter.

When there is no depositing of the relics of the saints, the bishop immediately says the prayer of dedication as indicated in no. 62 below.

Depositing of the Relics

61. Then, if relics of the martyrs or other saints are to be placed beneath the altar, the bishop approaches the altar. A deacon or priest brings them to the bishop, who places them in a suitably prepared aperture. Meanwhile, one of the following antiphons is sung with Psalm 15.

> *Saints of God, you have been enthroned at the foot of God's altar; pray for us to the Lord Jesus Christ.*

Or:

> *The bodies of the saints lie buried in peace, but their names will live on for ever (alleluia).*

Another appropriate song may be sung.

Meanwhile a stone mason closes the aperture and the bishop returns to the chair.

Prayer of Dedication

62. Then the bishop, standing without miter at the chair or near the altar, with hands extended, says:

> *Father in heaven,*
> *source of holiness and true purpose,*
> *it is right that we praise and glorify your name.*
>
> *For today we come before you,*
> *to dedicate to your lasting service*
> *this house of prayer, this temple of worship,*
> *this home in which we are nourished by your word and your sacraments.*
>
> *Here is reflected the mystery of the Church.*
>
> *The Church is fruitful,*
> *made holy by the blood of Christ:*
> *a bride made radiant with his glory,*

a virgin splendid in the wholeness of her faith,
a mother blessed through the power of the Spirit.

The Church is holy,
your chosen vineyard:
its branches envelop the world,
its tendrils, carried on the tree of the cross,
reach up to the kingdom of heaven.

The Church is favored,
the dwelling place of God on earth:
a temple built of living stones,
founded on the apostles
with Jesus Christ its cornerstone.

The Church is exalted,
a city set on a mountain:
a beacon to the whole world,
bright with the glory of the Lamb,
and echoing the prayers of her saints.

Lord,
send your Spirit from heaven
to make this church an ever-holy place,
and this altar a ready table for the sacrifice of Christ.

Here may the waters of baptism
overwhelm the shame of sin;
here may your people die to sin
and live again through grace as your children.

Here may your children,
gathered around your altar,
celebrate the memorial of the Paschal Lamb,
and be fed at the table
of Christ's word and Christ's body.

Here may prayer, the Church's banquet,
resound through heaven and earth
as a plea for the world's salvation.

Here may the poor find justice,
the victims of oppression, true freedom.

From here may the whole world
clothed in the dignity of the children of God,
enter with gladness your city of peace.

We ask this through our Lord Jesus Christ, your Son,
who lives and reigns with you and the Holy Spirit,
one God, for ever and ever.
R. Amen.

Anointing of the Altar and the Walls of the Church

63. Then the bishop, removing the chasuble if necessary and putting on a linen gremial, goes to the altar with the deacons and other ministers, one of whom carries the chrism. The bishop proceeds to anoint the altar and the walls of the church as described in no. 64 below.

If the bishop wishes to associate some of the concelebrating priests with him in the anointing of the walls, after the anointing of the altar, he hands them vessels of sacred chrism and goes with them to complete the anointings.

However, the bishop may give the task of anointing the walls to the priests alone; in that case, he hands the vessels of sacred chrism to them after he has anointed the altar.

64. The bishop, standing before the altar, says:

We now anoint this altar and this building.
May God in his power make them holy,
visible signs of the mystery of Christ and his Church.

Then he pours chrism on the middle of the altar and on each of its four corners, and it is recommended that he anoint the entire table of the altar with this.

When the altar has been anointed, the bishop anoints the walls of the church, signing with chrism the suitably distributed twelve or four crosses. He may have the assistance of two or four priests.

If the anointing of the walls is given to the priests, after the bishop has anointed the altar, they anoint the walls of the church signing the crosses with chrism.

Meanwhile one of the following antiphons is sung with Psalm 84.

See the place where God lives among his people; there the Spirit of God will make his home among you; the temple of God is holy and you are that temple (alleluia).

Or:

Holy is the temple of the Lord, it is God's handiwork, his dwelling place.

Another appropriate song may be sung.

65. When the altar and walls have been anointed, the bishop returns to the chair, sits, and washes his hands. Then the bishop takes off the gremial and puts on the chasuble. The priests also wash their hands after they have anointed the walls.

Incensation of the Altar and the Church

66. After the rite of anointing, a brazier is placed on the altar for burning incense or aromatic gums, or, if desired, a heap of incense mixed with small candles or wax tapers is made on the altar. The bishop puts incense into the brazier or he lights the heap of incense with a small candle handed to him by a minister, saying:

> *Lord,*
> *may our prayer ascend as incense in your sight.*
> *As this building is filled with fragrance*
> *so may your Church fill the world*
> *with the fragrance of Christ.*

67. Then the bishop puts incense into some censers and incenses the altar; he returns to the chair, is incensed, and then sits. Ministers, walking through the church, incense the people and the walls.

68. Meanwhile one of the following antiphons is sung with Psalm 138.

> *An angel stood by the altar of the temple, holding a golden censer.*

Or:

> *From the hand of the angel, clouds of incense rose in the presence of the Lord.*

Another appropriate song may be sung.

Lighting of the Altar and the Church.

69. After the incensation, a few ministers wipe the table of the altar with cloths, and, if need be, cover it with a waterproof linen. They then cover the altar with a cloth, and, if opportune, decorate it with flowers. They arrange in a suitable manner the candles needed for the celebration of Mass, and, if need be, the cross.

70. Then the bishop gives to the deacon a lighted candle, and says:

> *Light of Christ,*
> *shine forth in the Church*
> *and bring all nations*
> *to the fullness of truth.*

Then the bishop sits. The deacon goes to the altar and lights the candles for the celebration of the eucharist.

71. Then the festive lighting takes place: all the candles, including those at the places where the anointings were made, and the other lamps are lit as a sign of rejoicing. Meanwhile the following antiphon is sung with the canticle of Tobias.

> *Your light will come, Jerusalem; upon you the glory of the Lord will dawn and all nations will walk in your light, alleluia.*

Or, during Lent:

> *Jerusalem, city of God, you will shine with the light of God's splendor; all people on earth will pay you homage.*

Canticle of Tobias
(Vg. 13:10; 13 – 14ab; 14c – 15; 17)

> *Bless the Lord, all you saints of the Lord.*
> *Rejoice and give him thanks.*

(Repeat antiphon)

> *Jerusalem, city of God,*
> *you will shine with the light of God's splendor;*
> *all people on earth will pay you homage.*
> *Nations will come from afar,*
> *bearing gifts for the King of heaven;*
> *in you they will worship the Lord.*

(Repeat antiphon)

> *Nations will consider your land holy,*
> *for in you they will call upon the great name of the Lord.*
> *You will exult and rejoice over the children of the righteous,*
> *for they will be gathered together to praise the Lord.*

(Repeat antiphon)
Another appropriate song may be sung, especially one in honor of Christ, the light of the world.

Part IV

Liturgy of the Eucharist

72. The deacons and the ministers prepare the altar in the usual way. Then some of the congregation bring bread, wine, and water for the celebration of the Lord's sacrifice. The bishop receives the gifts at the chair. While the gifts are being brought, the following antiphon may be sung:

> *Lord God, in the simplicity of my heart I have joyously offered all things to you; with great joy I have looked upon your chosen people, Lord God, I have obeyed your will (alleluia).*

Another appropriate song may be sung.

73. When all is ready, the bishop goes to the altar, removes the miter, and kisses the altar. The Mass proceeds in the usual way; however, neither the gifts nor the altar are incensed.

Prayer over the Gifts

74. With hands extended, the bishop sings or says:

> *Lord,*
> *accept the gifts of a rejoicing Church.*
>
> *May your people,*
> *who are gathered in this sacred place,*
> *arrive at eternal salvation*
> *through the mysteries in which they share.*
> *Grant this through Christ our Lord.*
> *R. Amen.*

Eucharistic Prayer

74. Eucharistic Prayer I or III is said, with the following preface, which is an integral part of the rite of the dedication of a church. With hands extended the bishop sings or says:

> *The Lord be with you.*
> *R. And also with you.*
>
> *Lift up your hearts.*
> *R. We lift them up to the Lord.*
>
> *Let us give thanks to the Lord our God.*
> *R. It is right to give him thanks and praise.*

Father, all-powerful and ever-living God,
we do well always and everywhere to give you thanks.

The whole world is your temple,
shaped to resound with your name.
Yet you also allow us to dedicate to your service
places designed for your worship.

With hearts full of joy
we consecrate to your glory
this work of our hands, this house of prayer.

Here is foreshadowed the mystery of your true temple;
this church is the image on earth of your heavenly city:

For you made the body of your Son
born of the Virgin,
a temple consecrated to your glory,
the dwelling place of your godhead in all its fullness.

You have established the Church as your holy city,
founded on the apostles,
with Jesus Christ its cornerstone.

You continue to build your Church with chosen stones,
enlivened by the Spirit,
and cemented together by love.

In that holy city you will be all in all for endless ages,
and Christ will be its light for ever.

Through Christ we praise you, Lord,
with all the angels and saints in their song of joy:

Holy, holy, holy Lord, God of power and might,
heaven and earth are full of your glory.
> *Hosanna in the highest.*
Blessed is he who comes in the name of the Lord.
> *Hosanna in the highest.*

76. In Eucharistic Prayer I the special form of **Father, accept this offering** is said:

Father,
accept this offering
from your whole family,
and from your servants

who with heart and hand
have given and built this church
as an offering to you (in honor of N.).
Grant us your peace in this life,
save us from final damnation,
and count us among those you have chosen.

77. In the intercessions of Eucharistic Prayer III, after the words, **with . . . the entire people your Son has gained for you,** the following is said:

Father,
accept the prayers of those who dedicate this church to you.

May it be a place of salvation and sacrament
where your Gospel of peace is proclaimed
and your holy mysteries celebrated.

Guided by your word and secure in your peace
may your chosen people now journeying through life
arrive safely at their eternal home.

There may all your children
now scattered abroad
be settled at last in your city of peace.

78. While the bishop is receiving the body of Christ the communion song begins. One of the following antiphons is sung with Psalm 128.

My house shall be called a house of prayer, says the Lord: in it all who ask shall receive, all who seek shall find, and all who knock shall have the door opened to them (alleluia).

Or:

May the children of the Church be like olive branches around the table of the Lord (alleluia).

Another appropriate song may be sung.

If there is no inauguration of the blessed sacrament chapel, the Mass proceeds as follows, no. 83.

Inauguration of the Blessed Sacrament Chapel

79. The inauguration of a chapel where the blessed sacrament is to be reserved, is carried out appropriately in this way: after the communion the pyx containing the blessed sacrament is left on the table of the altar. The bishop goes to the chair, and all pray in silence for a brief period. Then the bishop says the following prayer after communion.

> *Let us pray.*

Pause for silent prayer, if this has not preceded.

> *Lord,*
> *through these gifts*
> *increase the vision of your truth in our minds.*
>
> *May we always worship you in your holy temple,*
> *and rejoice in your presence with all your saints.*
>
> *Grant this through Christ our Lord.*
> *R. Amen.*

80. When the prayer is completed, the bishop returns to the altar, genuflects, and incenses the blessed sacrament. Afterward, when he has received the humeral veil, he takes the pyx, which he covers with the veil itself. Then a procession is formed in which, preceded by the crossbearer and with lighted torches and incense, the blessed sacrament is carried through the main body of the church to the chapel of reservation. As the procession proceeds, the following antiphon is sung with Psalm 147:12 – 20.

> *Praise the Lord, Jerusalem.*

Another appropriate song may be sung.

81. When the procession comes to the chapel of reservation, the bishop places the pyx on the altar or in the tabernacle, the door of which remains open. Then he puts incense in the censer, kneels, and incenses the blessed sacrament. Finally, after a brief period during which all pray in silence, the deacon puts the pyx in the tabernacle or closes the door. A minister lights the lamp, which will burn perpetually before the blessed sacrament.

82. If the chapel where the blessed sacrament is reserved can be seen clearly by the congregation, the bishop immediately imparts the blessing of the Mass (see below, no. 84). Otherwise, the procession returns to the sanctuary by the shorter route and the bishop imparts the blessing either at the altar or at the chair.

Prayer after Communion

83. If there is no inauguration of the blessed sacrament chapel, when the communion of the congregation is finished, the bishop says:

Let us pray.

Pause for silent prayer, if this has not preceded.

Lord,
through these gifts
increase the vision of your truth in our minds.

May we always worship you in your holy temple,
and rejoice in your presence with all your saints.

Grant this through Christ our Lord.
R. Amen.

Blessing and Dismissal

84. The bishop receives the miter and says:

The Lord be with you.
R. And also with you.

Then the deacon, if appropriate, gives the invitation to the people in these or similar words:

Bow your heads and pray for God's blessing.

Then the bishop extends his hands over the people and blesses them, saying:

The Lord of heaven and earth
has assembled you before him this day
to dedicate this house of prayer.
May he fill you with the blessings of heaven.
R. Amen.

God the Father wills that all his children
scattered throughout the world
become one family in his Son.
May he make you his temple,
the dwelling place of his Holy Spirit.
R. Amen.

May God free you from every bond of sin,
dwell within you and give you joy.

May you live with him for ever
in the company of all his saints.
R. Amen.

The bishop takes the pastoral staff and continues:

May almighty God bless you,
the Father, and the Son, + and the Holy Spirit.
R. Amen.

85. Finally the deacon dismisses the people in the usual way.

Chapter Three

Dedication of a Church in Which Mass Is Already Being Celebrated Regularly

Introduction

1. In order to bring out fully the symbolism and the significance of the rite, the opening of a new church and its dedication should take place at one and the same time. For this reason, as was said before, care should be taken that, as far as possible, Mass is not celebrated in a new church before it is dedicated (see chapter two, nos. 8, 15, 17).

Nevertheless in the case of the rite of the dedication of a church where the sacred mysteries are already being celebrated regularly, the rite set out in this chapter must be used.

Moreover, a clear distinction exists in regard to these churches. In the case of those just built the reason for a dedication is obvious. In the case of those standing for some time the following requirements must be met for them to be dedicated:

— that the altar has not already been dedicated, since it is rightly forbidden both by custom and by liturgical law to dedicate a church without dedicating the altar, for the dedication of the altar is the principal part of the whole rite;

— that there be something new or notably altered about the edifice, relative either to its structure (for example, a total restoration) or its status in law (for example, the church's being ranked as a parish church).

2. All the directions given in the Introduction to chapter two apply to this rite, unless they are clearly extraneous to the situation which this rite envisages or other directions are given.

This rite differs chiefly from that described in chapter two on these points:

a) The rite of opening the doors of the church (see chapter two, no. 34 or no. 41) is omitted, since the church is already open to the community; consequently, the entrance rite takes the form of the simple entrance (see chapter two, nos. 43–47). However, in the case of dedicating a church closed for a long time and now being opened again for sacred celebrations, the rite of opening the doors may be carried out, since in this case it retains its point and significance.

b) The rite of handing over the church to the bishop (see chapter two, no. 33 or no. 40 or no. 47), depending on the situation, is either to be followed, omitted, or adapted in a way relevant to the condition of the church being dedicated (for example, it will be right to retain it in dedicating a church built recently; to omit it in dedicating an older church where nothing has been changed in the structure; to adapt it in dedicating an older church completely restored).

c) The rite of sprinkling the church walls with holy water (see chapter two, nos. 48–50), purificatory by its very nature, is omitted.

d) All the rites belonging to the first proclamation of the word of God in a church (see chapter two, no. 53) are omitted; thus the liturgy of the word takes place in the usual way. A different, pertinent reading is chosen in place of Nehemiah 8:1–4a and its responsorial psalm, Psalm 19b:8–9, 10, 15 (see chapter two, no. 54a).

OUTLINE OF THE RITE

INTRODUCTORY RITES
    Entrance into the Church
        Entrance Procession
        Greeting
        Handing Over the Building
    Blessing and Sprinkling of Water
    Hymn: Gloria
    Opening Prayer

LITURGY OF THE WORD
    First Reading
    Responsorial Psalm
    Second Reading
    Gospel Acclamation
    Gospel
    Homily
    Profession of Faith

PRAYER OF DEDICATION AND THE ANOINTINGS
    Invitation to Prayer
    Litany of the Saints
    Concluding Prayer
    [Depositing of the Relics]
    Prayer of Dedication
    Anointing of the Altar and the Walls of the Church
    Incensation of the Altar and the Church
    Lighting of the Altar and the Church

LITURGY OF THE EUCHARIST
    Preparation of the Altar and the Gifts
    Prayer over the Gifts
    Eucharistic Prayer
    _____

    Communion
    [Inauguration of the Blessed Sacrament Chapel
        Prayer after Communion
        Procession to the Chapel
        Incensation of the Eucharist]
    Prayer after Communion

CONCLUDING RITE
    Blessing and Dismissal

Rite of Dedication

Part I
Introductory Rites

Entrance into the Church

3. When the people are assembled, the bishop and the concelebrating priests, the deacons, and the ministers, each in appropriate vestments, preceded by the cross-bearer, go from the sacristy through the main body of the church to the sanctuary.

4. If there are relics of the saints to be placed beneath the altar, these are brought in the entrance procession to the sanctuary from the sacristy or the chapel where since the vigil they have been exposed for the veneration of the people. For a just cause, before the celebration begins, the relics may be placed between lighted torches in a suitable part of the sanctuary.

5. As the procession proceeds, the entrance antiphon is sung with Psalm 122.

> *God in his holy dwelling, God who has gathered us together in his house: he will strengthen and console his people.*

Or:

> *Let us go rejoicing to the house of the Lord.*

Another appropriate song may be sung.

6. When the procession reaches the sanctuary, the relics of the saints are placed between lighted torches in a suitable place. The concelebrating priests, the deacons, and the ministers go to the places assigned to them; the bishop, without kissing the altar, goes to the chair. Then, putting aside the pastoral staff and miter, he greets the people, saying:

> *The grace and peace of God*
> *be with all of you*
> *in his holy Church.*
> *R. And also with you.*

Other suitable words taken preferably from sacred Scripture may be used.

7. If circumstances dictate that the church is to be handed over to the bishop (see Introduction, no. 2b), representatives of those who have been involved in the building of the church (members of the parish or of the diocese, contributors, architects, workers) hand over the building to the bishop, offering him either the legal documents for possession of the building, or the keys, or the plan of the building, or the book in which the progress of the work is described and the names of those in charge of it and the names of the workers recorded. One of the representatives addresses the bishop and the community in a few words, pointing out, if need be, what the church expresses in its art and in its own special design.

Blessing and Sprinkling of Water

8. When the entrance rite is completed, the bishop blesses water with which to sprinkle the people as a sign of repentance and as a reminder of their baptism. The ministers return the vessel with the water to the bishop who stands at the chair. The bishop invites all to pray, in these or similar words:

Brothers and sisters in Christ in this solemn rite of dedication let us ask the Lord our God to bless this water, created by his hand.

It is a sign of our repentance and a reminder of our baptism.

May the grace of God help us to remain faithful members of his Church, open to the Spirit we have received.

All pray in silence for a brief period. The bishop then continues:

God of mercy,
you call every creature to the light of life,
and surround us with such great love
that when we stray
you continually lead us back to Christ our head.

For you have established an inheritance of such mercy,
that those sinners, who pass through water made sacred,
die with Christ and rise restored
as members of his body
and heirs of his eternal covenant.

Bless + this water;
sanctify it.

As it is sprinkled upon us and throughout this church
make it a sign of the saving waters of baptism,
by which we become one in Christ, the temple of your Spirit.

May all here today,
and all those in days to come,
who will celebrate your mysteries in this church
be united at last in the holy city of your peace.

We ask this in the name of Jesus the Lord.
R. Amen.

9. The bishop, accompanied by the deacons, sprinkles the people with holy water, then if the altar is completely new he sprinkles it too. Meanwhile the following antiphon is sung.

I saw water flowing from the right side of the temple, alleluia. It brought God's
life and his salvation, and the people sang in joyful praise: alleluia, alleluia.

Or, during Lent:

I will pour clean water over you and wash away all your defilement. A new
heart will I give you, says the Lord.

Another appropriate song may be sung.

10. After the sprinkling the bishop returns to the chair and, when the singing is finished, standing with hands joined, says:

May God, the Father of mercies,
dwell in this house of prayer.
May the grace of the Holy Spirit cleanse us,
for we are the temple of his presence.
R. Amen.

Hymn

11. Then the Gloria is sung.

Opening Prayer

12. When the hymn is finished, the bishop, with hands joined, says:

Let us pray.

All pray in silence for a brief period. Then the bishop, with hands extended, says:

Lord,
fill this place with your presence,
and extend your hand
to all those who call upon you.

May your word here proclaimed
and your sacraments here celebrated
strengthen the hearts of all the faithful.

We ask this through our Lord Jesus Christ, your Son,
who lives and reigns with you and the Holy Spirit,
one God, for ever and ever.
R. Amen.

Part II
Liturgy of the Word

13. The bishop sits and receives the miter; the people also are seated. Then the liturgy of the word takes place; the readings are taken from texts in *The Lectionary* (nos. 701 and 706) for the rite of the dedication of a church.

14. Neither lights nor incense are carried at the gospel.

15. After the gospel the bishop gives the homily, in which he explains the biblical readings and the meaning of the rite.

16. The profession of faith is said. The general intercessions are omitted since in their place the litany of the saints is sung.

Part III
Prayer of Dedication and the Anointings

Invitation to Prayer

17. Then all stand, and the bishop, without his miter, invites the people to pray in these or similar words:

> *Let us ask the saints to support our prayers to God the Father almighty,*
> *who has made the hearts of his people faithful temples of his Spirit.*

Deacon (except on Sundays and during the Easter season):

> *Let us kneel.*

Litany of the Saints

18. Then the litany of the saints is sung, with all responding. On Sundays and also during the Easter season, all stand; on other days, all kneel.

19. The cantors begin the litany (appendix, p. 215); they add, at the proper place, names of other saints (the titular of the church, the patron saint of the place, and the saints whose relics are to be deposited, if this is to take place) and petitions suitable to the occasion.

20. When the litany is finished, the bishop, standing with hands extended, says:

> *Lord,*
> *may the prayers of the Blessed Virgin Mary*
> *and of all the saints*
> *make our prayers acceptable to you.*
>
> *May this building,*
> *which we dedicate to your name,*
> *be a house of salvation and grace*
> *where Christians gathered in fellowship*
> *may worship you in spirit and truth*
> *and grow together in love.*
>
> *Grant this through Christ our Lord.*
> *R. Amen.*

If it is applicable, the deacon says:

> *Let us stand.*

All rise. The bishop receives the miter.

When there is no depositing of the relics of the saints, the bishop immediately says the prayer of dedication as indicated in no. 22 below.

Depositing of the Relics

21. Then, if relics of the martyrs or other saints are to be placed beneath the altar, the bishop approaches the altar. A deacon or priest brings them to the bishop, who places them in a suitably prepared aperture. Meanwhile one of the following antiphons is sung with Psalm 15.

> *Saints of God, you have been enthroned at the foot of God's altar; pray for us to the Lord Jesus Christ.*

Or:

> *The bodies of the saints lie buried in peace, but their names will live on for ever (alleluia).*

Another appropriate song may be sung.
Meanwhile a stone mason closes the aperture and the bishop returns to the chair.

Prayer of Dedication

22. Then the bishop, standing without miter at the chair or near the altar, with hands extended, says:

Father in heaven,
source of holiness and true purpose,
it is right that we praise and glorify your name.

For today we come before you,
to dedicate to your lasting service
this house of prayer, this temple of worship,
this home in which we are nourished by your word and your sacraments.

Here is reflected the mystery of the Church.

The Church is fruitful,
made holy by the blood of Christ:
a bride made radiant with his glory,
a virgin splendid in the wholeness of her faith,
a mother blessed through the power of the Spirit.

The Church is holy,
your chosen vineyard:
its branches envelop the world,
its tendrils, carried on the tree of the cross,
reach up to the kingdom of heaven.

The Church is favored,
the dwelling place of God on earth:
a temple built of living stones,
founded on the apostles
with Jesus Christ its cornerstone.

The Church is exalted,
a city set on a mountain:
a beacon to the whole world,
bright with the glory of the Lamb,
and echoing the prayers of her saints.

Lord,
send your Spirit from heaven
to make this church an ever-holy place,
and this altar a ready table for the sacrifice of Christ.

Here may the waters of baptism
overwhelm the shame of sin;
here may your people die to sin
and live again through grace as your children.

Here may your children,
gathered around your altar,
celebrate the memorial of the Paschal Lamb,
and be fed at the table
of Christ's word and Christ's body.

Here may prayer, the Church's banquet,
resound through heaven and earth
as a plea for the world's salvation.

Here may the poor find justice,
the victims of oppression, true freedom.

From here may the whole world
clothed in the dignity of the children of God,
enter with gladness your city of peace.

We ask this through our Lord Jesus, your Son,
who lives and reigns with you and the Holy Spirit,
one God for ever and ever.
R. Amen.

Anointing of the Altar and the Walls of the Church

23. Then the bishop, removing the chasuble if necessary and putting on a linen gremial, goes to the altar with the deacons and other ministers, one of whom carries the chrism. The bishop proceeds to anoint the altar and the walls of the church as described in no. 24 below.

If the bishop wishes to associate some of the concelebrating priests with him in the anointing of the walls, after the anointing of the altar, he hands them vessels of sacred chrism and goes with them to complete the anointings.

However, the bishop may give the task of anointing the walls to the priests alone; in that case, he hands the vessels of sacred chrism to them after he has anointed the altar.

24. The bishop, standing before the altar, says:

We now anoint this altar and this building.
May God in his power make them holy,
visible signs of the mystery of Christ and his Church.

Then he pours chrism on the middle of the altar and on each of its four corners, and it is recommended that he anoint the entire table of the altar with this.

When the altar has been anointed, the bishop anoints the walls of the church, signing with chrism the suitably distributed twelve or four crosses. He may have the assistance of two or four priests.

If the anointing of the walls is given to the priests, after the bishop has anointed the altar, they anoint the walls of the church signing the crosses with chrism.

Meanwhile one of the following antiphons is sung with Psalm 84.

See the place where God lives among his people; there the Spirit of God will make his home among you; the temple of God is holy and you are that temple (alleluia).

Or:

Holy is the temple of the Lord, it is God's handiwork, his dwelling place.

Another appropriate song may be sung.

25. When the altar and walls have been anointed, the bishop returns to the chair, sits, and washes his hands. Then the bishop takes off the gremial and puts on the chasuble. The priests also wash their hands after they have anointed the walls.

Incensation of the Altar and the Church

26. After the rite of anointing, a brazier is placed on the altar for burning incense or aromatic gums, or, if desired, a heap of incense mixed with small candles or wax tapers is made on the altar. The bishop puts incense into the brazier or he lights the heap of incense with a small candle handed to him by a minister, saying:

Lord,
may our prayer ascend as incense in your sight.
As this building is filled with fragrance
so may your Church fill the world
with the fragrance of Christ.

27. Then the bishop puts incense into some censers and incenses the altar; he returns to the chair, is incensed, and then sits. Ministers, walking through the church, incense the people and the walls.

28. Meanwhile one of the following antiphons is sung with Psalm 138.

An angel stood by the altar of the temple, holding a golden censer.

Or:

From the hand of the angel, clouds of incense rose in the presence of the Lord.

Another appropriate song may be sung.

Lighting of the Altar and the Church

29. After the incensation, a few ministers wipe the table of the altar with cloths, and, if need be, cover it with a waterproof linen. They then cover the altar with a cloth, and, if opportune, decorate it with flowers. They arrange in a suitable manner the candles needed for the celebration of Mass, and, if need be, the cross.

30. Then the bishop gives to the deacon a lighted candle and says:

Light of Christ,
shine forth in the Church
and bring all nations
to the fullness of truth.

Then the bishop sits. The deacon goes to the altar and lights the candles for the celebration of the eucharist.

31. Then the festive lighting takes place: all the candles, including those at the places where the anointings were made, and the other lamps are lit as a sign of rejoicing. Meanwhile the following antiphon is sung with the canticle of Tobias.

Your light will come, Jerusalem; upon you the glory of the Lord will dawn
and all nations will walk in your light, alleluia.

Or, during Lent:

Jerusalem, city of God, you will shine with the light of God's splendor; all
people on earth will pay you homage.

Canticle of Tobias
(Vg. 13:10; 13 – 14ab; 14c – 15; 17)

Bless the Lord, all you saints of the Lord.
Rejoice and give him thanks.

(Repeat antiphon)

Jerusalem, city of God,
you will shine with the light of God's splendor;
all people on earth will pay you homage.
Nations will come from afar,
bearing gifts for the King of heaven;
in you they will worship the Lord.

(Repeat antiphon)

Nations will consider your land holy,
for in you they will call upon the great name of the Lord.
You will exult and rejoice over the children of the righteous,
for they will be gathered together to praise the Lord.

(Repeat antiphon)
Another appropriate song may be sung, especially one in honor of Christ, the light of the world.

Part IV

Liturgy of the Eucharist

32. The deacons and the ministers prepare the altar in the usual way. Then some of the congregation bring bread, wine, and water for the celebration of the Lord's sacrifice. The bishop receives the gifts at the chair. While the gifts are being brought, the following antiphon may be sung:

Lord God, in the simplicity of my heart I have joyously offered all things to you; with great joy I have looked upon your chosen people; Lord God, I have obeyed your will (alleluia).

Another appropriate song may be sung.

33. When all is ready, the bishop goes to the altar, removes the miter, and kisses the altar. The Mass proceeds in the usual way; however, neither the gifts nor the altar are incensed.

Prayer over the Gifts

34. With hands extended, the bishop sings or says:

Lord,
accept the gifts of a rejoicing Church.

May your people,
who are gathered in this sacred place,
arrive at eternal salvation
through the mysteries in which they share.

Grant this through Christ our Lord.
R. Amen.

Eucharistic Prayer

35. Eucharistic Prayer I or III is said, with the following preface. With hands extended the bishop sings or says:

The Lord be with you.
R. And also with you.

Lift up your hearts.
R. We lift them up to the Lord.

Let us give thanks to the Lord our God.
R. It is right to give him thanks and praise.

Father of holiness and power,
we give you thanks and praise
through Jesus Christ, your Son.

For you have blessed this work of our hands
and your presence makes it a house of prayer;
nor do you ever refuse us welcome
when we come in before you as your pilgrim people.

In this house you realize the mystery of your dwelling among us:
for in shaping us here as your holy temple
you enrich your whole Church,
which is the very body of Christ,
and thus bring closer to fulfillment
the vision of your peace,
the heavenly city of Jerusalem.

And so, with all your angels and saints,
who stand in your temple of glory,
we praise you and give you thanks, as we sing:

Holy, holy, holy Lord, God of power and might,
heaven and earth are full of your glory.
> *Hosanna in the highest.*
Blessed is he who comes in the name of the Lord.
> *Hosanna in the highest.*

36. While the bishop is receiving the body of Christ the communion song begins. One of the following antiphons is sung with Psalm 128.

> *My house shall be called a house of prayer, says the Lord: in it all who ask shall receive, all who seek shall find, and all who knock shall have the door opened to them (alleluia).*

Or:

> *May the children of the Church be like olive branches around the table of the Lord (alleluia).*

Another appropriate song may be sung.

If there is no inauguration of the blessed sacrament chapel, the Mass proceeds as below, no. 38.

Inauguration of the Blessed Sacrament Chapel

37. [79] The inauguration of a chapel where the blessed sacrament is to be reserved, is carried out appropriately in this way: after the communion the pyx containing the blessed sacrament is left on the table of the altar. The bishop goes to the chair, and all pray in silence for a brief period. Then the bishop says the following prayer after communion:

> *Let us pray.*

Pause for silent prayer, if this has not preceded.

> *Lord,*
> *through these gifts*
> *increase the vision of your truth in our minds.*
>
> *May we always worship you in your holy temple,*
> *and rejoice in your presence with all your saints.*
>
> *Grant this through Christ our Lord.*
> *R. Amen.*

[80] When the prayer is completed, the bishop returns to the altar, genuflects, and incenses the blessed sacrament. Afterward, when he has received the humeral veil,

he takes the pyx, which he covers with the veil itself. Then a procession is formed in which, preceded by the crossbearer and with lighted torches and incense, the blessed sacrament is carried through the main body of the church to the chapel of reservation. As the procession proceeds, the following antiphon is sung with Psalm 147:12–20.

Praise the Lord, Jerusalem.

Another appropriate song may be sung.

[81] When the procession comes to the chapel of reservation, the bishop places the pyx on the altar or in the tabernacle, the door of which remains open. Then he puts incense in the censer, kneels, and incenses the blessed sacrament. Finally, after a brief period during which all pray in silence the deacon puts the pyx in the tabernacle or closes the door. A minister lights the lamp, which will burn perpetually before the blessed sacrament.

[82] If the chapel where the blessed sacrament is reserved can be seen clearly by the congregation, the bishop immediately imparts the blessing of the Mass (see below, no. 39). Otherwise the procession returns to the sanctuary by the shorter route and the bishop imparts the blessing either at the altar or at the chair.

Prayer after Communion

38. If there is no inauguration of the blessed sacrament chapel, when the communion of the congregation is finished, the bishop says:

Let us pray.

Pause for silent prayer, if this has not preceded.

Lord,
through these gifts
increase the vision of your truth in our minds.

May we always worship you in your holy temple,
and rejoice in your presence with all your saints.

Grant this through Christ our Lord.
R. Amen.

Blessing and Dismissal

39. The bishop receives the miter and says:

The Lord be with you.
R. And also with you.

Then the deacon, if appropriate, gives the invitation to the people in these or similar words:

Bow your heads and pray for God's blessing.

Then the bishop extends his hands over the people and blesses them, saying:

The Lord of earth and heaven
has assembled you before him this day
to dedicate this house of prayer.
May he fill you with the blessings of heaven.
R. Amen.

God the Father wills that all his children
scattered through the world
become one family in his Son.
May he make you his temple,
the dwelling place of his Holy Spirit.
R. Amen.

May God free you from every bond of sin,
dwell within you and give you joy.
May you live with him for ever
in the company of all his saints.
R. Amen.

The bishop takes the pastoral staff and continues:

May almighty God bless you,
the Father, and the Son, + and the Holy Spirit.
R. Amen.

40. Finally the deacon dismisses the people in the usual way.

Chapter Four

Rite of Dedication of an Altar

Introduction

I. Nature and Dignity of the Altar

1. From meditating on God's word, the ancient Fathers of the Church did not hesitate to assert that Christ was the victim, priest, and altar of his own sacrifice.[1] For in the Letter to the Hebrews Christ is presented as the High Priest who is also the living altar of the heavenly temple,[2] and in the Book of Revelation our Redeemer appears as the Lamb who has been sacrificed[3] and whose offering is taken by the holy angel to the altar in heaven.[4]

The Christian Is Also a Spiritual Altar

2. Since Christ, Head and Teacher, is the true altar, his members and disciples are also spiritual altars on which the sacrifice of a holy life is offered to God. The Fathers seem to have this in mind. St. Ignatius of Antioch asks the Romans quite plainly: "Grant me only this favor: let my blood be spilled in sacrifice to God, while there is still an altar ready."[5] St. Polycarp exhorts widows to lead a life of holiness, for "they are God's altar."[6] Among others, St. Gregory the Great echoes these words when he says: "What is God's altar if not the souls of those who lead good lives? . . . Rightly, then, the heart of the just is said to be the altar of God."[7]

In another image frequently used by the writers of the Church, Christians who give themselves to prayer, offer petitions to God, and present sacrifices of supplication, are the living stones out of which the Lord Jesus builds the Church's altar.[8]

The Altar, Table of the Sacrifice and the Paschal Meal

3. By instituting in the form of a sacrificial meal the memorial of the sacrifice he was about to offer the Father on the altar of the cross, Christ made holy the table where the community would come to celebrate their Passover. Therefore the altar is the table for a sacrifice and for a banquet. At this table the priest, representing Christ the Lord, accomplishes what the Lord himself did and what he handed on to his disciples to do in his memory. The Apostle clearly intimates this: "The blessing cup that we bless is a communion with the blood of Christ and the bread that we break is a communion with the body of Christ. The fact that there is only one loaf

means that though there are many of us, we form a single Body because we all have a share in this one loaf."[9]

The Altar, Sign of Christ

4. The Church's children have the power to celebrate the memorial of Christ and take their place at the Lord's table anywhere that circumstances might require. But it is in keeping with the Eucharistic mystery that the Christian people erect a permanent altar for the celebration of the Lord's Supper and they have done so from the earliest times.

The Christian altar is by its very nature properly the table of sacrifice and of the paschal banquet. It is:

— a unique altar on which the sacrifice of the cross is perpetuated in mystery throughout the ages until Christ comes;

— a table at which the church's children gather to give thanks to God and receive the body and blood of Christ.

In every church, then, the altar "is the center of the thanksgiving that the eucharist accomplishes"[10] and around which the Church's other rites are, in a certain manner, arrayed.[11]

At the altar the memorial of the Lord is celebrated and his body and blood given to the people. Therefore the Church's writers have seen in the altar a sign of Christ himself. This is the basis for the saying: "The altar is Christ."

The Altar as Honoring Martyrs

5. All the dignity of the altar rests on its being the Lord's table. Thus the martyr's body does not bring honor to the altar; rather the altar does honor to the martyr's tomb. For it is altogether proper to erect altars over the burial place of martyrs and other saints or to deposit their relics beneath altars as a mark of respect and as a symbol of the truth that the sacrifice of the members has its source in the sacrifice of the Head.[12] Thus "the triumphant victims come to their rest in the place where Christ is victim: he, however, who suffered for all is on the altar; they who have been redeemed by his sufferings are beneath the altar."[13] This arrangement would seem to recall in a certain manner the spiritual vision of the Apostle John in the Book of Revelation: "I saw underneath the altar the souls of all the people who have been killed on account of the word of God, for witnessing to it."[14] His meaning is that although all the saints are rightly called Christ's witnesses, the witness of blood has a special significance that only the relics of the martyrs beneath the altar express in its entirety.

II. Erecting an Altar

6. It is desirable that in every church there be a fixed altar and that in other places set apart for sacred celebrations there be either a fixed or a movable altar.

A fixed altar is one so constructed that it is attached to the floor so that it cannot be moved; a movable altar can be transferred from place to place.[15]

7. In new churches it is better to erect only one altar so that in the one assembly of the people of God the single altar signifies the one Savior Jesus Christ and the one eucharist of the Church.

But an altar may also be erected in a chapel (somewhat separated, if possible, from the body of the church) where the tabernacle for the reservation of the blessed sacrament is situated. On weekdays when there is a small gathering of people Mass may be celebrated at this altar.

The merely decorative erection of several altars in a church must be entirely avoided.

8. The altar should be freestanding so that the priest can easily walk around it and celebrate Mass facing the people. "It should be so placed as to be a focal point on which the attention of the whole congregation centers naturally."[16]

9. In accordance with received custom in the Church and the biblical symbolism connected with an altar, the table of a fixed altar should be of stone, indeed of natural stone. But, at the discretion of the conference of bishops, any becoming, solid, and finely wrought material may be used in erecting an altar.

The pedestal or base of the table may be of any sort of material, provided it is becoming and solid.[17]

10. The altar is of its very nature dedicated to the one God, for the eucharistic sacrifice is offered to the one God. This is the sense in which the Church's practice of dedicating altars to God in honor of the saints must be understood. St. Augustine expresses it well: "It is not to any of the martyrs, but to the God of the martyrs, though in memory of the martyrs, that we raise our altars."[18]

This should be made clear to the people. In new churches statues and pictures of saints may not be placed above the altar.

Likewise, when relics of saints are exposed for veneration, they should not be placed on the table of the altar.

11. It is fitting to continue the tradition in the Roman liturgy of placing relics of martyrs or other saints beneath the altar.[19] But the following should be noted.

a) Such relics should be of a size sufficient for them to be recognizable as parts of human bodies. Hence excessively small relics of one or more saints must not be placed beneath an altar.

b) The greatest care must be taken to determine whether the relics in question are authentic. It is better for an altar to be dedicated without relics than to have relics of doubtful authenticity placed beneath it.

c) A reliquary must not be placed on the altar or set into the table of the altar, but placed beneath the table of the altar, as the design of the altar permits.

When the rite of depositing relics takes place, it is highly recommended to keep a vigil at the relics of the martyr or saint, in accordance with the provisions of chapter two, no. 10.

III. Celebration of the Dedication

Minister of the Rite

12. Since the bishop has been entrusted with the care of the particular Church, it is his responsibility to dedicate to God new altars built in his diocese.

If he cannot himself preside at the rite, he shall entrust the function to another bishop, especially to one who is his associate and assistant in the pastoral care of the community for which the new altar has been erected or, in altogether special circumstances, to a priest, to whom he shall give a special mandate.

Choice of Day

13. Since an altar becomes sacred principally by the celebration of the eucharist, in fidelity to this truth the celebration of Mass on a new altar before it has been dedicated is to be carefully avoided, so that the Mass of dedication may also be the first eucharist celebrated on the altar.

14. A day should be chosen for the dedication of a new altar when the people can be present in large numbers, especially a Sunday, unless pastoral considerations suggest otherwise. However, the rite of the dedication of an altar may not be celebrated during the Easter triduum, on Ash Wednesday, the weekdays of Holy Week, and All Souls.

Mass of the Dedication

15. The celebration of the eucharist is inseparably bound up with the rite of the dedication of an altar. The Mass is the Mass for the dedication of an altar. On Christmas, Epiphany, Ascension, Pentecost, and on the Sundays of Advent, Lent, and the Easter season, the Mass is the Mass of the day, with the exception of the prayer over the gifts and the preface, which are closely interwoven with the rite itself.

16. It is fitting that the bishop concelebrate the Mass with the priests present, especially with those who have been given charge over the parish or the community for which the altar has been erected.

Parts of the Rite

A. Introductory Rites

17. The introductory rites of the Mass of the dedication of an altar take place in the usual way except that in place of the penitential rite the bishop blesses water and with it sprinkles the people and the new altar.

B. Liturgy of the Word

18. It is commendable to have three readings in the liturgy of the word, chosen, according to the rubrical norm, either from the liturgy of the day (see no. 15) or from those in the Lectionary for the rite of the dedication of an altar (nos. 704 and 706).

19. After the readings, the bishop gives the homily, in which he explains the biblical readings and the meaning of the dedication of an altar.

After the homily, the profession of faith is said. The general intercessions are omitted, since the Litany of the Saints is sung in their place.

C. Prayer of Dedication and the Anointing of the Altar

Depositing of the Relics of the Saints

20. If it is to take place, the relics of martyrs or other saints are placed beneath the altar after the Litany of the Saints. The rite is meant to signify that all who have been baptized in the death of Christ, especially those who have shed their blood for the Lord, share in Christ's passion (see no. 5).

Prayer of Dedication

21. The celebration of the eucharist is the most important and the one necessary rite for the dedication of an altar. Nevertheless, in accordance with the universal tradition of the Church in both East and West, a special prayer of dedication is also said. This prayer is a sign of the intention to dedicate the altar to the Lord for all times and a petition for his blessing.

Rites of Anointing, Incensing, Covering, and Lighting the Altar

22. The rites of anointing, incensing, covering, and lighting the altar express in visible signs several aspects of the invisible work that the Lord accomplishes through the Church in its celebration of the divine mysteries, especially the eucharist.

a) *Anointing* of the altar: The anointing with chrism makes the altar a symbol of Christ, who, before all others, is and is called "The Anointed One"; for the Father anointed him with the Holy Spirit and constituted him the High Priest so that on the altar of his body he might offer the sacrifice of his life for the salvation of all.

b) *Incense* is burned on the altar to signify that Christ's sacrifice, there perpetuated in mystery, ascends to God as an odor of sweetness, and also to signify that the people's prayers rise up pleasing and acceptable, reaching the throne of God.[20]

c) *The covering of the altar* indicates that the Christian altar is the altar of the eucharistic sacrifice and the table of the Lord; around it priests and people, by one and the same rite but with a difference of function, celebrate the memorial of Christ's death and resurrection and partake of his supper. For this reason the altar is prepared as the table of the sacrificial banquet and adorned as for a feast. Thus the dressing of the altar clearly signifies that it is the Lord's table at which all God's people joyously meet to be refreshed with divine food, namely, the body and blood of Christ sacrificed.

d) *The lighting of the altar* teaches us that Christ is "a light to enlighten the nations";[21] his brightness shines out in the Church and through it in the whole human family.

D. Celebration of the Eucharist

23. After the altar has been prepared, the bishop celebrates the eucharist, the principal and the most ancient part of the whole rite,[22] because the celebration of the eucharist is in the closest harmony with the rite of the dedication of an altar:

— For the celebration of the eucharistic sacrifice achieves the end for which the altar was erected and expresses this end by particularly clear signs.

— Furthermore, the eucharist, which sanctifies the hearts of those who receive it, in a sense consecrates the altar, as the ancient Fathers of the Church often assert: "This altar should be an object of awe: by nature it is stone, but it is made holy when it receives the body of Christ."[23]

— Finally, the bond closely connecting the dedication of an altar with the celebration of the eucharist is likewise evident from the fact that the Mass for the dedication has its own preface, which is a central part of the rite itself.

IV. Adaptation of the Rite

Adaptations within the Competence of the Conferences of Bishops

24. The conferences of bishops may adapt this rite, as required, to the character of each region, but in such a way that nothing of its dignity and solemnity is lost.

However, the following are to be respected:

a) The celebration of Mass with the proper preface and prayer for a dedication must never be omitted.

b) Rites that have a special meaning and force from liturgical tradition (see no. 22) must be retained, unless weighty reasons stand in the way, but the wording may be suitably adapted if necessary.

With regard to adaptations, the competent ecclesiastical authority is to consult the Holy See and introduce adaptations with its consent.[24]

Adaptations within the Competence of the Ministers

25. It is for the bishop and for those in charge of the celebration of the rite to decide whether to have the depositing of relics of the saints; in so doing, they are to follow what is laid down in no. 11 and they are to take as the decisive consideration the spiritual good of the community and a proper sense of liturgy.

It is for the rector of the church in which the altar is to be dedicated, helped by those who assist him in the pastoral work, to decide and prepare everything concerning the readings, singing, and other pastoral aids to foster the fruitful participation of the people and to ensure a dignified celebration.

V. Pastoral Preparation

26. The people are to be informed in good time about the dedication of a new altar and they are to be properly prepared to take an active part in the rite. Accordingly, they should be taught what each rite means and how it is carried out. For the purpose of giving this instruction, use may be made of what has been said earlier about the nature and dignity of an altar and the meaning and import of the rites. In this way the people will be imbued with the rightful love that is owed to the altar.

VI. Requisites for the Dedication of an Altar

27. For the celebration of the rite the following should be prepared:
— The Roman Missal;
— The Lectionary;
— The Roman Pontifical;
— the cross and the Book of the Gospels to be carried in the procession;
— container of water to be blessed and sprinkler;
— container with the holy chrism;
— towels for wiping the table of the altar;
— if needed, a waxen linen cloth or waterproof covering of the same size as the altar;
— basin and jug of water, towels, and all that is needed for washing the bishop's hands;
— linen gremial;
— brazier for burning incense or aromatic spices; or grains of incense and small candles to burn on the altar;
— censer, incense boat and spoon;
— chalice, corporal, purificators, and hand towel;

— bread, wine, and water for the celebration of Mass;
— altar cross, unless there is already a cross in the sanctuary, or the cross that is carried in the entrance procession is to be placed near the altar;
— altar cloth, candles, and candlesticks;
— flowers, if opportune.

28. For the Mass of the dedication the vestments are white or of some festive color. The following should be prepared:
— for the bishop: alb, stole, chasuble, miter, pastoral staff, and pallium, if the bishop has the right to wear one;
— for the concelebrating priests: the vestments for concelebrating Mass;
— for the deacons: albs, stoles, and dalmatics;
— for other ministers: albs or other lawfully approved dress.

29. If relics of the saints are to be placed beneath the altar, the following should be prepared:
a) *In the place from which the procession begins:*
— a reliquary containing the relics, placed between flowers and lights. But as circumstances dictate, the reliquary may be placed in a suitable part of the sanctuary before the rite begins;
— for the deacons who will carry the relics to be deposited: albs, red stoles, if the relics are those of a martyr, or white in other cases, and, if available, dalmatics. If the relics are carried by priests, then, in place of dalmatics, chasubles should be prepared. Relics may also be carried by other ministers, vested in albs or other lawfully approved dress.
b) *In the sanctuary:*
— a small table on which the reliquary is placed during the first part of the dedication rite.
c) *In the sacristy:*
— a sealant or cement to close the cover of the aperture. In addition, a stonemason should be on hand to close the depository of the relics at the proper time.

30. It is fitting to observe the custom of enclosing in the reliquary a parchment on which is recorded the day, month, and year of the dedication of the altar, the name of the bishop who celebrated the rite, the titular of the church, and the names of the martyrs or saints whose relics are deposited beneath the altar.

A record of the dedication of the church is to be drawn up in duplicate and signed by the bishop, the rector of the church, and representatives of the local community; one copy is to be kept in the diocesan archives, the other in the archives of the church.

OUTLINE OF THE RITE

INTRODUCTORY RITES
Entrance into the Church
 Entrance Procession
 Greeting
Blessing and Sprinkling of Water
Hymn: Gloria
Opening Prayer

LITURGY OF THE WORD
First Reading
Responsorial Psalm
Second Reading
Gospel Acclamation
Gospel
Homily
Profession of Faith

PRAYER OF DEDICATION AND THE ANOINTINGS
Invitation to Prayer
Litany of the Saints
Concluding Prayer
[Depositing of the Relics]
Prayer of Dedication
Anointing of the Altar
Incensation of the Altar
Lighting of the Altar

LITURGY OF THE EUCHARIST
Preparation of the Altar and the Gifts
Prayer over the Gifts
Eucharistic Prayer

Communion
Prayer after Communion

CONCLUDING RITE
Blessing and Dismissal

Rite of Dedication

Part I

Introductory Rites

Entrance into the Church

31. When the people are assembled, the bishop and the concelebrating priests, the deacons, and the ministers, each in appropriate vestments, preceded by the cross-bearer, go from the sacristy through the main body of the church to the sanctuary.

32. If there are relics of the saints to be placed beneath the altar, these are brought in the entrance procession to the sanctuary from the sacristy or the chapel where since the vigil they have been exposed for the veneration of the people. For a just cause, before the celebration begins, the relics may be placed between lighted torches in a suitable part of the sanctuary.

33. As the procession proceeds, the entrance antiphon is sung with Psalm 43.

> *O God, our shield, look with favor on the face of your anointed; one day within your courts is better than a thousand elsewhere (alleluia).*

Or:

> *I will go to the altar of God, the God of my joy.*

Another appropriate song may be sung.

34. When the procession reaches the sanctuary, the relics of the saints are placed between lighted torches in a suitable place. The concelebrating priests, the deacons, and the ministers go to the places assigned to them; the bishop, without kissing the altar, goes to the chair. Then, putting aside the pastoral staff and miter, he greets the people, saying:

> *The grace and peace of God*
> *be with all of you*
> *in his holy Church*
> *R. And also with you.*

Other suitable words taken preferably from sacred Scripture may be used.

Blessing and Sprinkling of Water

35. When the entrance rite is completed, the bishop blesses water with which to sprinkle the people as a sign of repentance and as a reminder of their baptism, and to purify the altar. The ministers bring the vessel with the water to the bishop who stands at the chair. The bishop invites all to pray, in these or similar words:

> Brothers and sisters in Christ, this is a day of rejoicing: we have come together to dedicate this altar by offering the sacrifice of Christ.
> May we respond to these holy rites, receive God's word with faith, share at the Lord's table with joy, and raise our hearts in hope.
> Gathered around this one altar we draw nearer to Christ, the living stone, in whom we become God's holy temple.
> But first let us ask God to bless this gift of water. As it is sprinkled upon us and upon this altar, may it be a sign of our repentance and a reminder of our baptism.

All pray in silence for a brief period. The bishop then continues:

> God of mercy,
> you call every creature to the light of life,
> and surround us with such great love
> that when we stray
> you continually lead us back to Christ our head.
>
> For you have established an inheritance of such mercy,
> that those sinners, who pass through water made sacred,
> die with Christ to rise restored
> as members of his body
> and heirs of his eternal covenant.
>
> Bless + this water;
> sanctify it.
>
> As it is sprinkled upon us and upon this altar
> make it a sign of the saving waters of baptism,
> by which we become one in Christ, the temple of your Spirit.
>
> May all here today,
> and all those in days to come,
> who will celebrate your mysteries on this altar,
> be united at last in the holy city of your peace.
>
> We ask this in the name of Jesus the Lord.
> R. Amen.

36. When the invocation over the water is finished, the bishop, accompanied by the deacons, passes through the main body of the church, sprinkling the people with the holy water; then, when he has returned to the sanctuary, he sprinkles the altar. Meanwhile the following antiphon is sung.

I saw water flowing from the right side of the temple: alleluia. It brought God's life and his salvation, and the people sang in joyful praise: alleluia, alleluia.

Or, during Lent:

I will pour clean water over you and wash away all your defilement. A new heart will I give you, says the Lord.

Another appropriate song may be sung.

37. After the sprinkling the bishop returns to the chair and, when the singing is finished, standing with hands joined, says:

May God, the Father of mercies,
to whom we dedicate this altar on earth,
forgive us our sins
and enable us to offer
an unending sacrifice of praise
on his altar in heaven.
R. Amen.

Hymn
38. Then the Gloria is sung.

Opening Prayer
39. When the hymn is finished, the bishop, with hands joined, says:

Let us pray.

All pray in silence for a brief period. then the bishop, with hands extended, says:

Lord,
you willed that all things be drawn to your Son,
mounted on the altar of the cross.

Bless those who dedicate this altar to your service.

May it be the table of our unity,
a banquet of plenty,
and a source of the Spirit,
in whom we grow daily as your faithful people.

We ask this through our Lord Jesus Christ, your Son,
who lives and reigns with you and the Holy Spirit,
one God, for ever and ever.
R. Amen.

Part II

Liturgy of the Word

40. In the liturgy of the word everything takes place in the usual way. The readings and the gospel are taken, in accordance with the rubrics, either from the texts in *The Lectionary* (nos. 704 and 706) for the rite of the dedication of an altar or from the Mass of the day.

41. After the gospel the bishop gives the homily, in which he explains the biblical readings and the meaning of the rite.

42. The profession of faith is said. The general intercessions are omitted since in their place the litany of the saints is sung.

Part III

Prayer of Dedication and the Anointings

Invitation to Prayer

43. Then all stand, and the bishop, without his miter, invites the people to pray in these or similar words:

> *Let our prayers go forth to God the Father through Jesus Christ, his Son, with whom are joined all the saints who have shared in his suffering and now sit at his table of glory.*

Deacon (except on Sundays and during the Easter season):

> *Let us kneel.*

Litany of the Saints

44. Then the litany of the saints is sung, with all responding. On Sunday and also during the Easter season, all stand; on other days, all kneel.

45. The cantors begin the litany (appendix, p. 215); they add, at the proper place, names of other saints (the titular of the church, the patron saint of the place, and the saints whose relics are to be deposited, if this is take place) and petitions suitable to the occasion.

46. When the litany is finished, the bishop, standing with hands extended, says:

> *Lord,*
> *may the prayers of the Blessed Virgin Mary*
> *and of all the saints*
> *make our prayers acceptable to you.*
>
> *May this altar be the place*
> *where the great mysteries of redemption are accomplished:*
> *a place where your people offer their gifts,*
> *unfold their good intentions,*
> *pour out their prayers,*
> *and echo every meaning of their faith and devotion.*
>
> *Grant this through Christ our Lord.*
> *R. Amen.*

If it is applicable, the deacon says:

> *Let us stand.*

All rise. The bishop receives the miter.
When there is no depositing of the relics of the saints, the bishop immediately says the prayer of dedication as indicated in no. 48 below.

Depositing of the Relics

47. Then, if relics of the martyrs or other saints are to be placed beneath the altar, the bishop approaches the altar. A deacon or priest brings them to the bishop, who places them in a suitably prepared aperture. Meanwhile one of the following antiphons is sung with Psalm 15.

> *Saints of God, you have been enthroned at the foot of God's altar; pray for us to the Lord Jesus Christ.*

Or:

> *The bodies of the saints lie buried in peace, but their names will live on for ever (alleluia).*

Another appropriate song may be sung.

Meanwhile a stone mason closes the aperture and the bishop returns to the chair.

Prayer of Dedication

48. Then the bishop, standing without miter at the chair or near the altar, with hands extended, says:

> Father,
> we praise you and give you thanks,
> for you have established the sacrament of true worship
> by bringing to perfection in Christ
> the mystery of the one true altar
> prefigured in those many altars of old.
>
> Noah,
> the second father of the human race,
> once the waters fell and the mountains peaked again,
> built an altar in your name.
> You, Lord, were appeased by his fragrant offering
> and your rainbow bore witness
> to a covenant refounded in love.
>
> Abraham,
> our father in faith,
> wholeheartedly accepted your word
> and constructed an altar on which to slay
> Isaac, his only son.
> But you, Lord, stayed his hand
> and provided a ram for his offering.
>
> Moses,
> mediator of the old law,
> built an altar
> on which was cast the blood of a lamb:
> so prefiguring the altar of the cross.
>
> All this Christ has fulfilled in the paschal mystery:
> as priest and victim he freely mounted the tree of the cross
> and gave himself to you, Father, as the one perfect oblation.

In his sacrifice the new covenant is sealed,
in his blood sin is engulfed.

Lord, we therefore stand before you in prayer.

Bless this altar built in the house of the Church,
that it may ever be reserved for the sacrifice of Christ,
and stand for ever as the Lord's table,
where your people will find nourishment and strength.

Make this altar a sign of Christ
from whose pierced side flowed blood and water,
which ushered in the sacraments of the Church.

Make it a table of joy,
where the friends of Christ may hasten
to cast upon you their burdens and cares
and take up their journey restored.

Make it a place of communion and peace,
so that those who share the body and blood of your Son
may be filled with his Spirit
and grow in your life of love.

Make it a source of unity and friendship,
where your people may gather as one
to share your spirit of mutual love.

Make it the center of our praise and thanksgiving
until we arrive at the eternal tabernacle,
where, together with Christ,
high priest and living altar,
we will offer you an everlasting sacrifice of praise.

We ask this through our Lord Jesus Christ, your Son,
who lives and reigns with you and the Holy Spirit,
one God, for ever and ever.
R. Amen.

Anointing of the Altar

49. When the above is finished, the bishop, removing the chasuble if necessary and putting on a linen gremial, goes to the altar with the deacon or another minister, one of whom carries the chrism. Standing before the altar, the bishop says:

We now anoint this altar.
May God in his power make it holy,
a visible sign of the mystery of Christ,
who offered himself for the life of the world.

Then he pours chrism on the middle of the altar and on each of its four corners, and it is recommended that he anoint the entire table of the altar with this.

50. During the anointing, outside the Easter Season, the following antiphon is sung (see below, no.51) with Psalm 45.

God, your God, has anointed you with the oil of gladness.

Another appropriate song may be sung.

51. During the Easter Season the following antiphon is sung with Psalm 118.

The stone which the builders rejected has become the keystone of the building, alleluia.

Another appropriate song may be sung.

52. When the altar has been anointed, the bishop returns to the chair, sits, and washes his hands. Then the bishop takes off the gremial and puts on the chasuble.

Incensation of the Altar

53. After the rite of anointing, a brazier is placed on the altar for burning incense or aromatic gums, or, if desired, a heap of incense mixed with small candles or wax tapers is made on the altar. The bishop puts incense into the brazier or he lights the heap of incense with a small candle handed to him by a minister, saying:

Lord,
may our prayer ascend as incense in your sight.
As this building is filled with fragrance
so may your Church fill the world
with the fragrance of Christ.

Then the bishop puts incense into the censer and incenses the altar; he returns to the chair, is incensed, and then sits. A minister incenses the people. Meanwhile one of the following antiphons is sung with Psalm 138.

An angel stood by the altar of the temple, holding a golden censer.

Or:

From the hand of the angel, clouds of incense rose in the presence of the Lord.

Another appropriate song may be sung.

Lighting of the Altar

54. After the incensation, a few ministers wipe the table of the altar with cloths, and, if need be, cover it with a waterproof linen. They then cover the altar with a cloth, and, if opportune, decorate it with flowers. They arrange in a suitable manner the candles needed for the celebration of Mass, and, if need be, the cross.

55. Then the bishop gives to the deacon a lighted candle, and says:

> *Light of Christ,*
> *shine on this altar*
> *and be reflected by those*
> *who share at this table.*

Then the bishop sits. The deacon goes to the altar and lights the candles for the celebration of the eucharist.

56. Then the festive lighting takes place: as a sign of rejoicing all the lamps around the altar are lit. Meanwhile the following antiphon is sung.

> *In you, O Lord, is the fountain of life; in your light we shall see light.*

Another appropriate song may be sung, especially one in honor of Christ, the light of the world.

Part IV

Liturgy of the Eucharist

57. The deacons and the ministers prepare the altar in the usual way. Then some of the congregation bring bread, wine, and water for the celebration of the Lord's sacrifice. The bishop receives the gifts at the chair. While the gifts are being brought, one of the following antiphons may be sung.

> *If you are bringing your gift to the altar, and there you remember that your neighbor has something against you, leave your gift in front of the altar; go at once and make peace with your neighbor, and then come back and offer your gift, alleluia.*

Or:

*Moses consecrated the altar to the Lord and offered sacrifices and burnt
offerings; he made an evening sacrifice of sweet fragrance to the Lord God
in the sight of the children of Israel.*

Another appropriate song may be sung.

58. When all is ready, the bishop goes to the altar, removes the miter, and kisses the
altar. The Mass proceeds in the usual way; however, neither the gifts nor the altar
are incensed.

Prayer over the Gifts

59. With hands extended, the bishop sings or says:

*Lord,
send your Spirit upon this altar
to sanctify these gifts;
may he prepare our hearts
to receive them worthily.*

*Grant this through Christ our Lord.
R. Amen.*

Eucharistic Prayer

60. Eucharistic Prayer I or III is said, with the following preface, which is an integral
part of the rite of the dedication of an altar:

*The Lord be with you.
R. And also with you.*

*Lift up your hearts.
R. We lift them up to the Lord.*

*Let us give thanks to the Lord our God.
R. It is right to give him thanks and praise.*

*Father, all-powerful and ever-living God,
we do well always and everywhere to give you thanks
through Jesus Christ our Lord.*

*True priest and true victim,
he offered himself to you
on the altar of the cross*

and commanded us to celebrate
that same sacrifice,
until he comes again.

Therefore your people have built this altar
and have dedicated it to your name
with grateful hearts.

This is a truly sacred place.

Here the sacrifice of Christ is offered in mystery,
perfect praise is given to you,
and our redemption is made continually present.

Here is prepared the Lord's table,
at which your children,
nourished by the body of Christ,
are gathered into a Church, one and holy.

Here your people drink of the Spirit,
the stream of living water,
flowing from the rock of Christ.
They will become, in him,
a worthy offering and a living altar.

We praise you, Lord,
with all the angels and saints in their song of joy:

Holy, holy, holy Lord, God of power and might,
heaven and earth are full of your glory.
    Hosanna in the highest.
Blessed is he who comes in the name of the Lord.
    Hosanna in the highest.

61. While the bishop is receiving the body of Christ the communion song begins. One of the following antiphons is sung with Psalm 128.

Even the sparrow finds a home and the swallow a nest wherein she places her young: near to your altars, O Lord of Hosts, my King and my God.

Or:

May the children of the Church be like olive branches around the table of the Lord (alleluia).

Another appropriate song may be sung.

Prayer after Communion

62. Then, standing at the chair or the altar, the bishop sings or says:

Let us pray.

Pause for silent prayer, if this has not preceded.

Lord,
may we always be drawn
to this altar of sacrifice.

United in faith and love,
may we be nourished by the body of Christ
and transformed into his likeness,
who lives and reigns with you and the Holy Spirit,
one God, for ever and ever.
R. Amen.

Blessing and Dismissal

63. The bishop receives the miter and says:

The Lord be with you.
R. And also with you.

Then the deacon, if appropriate, gives the invitation to the people in these or similar words:

Bow your heads and pray for God's blessing.

Then the bishop extends his hands over the people and blesses them, saying:

May God, who has given you the dignity
of a royal priesthood,
strengthen you in your holy service
and make you worthy to share in his sacrifice.
R. Amen.

May he, who invites you to the one table
and feeds you with the one bread,
make you one in heart and mind.
R. Amen.

May all to whom you proclaim Christ
be drawn to him

by the example of your love.
R. Amen.

The bishop takes the pastoral staff and continues:

May almighty God bless you,
the Father, and the Son, + and the Holy Spirit.
R. Amen.

64. Finally the deacon dismisses the people in the usual way.

Chapter Five

Rite of Blessing a Church

Introduction

1. Since sacred edifices, that is, churches, are permanently set aside for the celebration of the divine mysteries, it is right for them to receive a dedication to God. This is done according to the rite in chapters two and three for dedicating a church, a rite impressive for its striking ceremonies and symbols.

    Oratories, chapels, or other sacred edifices set aside only temporarily for divine worship because of special conditions, more properly receive a blessing, according to the rite described below.

2. As to the structure of the liturgy, the choice of a titular, and the pastoral preparation of the people, what is said in the Introduction to chapter two, nos. 4–5, 7, 20, is to be followed, with the necessary modifications.

    A church or an oratory is blessed by the bishop of the diocese or by a priest delegated by him.

3. A church or an oratory may be blessed on any day, apart from the Easter triduum. As far as possible a day should be chosen when the people can be present in large numbers, especially a Sunday, unless pastoral considerations suggest otherwise.

4. On days mentioned in the Table of Liturgical Days, nos. 1–4, the Mass is the Mass of the day; but on other days the Mass is either the Mass of the day or the Mass of the titular of the church or oratory.

5. For the rite of the blessing of a church or an oratory all things needed for the celebration of Mass are prepared. But even though it may have already been blessed or dedicated, the altar should be left bare until the beginning of the liturgy of the eucharist. In a suitable place in the sanctuary the following also should be prepared:
    — container of water to be blessed and sprinkler;
    — censer, incense boat and spoon;
    — The Roman Pontifical;
    — altar cross, unless there is already a cross in the sanctuary, or the cross that is carried in the entrance procession is to be placed near the altar;
    — altar cloth, candles, candlesticks, and flowers, if opportune.

6. When at the same time as the church is blessed the altar is to be consecrated, all those things should be prepared that are listed in chapter four, no. 27 and no. 29, if relics of the saints are to be deposited beneath the altar.

7. For the Mass of the blessing of a church the vestments are white or some festive color. The following should be prepared:
— for the bishop: alb, stole, chasuble, miter, pastoral staff;
— for a priest: the vestments for celebrating Mass;
— for the concelebrating priests: the vestments for concelebrating Mass;
— for the deacons: albs, stoles, and dalmatics;
— for other ministers: albs or other lawfully approved dress.

OUTLINE OF THE RITE

INTRODUCTORY RITES
Entrance into the Church
   Greeting
Blessing and Sprinkling of Water
Hymn: Gloria
Opening Prayer

LITURGY OF THE WORD
First Reading
Responsorial Psalm
Second Reading
Gospel Acclamation
Gospel
Homily
[Profession of Faith]

BLESSING OF THE ALTAR
Prayer of Blessing
Incensation of the Altar and People

LITURGY OF THE EUCHARIST
Preparation of the Altar
Presentation of the Gifts
Eucharistic Prayer

Communion
[Inauguration of the Blessed Sacrament Chapel]
Prayer after Communion

CONCLUDING RITE
Blessing and Dismissal

Rite of Blessing

Part I
Introductory Rites

Entrance into the Church

8. When the people are assembled, while the entrance song is being sung, the bishop and the concelebrating priests, the deacons, and the ministers, each in appropriate vestments, preceded by the crossbearer, go from the sacristy through the main body of the church to the sanctuary.

When the procession arrives at the sanctuary, the bishop without kissing or incensing the altar, goes immediately to the chair; the others go to the places assigned to them.

9. The bishop puts aside the pastoral staff and miter, and when the singing is finished, he greets the people, saying:

> *The grace and peace of God*
> *be with all of you*
> *in his holy Church.*
> *R. And also with you.*

Other suitable words taken preferably from sacred Scripture may be used.

Blessing and Sprinkling of Water

10. Then the bishop blesses water with which to sprinkle the people as a sign of repentance and as a reminder of their baptism, and to purify the walls of the new church or oratory. The ministers bring the vessel with the water to the bishop who stands at the chair. The bishop invites all to pray, in these or similar words:

> *Brothers and sisters in Christ, this is a day of rejoicing. For we have come together to offer this new church to God.*
> *We ask that he bless us with his grace and, by his power, bless this gift of water.*
> *As it is sprinkled upon us and throughout this new church, may it become a sign of our repentance, a reminder of our baptism, and a symbol of the cleansing of these walls.*

> *But first let us call to mind that we ourselves, who are bound here in faith and love, are the living Church, set in the world, as a sign and witness of God's love for all.*

11. All pray in silence for a brief period. The bishop then continues:

> *God of mercy,*
> *you call every creature to the light of life,*
> *and surround us with such great love*
> *that when we stray*
> *you continually lead us back to Christ our head.*
>
> *For you have established an inheritance of such mercy,*
> *that those sinners, who pass through water made sacred,*
> *die with Christ and rise restored*
> *as members of his body*
> *and heirs of his eternal covenant.*
>
> *Bless + this water;*
> *sanctify it.*
>
> *As it is sprinkled upon us and throughout this church*
> *make it a sign of the saving waters of baptism,*
> *by which we become one in Christ, the temple of your Spirit.*
>
> *May all here today,*
> *and all those in days to come,*
> *who will celebrate your mysteries in this church,*
> *be united at last in the holy city of your peace.*
>
> *We ask this in the name of Jesus the Lord.*
> *R. Amen.*

12. When the invocation over the water is finished, the bishop, accompanied by the deacons, passes through the main body of the church, sprinkling the people and the walls with the holy water; then, when he has returned to the sanctuary, he sprinkles the altar, unless it is already blessed or dedicated (see above, no. 5). Meanwhile the following antiphon is sung.

> *I saw water flowing from the right side of the temple, alleluia. It brought God's life and his salvation, and the people sang in joyful praise: alleluia, alleluia.*

Or, during Lent:

> *I will pour clean water over you and wash away all your defilement. A new*
> *heart will I give you, says the Lord.*

Another appropriate song may be sung.

13. After the sprinkling the bishop returns to the chair and, when the singing is finished, standing with hands joined, says:

> *May God, the Father of mercies,*
> *dwell in this house of prayer.*
> *May the grace of the Holy Spirit cleanse us,*
> *for we are the temple of his presence.*
> *R. Amen.*

Hymn

14. Then, except on Sundays or weekdays of Advent and Lent, the Gloria is sung.

Opening Prayer

15. When the hymn is finished, the following prayer is said except on the days listed in the Table of Liturgical Days, nos. 1–4, when the prayer of the day is used. The bishop, with hands joined, says:

> *Let us pray.*

All pray in silence for a brief period. Then the bishop, with hands extended, says:

> *Lord,*
> *bless this church,*
> *which we have been privileged to build with your help.*
>
> *May all who gather here in faith*
> *to listen to your word*
> *and celebrate your sacraments,*
> *experience the presence of Christ,*
> *who promised to be with those*
> *gathered in his name,*
> *for he lives and reigns with you and the Holy Spirit,*
> *one God, for ever and ever.*
> *R. Amen.*

Part II

Liturgy of the Word

16. The readings are taken, in accordance with the rubrics (see above no. 4), either from the texts in *The Lectionary* (nos. 704 and 706) for the rite of the dedication of a church or from the Mass of the day.

17. Neither lights nor incense are carried at the gospel.

18. After the gospel the bishop gives the homily, in which he explains the biblical readings and the meaning of the rite.

19. The profession of faith and the general intercessions are said in the usual way.

Part III

Blessing of the Altar

20. Then the bishop goes to bless the altar. Meanwhile the following antiphon is sung.

> *May the children of the Church be like olive branches around the table of the Lord (alleluia).*

Another appropriate song may be sung.

21. When the singing is finished, the bishop, standing without miter, speaks to the people in these or similar words:

> *Brothers and sisters, our community rejoices as it comes together to bless this altar. Let us ask God to look kindly on the Church's offering placed upon it and to receive his people as an everlasting gift.*

All pray in silence for a brief period. Then the bishop, with hands extended, says:

Blessed are you, Lord our God,
who accepted the sacrifice of Christ,
offered on the altar of the cross
for the salvation of the world.

Now with a Father's love,
you call your people to celebrate his memory
by coming together at his table.

May this altar,
which we have built for your holy mysteries,
be the center of our praise and thanksgiving.

May it be the table
at which we break the bread which gives us life
and drink the cup which makes us one.

May it be the fountain
of the unfailing waters of salvation.

Here may we draw close to Christ,
the living stone,
and, in him, grow into a holy temple.

Here may our lives of holiness
become a pleasing sacrifice to your glory.
R. Blessed be God for ever.

The bishop puts incense into some censers and incenses the altar; receiving the miter, he returns to the chair, is incensed, and then sits. Ministers, walking through the church, incense the people and the main body of the church.

---

22. If the altar is to be dedicated, the profession of faith is said, and the general intercessions are omitted, and what is laid down in Chapter Four, nos. 43 – 56, is observed.

But if the altar is to be neither blessed nor consecrated (for example, because an altar already blessed or dedicated has been transferred to the new church), after the general intercessions the Mass proceeds as in no. 23 below.

Part IV

Liturgy of the Eucharist

23. Ministers cover the altar with a cloth, and, if opportune, decorate it with flowers. They arrange in a suitable manner the candles needed for the celebration of Mass, and, if need be, the cross.

24. When the altar is ready, some of the congregation bring bread, wine, and water for the celebration of the Lord's sacrifice. The bishop receives the gifts at the chair. While the gifts are being brought, one of the following antiphons may be sung.

If you are bringing your gift to the altar, and there you remember that your
neighbor has something against you, leave your gift in front of the altar; go
at once and make peace with your neighbor, and then come back and offer
your gift, alleluia.

Or:

Moses consecrated the altar to the Lord and offered sacrifices and burnt offerings; he made an evening sacrifice of sweet fragrance to the Lord God in the sight of the children of Israel.

Another appropriate song may be sung.

25. When all is ready, the bishop goes to the altar, removes the miter, and kisses the altar. The Mass proceeds in the usual way; however, neither the gifts nor the altar are incensed. But if the altar was not blessed or dedicated in this celebration, the incensation takes place in the usual way.

26. If a chapel of the blessed sacrament is to be inaugurated, when the communion of the congregation is finished, everything takes place as described in Chapter Two, nos. 79–82.

Blessing and Dismissal

27. The bishop receives the miter and says:

The Lord be with you.
R. And also with you.

Then the deacon, if appropriate, gives the invitation to the people in these or similar words:

Bow your heads and pray for God's blessing.

Then the bishop extends his hands over the people and blesses them, saying:

The Lord of earth and heaven
has assembled you before him this day
to bless this house of prayer.
May he fill you with the blessings of heaven.
R. Amen.

God the Father wills that all his children
scattered through the world
become one family in his Son.
May he make you his temple,
the dwelling place of his Holy Spirit.
R. Amen.

May God free you from every bond of sin,
dwell within you and give you joy.
May you live with him for ever
in the company of all his saints.
R. Amen.

The bishop takes the pastoral staff and continues:

May almighty God bless you,
the Father, and the Son, + and the Holy Spirit.
R. Amen.

28. Finally the deacon dismisses the people in the usual way.

Chapter Six

Rite of Blessing an Altar

Introduction

1. "A fixed altar is one so constructed that it is attached to the floor so that it cannot be moved; a movable altar can be transferred from place to place."[1]

A fixed altar is to be dedicated according to the rite described in chapter four. A movable altar also deserves religious respect because it is a table set aside solely and permanently for the eucharistic banquet. Consequently, before a movable altar is put to use, if it is not dedicated, it should at least be blessed with the following rite.[2]

2. A movable altar may be constructed of any solid material that the traditions and culture of different regions determine to be suitable for liturgical use.[3]

3. To erect a movable altar what is laid down in the Introduction to chapter four, nos. 6–10, is to be followed, with the necessary modifications. However, it is not permissible to place the relics of saints in the base of a movable altar.

4. It is appropriate that a movable altar be blessed by the bishop of the diocese or by the priest who is rector of the church.

5. A movable altar may be blessed on any day, except Good Friday and Holy Saturday. As far as possible, a day should be chosen when the people can be present in large numbers, especially a Sunday, unless pastoral considerations suggest otherwise.

6. In the rite of blessing a movable altar the Mass is the Mass of the day.

7. The altar should be left bare until the beginning of the liturgy of the eucharist. Hence a cross (if need be), and altar cloth, candles, and everything else necessary to prepare the altar should be on hand at a convenient place in the sanctuary.

OUTLINE OF THE RITE

INTRODUCTORY RITES

LITURGY OF THE WORD
First Reading
Responsorial Psalm
[Second Reading]
Gospel Acclamation
Gospel
Homily
[Profession of Faith]
General Intercessions

BLESSING OF THE ALTAR
Invitation to Prayer
Prayer of Blessing
Sprinkling and Incensation of the Altar

LITURGY OF THE EUCHARIST
Preparation of the Altar
Presentation of the Gifts
Eucharistic Prayer

———————————

Communion
Prayer after Communion

CONCLUDING RITE
Blessing and Dismissal

Rite of Blessing

8. During Mass everything takes place in the usual way. When the general intercessions are finished the bishop goes to bless the altar. Meanwhile the following antiphon is sung.

> *May the children of the Church be like olive branches around the table of the Lord (alleluia).*

Another appropriate song may be sung.

9. When the singing is finished, the bishop, standing without miter, speaks to the people in these or similar words:

> *Brothers and sisters, our community rejoices as it comes together to bless this altar. Let us ask God to look kindly on the Church's offering placed upon it and to receive his people as an everlasting gift.*

All pray in silence for a brief period. Then the bishop, with hands extended, says:

Blessed are you, Lord our God,
who accepted the sacrifice of Christ,
offered on the altar of the cross
for the salvation of the world.

Now with a Father's love,
you call your people to celebrate his memory
by coming together at his table.

May this altar,
which we have built for your holy mysteries,
be the center of our praise and thanksgiving.

May it be the table
at which we break the bread which gives us life
and drink the cup which makes us one.

May it be the fountain
of the unfailing waters of salvation.

Here may we draw close to Christ,
the living stone,
and, in him, grow into a holy temple.

Here may our lives of holiness
become a pleasing sacrifice to your glory.
R. Blessed be God for ever.

10. The bishop then sprinkles the altar with holy water and incenses it. Then he returns to the chair, receives the miter, is incensed, and then sits. A minister incenses the people.

11. Ministers cover the altar with a cloth, and, if opportune, decorate it with flowers; they arrange in a suitable manner the candles needed for the celebration of Mass, and, if need be, the cross.

12. When the altar is ready, some of the congregation bring bread, wine, and water for the celebration of the Lord's sacrifice. The bishop receives the gifts at the chair. While the gifts are being brought, the following antiphon may be sung.

> *If you are bringing your gift to the altar, and there you remember that your neighbor has something against you, leave your gift in front of the altar; go at once and make peace with your neighbor, and then come back and offer your gift, alleluia.*

Another appropriate song may be sung.

13. When all is ready, the bishop goes to the altar, removes the miter, and kisses the altar. The Mass proceeds in the usual way; however, neither the gifts nor the altar are incensed.

Chapter Seven

Rite of Blessing a Chalice and Paten

Introduction

1. The chalice and paten for offering, consecrating, and receiving the bread and wine[1] have as their sole and permanent purpose the celebration of the eucharist and are therefore "sacred vessels."

2. The intention to devote these vessels entirely to the celebration of the eucharist is expressed in the presence of the community through a special blessing, which is preferably to be imparted within Mass.

3. Any priest may bless a chalice and paten, provided they have been made in conformity with the norms given in the General Instruction of the Roman Missal, nos. 290–295.

4. If only a chalice or only a paten is to be blessed, the text should be modified accordingly.

OUTLINE OF THE RITE

INTRODUCTORY RITES
    Liturgy of the Word
    Readings
    Homily
    General Intercessions

BLESSING OF THE CHALICE AND PATEN
    Placing of the Chalice and Paten on the Altar
    Prayer of Blessing

LITURGY OF THE EUCHARIST
    Preparation of the Altar
    Presentation of the Gifts
    Eucharistic Prayer

    Communion
    Prayer after Communion

CONCLUDING RITE
    Blessing and Dismissal

Rite of Blessing within Mass

5. In the liturgy of the word, apart from the days listed on the Table of Liturgical Days, nos. 1 – 9, one or two readings may be taken from those given below in nos. 6 – 8.

Readings from Sacred Scripture

6.   1. 1 Corinthians 10:14 – 22a (Gr. 10 – 22) "Our blessing-cup is a communion with the blood of Christ."
       2. 1 Corinthians 11:23 – 26 "This cup is the new covenant in my blood."

Responsorial Psalms

7.   1. Psalm 16:5 and 8, 9 – 10, 11
       R. (5a) The Lord is my inheritance and my cup.
       2. Psalm 23:1 – 3a, 3b – 4, 5, 6
       R. (5a, d) You prepared a banquet before me; my cup overflows.

Gospels

8.   1. Matthew 20:20 – 28 "You shall indeed drink my cup."
       2. Mark 14:12 – 16, 22 – 26 "This is my body. This is my my blood."

9. After the reading of the word of God the homily is given in which the celebrant explains the biblical readings and the meaning of the blessing of a chalice and paten that are used in the celebration of the Lord's Supper.

10. When the general intercessions are finished, ministers or representatives of the community that are presenting the chalice and paten place them on the altar. The celebrant then approaches the altar. Meanwhile the following antiphon is sung.

> *I will take the cup of salvation and call on the name of the Lord.*

Another appropriate song may be sung.

11. When the singing is finished, the celebrant says:

> *Let us pray.*

All pray in silence for a brief period. The celebrant then continues:

> *Lord,*
> *with joy we place on your altar*
> *this cup and this paten,*
> *vessels with which we will celebrate*
> *the sacrifice of Christ's new covenant.*

May they be sanctified,
for in them the body and blood of Christ
will be offered, consecrated, and received.

Lord,
when we celebrate Christ's faultless sacrifice on earth,
may we be renewed in strength
and filled with your Spirit,
until we join with your saints
at your table in heaven.

Glory and honor be yours for ever and ever.
R. Blessed be God for ever.

12. Afterward the ministers place a corporal on the altar. Some of the congregation bring bread, wine, and water for the celebration of the Lord's sacrifice. The celebrant puts the gifts in the newly blessed paten and chalice and offers them in the usual way. Meanwhile the following antiphon may be sung with Psalm 116:10 – 19.

I will take the cup of salvation and offer a sacrifice of praise (alleluia).

Another appropriate song may be sung.

13. When he has said the prayer **Lord God, we ask you to receive us,** the celebrant may incense the gifts and the altar.

14. If the circumstances of the celebration permit, it is appropriate that the congregation should receive the blood of Christ from the newly blessed chalice.

OUTLINE OF THE RITE

INTRODUCTORY RITES
 Greeting
 Brief Address

LITURGY OF THE WORD
 Reading(s)
 Homily

BLESSING OF THE CHALICE AND PATEN
 Placing of the Chalice and Paten on the Altar
 Prayer of Blessing
 General Intercessions
 Lord's Prayer
 Concluding Prayer

CONCLUDING RITE
 Blessing and Dismissal

Rite of Blessing outside Mass

15. After the people have assembled, the celebrant, with alb or surplice and stole, goes to the chair. Meanwhile, an antiphon with Psalm 116:10–19 (see above, no. 12) may be sung or another appropriate song.

16. The celebrant greets the people saying:

> *The grace of our Lord Jesus Christ,*
> *who offered for us his body and blood,*
> *the love of God,*
> *and the fellowship of the Holy Spirit*
> *be with you all.*
> *R. And also with you.*

 Other suitable words taken preferably from sacred Scripture may be used.

17. Then the celebrant briefly addresses the people, preparing them to take part in the celebration and explaining to them the meaning of the rite.

18. Afterward one or more texts from sacred Scripture are read, especially from those proposed above, with a suitable intervening responsorial psalm (see above, nos. 6–8) or a period of silence.

19. After the reading of the word of God the homily is given, in which the celebrant explains the biblical readings and the meaning of the blessing of a chalice and paten that are used in the celebration of the Lord's Supper.

20. After the homily the ministers or representatives of the community that are presenting the chalice and paten place them on the altar. The celebrant then approaches the altar. Meanwhile the following antiphon may be sung.

I will take the cup of salvation and call on the name of the Lord.

Another appropriate song may be sung.

21. Then the celebrant says:

Let us pray.

All pray in silence for a brief period. The celebrant then continues:

Father,
look kindly upon your children,
who have placed on your altar
this cup and this paten.

May these vessels be sanctified + by your blessing,
for with them we will celebrate
the sacrifice of Christ's new covenant.

And may we who celebrate these mysteries on earth
be renewed in strength
and filled with your Spirit
until we join with your saints
at your table in heaven.

Glory and honor be yours for ever and ever.
R. Blessed be God for ever.

22. Afterward the general intercessions take place either in the usual way or as indicated below:

Let us pray to the Lord Jesus who continuously offers himself for the Church, as the bread of life and the cup of salvation. With confidence we make our prayer:
Christ Jesus, bread of heaven, grant us eternal life.

Savior of all, in obedience to the Father's will, you drank the cup of suffering,
—grant that we may share in the mystery of your death and thus win the promise of eternal life.

Priest of the most high, hidden yet present in the sacrament of the altar,
—grant that we may discern by faith what is concealed from our eyes.

Good shepherd, you give yourself to your disciples as food and drink,
—grant that, fed by this mystery, we may be transformed into your likeness.

Lamb of God, you commanded your Church to celebrate the paschal mystery
under the signs of bread and wine,
—grant that this memorial may be the summit and source of holiness for all
who believe.

Son of God, you wondrously satisfy the hunger and thirst of all who eat and
drink at your table,
—grant that through the mystery of the eucharist we may learn to live your
command of love.

Then the celebrant may introduce the Lord's Prayer in these or similar words:

Fastened to the cross, Christ was the way of salvation; in fulfilling the
will of the Father he is acclaimed the master of prayer; let his prayer be the
source of ours as we say:

All:

Our Father . . .

The celebrant immediately continues:

Lord,
by the death and resurrection of your Son
you have brought redemption to the entire world.

Continue in us the work of your grace,
so that, ever recalling the mystery of Christ,
we may finally rejoice at your table in heaven.

Grant this through Christ our Lord.
R. Amen.

23. Then the celebrant blesses the people in the usual way and dismisses them saying:

Go in peace.
R. Thanks be to God.

Appendix

Litany of the Saints

The cantors begin the litany; they add, at the proper place, names of other saints (the titular of the church, the patron saint of the place, and the saints whose relics are to be deposited, if this is to take place) and petitions suitable to the occasion.

Lord, have mercy	Lord, have mercy
Christ, have mercy	Christ, have mercy
Lord, have mercy	Lord, have mercy
Holy Mary, Mother of God	pray for us
Saint Michael	pray for us
Holy angels of God	pray for us
Saint John the Baptist	pray for us
Saint Joseph	pray for us
Saint Peter and Saint Paul	pray for us
Saint Andrew	pray for us
Saint John	pray for us
Saint Mary Magdalene	pray for us
Saint Stephen	pray for us
Saint Ignatius of Antioch	pray for us
Saint Lawrence	pray for us
Saint Perpetua and Saint Felicity	pray for us
Saint Agnes	pray for us
Saint Gregory	pray for us
Saint Augustine	pray for us
Saint Athanasius	pray for us
Saint Basil	pray for us
Saint Martin	pray for us
Saint Benedict	pray for us
Saint Francis and Saint Dominic	pray for us
Saint Francis Xavier	pray for us
Saint John Vianney	pray for us
Saint Catherine	pray for us
Saint Teresa of Jesus	pray for us
All holy men and women	pray for us

Lord, be merciful	Lord, save your people
From all evil	Lord, save your people
From every sin	Lord, save your people
From everlasting death	Lord, save your people
By your coming as man	Lord, save your people
By your death and rising to new life	Lord, save your people
By your gift of the Holy Spirit	Lord, save your people

Be merciful to us sinners — Lord, hear our prayer

Guide and protect your holy Church — Lord, hear our prayer

Keep the pope and all the clergy
    in faithful service to your Church — Lord, hear our prayer

Bring all peoples together
    in trust and peace — Lord, hear our prayer

Strengthen us in your service — Lord, hear our prayer

Make this church (altar) holy
    and consecrate it to your worship — Lord, hear our prayer

Jesus, Son of the living God — Lord, hear our prayer

Christ, hear us — Christ, hear us

Lord Jesus, hear our prayer — Lord Jesus, hear our prayer

Notes to Chapter 1

1. See 1 Corinthians 3:9; LG, 6.

Notes to Chapter 2

1. See John 2:21.
2. See Cyprian, *De oratione dominica* 23: PL 4, 553; LG, no. 4: AAS 57 (1965) 7; ConstDecrDel 96.
3. See John 4:23.
4. See GIRM, nos. 253, 257, 258, 259–267, 271, 272, 276–277. See also Roman Ritual, *Holy Communion and Worship of the Eucharist outside Mass,* nos. 6 and 9–11.
5. See *Rite of Baptism for Children,* no. 25; *Rite of Penance,* no. 12.
6. See GIRM, no. 266.
7. See GILH, nos. 70–73.
8. See RM, Common of Martyrs 8, prayer over the gifts. Ambrose, *Epistula* 22:13: PL 16, 1023: "Let the triumphant victims rest in the place where Christ is victim: he however, who suffered for all, upon the altar; they, who have been redeemed by his sufferings, beneath the altar." See Ps. Maximus of Turin, *Sermo* 78: PL 57, 689–690. Revelation 6:9, "I saw underneath the altar the souls of all people who had been killed on account of the word of God, for witnessing to it."
9. See Revelation 8:3–4.
10. See Romans 12:1.
11. Luke 2:32.
12. See Pope Vigilius, *Epistula ad Profuturum episcopum* 4: PL 84, 832.
13. John Chrysostom, *Homilia 20 in 2 Cor* 3: PG 61, 540.
14. See SC, art. 40.
15. See GNLYC, Table of Liturgical Days, I, 4b and II, 8b.
16. See GNLYC, Table of Liturgical Days, I, 4b.

Notes to Chapter 4

1. See Epiphanius, *Panarium* 2, 1, *Haeresis* 55: PG 41, 979. Cyril of Alexandria, *De adoratione in spiritu et veritate* 9: PG 68, 647.
2. See Hebrews 4:14; 13:10.
3. See Revelation 5:6.
4. See RM, Order of Mass, no. 96.
5. Ignatius of Antioch, *Ad Romanos* 2:2: Funk PA 1:255.
6. Polycarp, *Ad Philippenses* 4:3: Funk PA 1:301.
7. Gregory the Great, *Homilarium in Ezechielem* 10, 19: PL 76, 1069.
8. See Origen, *In librum Iesu Nave,* Homilia 9, 1: SC 71, 244 and 246.

9. See 1 Corinthians 10:16 – 17.
10. GIRM, no. 259.
11. See Pius XII, Encycl. *Mediator Dei:* AAS 39 (1947) 529.
12. See RM, Common of Martyrs 8, prayer over the gifts.
13. Ambrose, *Epistula* 22, 13: PL 16, 1023. See Ps. Maximus of Turin, *Sermo* 78: PL 57, 689 – 690.
14. Revelation 6:9.
15. See GIRM, nos. 265, 261.
16. GIRM, no. 262.
17. See GIRM, no. 263.
18. Augustine, *Contra Faustum* 20, 21: PL 42, 384.
19. See GIRM, no. 266.
20. See Revelation 8:3 – 4: An angel "who had a golden censer, came and stood at the altar. A large quantity of incense was given to him to offer with the prayers of all the saints on the golden altar that stood in front of the throne; and so from the angel's hand the smoke of the incense went up in the presence of God and with it the prayers of the saints."
21. Luke 2:32.
22. See Pope Vigilius, *Epistula ad Profuturum episcopum,* 4: PL 84, 832.
23. John Chrysostom, *Homilia 20 in 2 Cor* 3: PG 61, 540.
24. See SC, art. 40.

Notes to Chapter 6

1. GIRM, no. 261.
2. See GIRM, no. 265.
3. See GIRM, no. 264.

Notes to Chapter 7

1. See GIRM, no. 289.